Midwives of the Revolution

D1283839

Midwives of the Revolution
Female Bolsheviks and
Women Workers in 1917

Jane McDermid and Anna Hillyar

Ohio University Press
Athens

Published in the United States of America by Ohio University Press,
Athens, Ohio 45701

First published in 1999 by UCL Press
The name of University College London (UCL) is a registered trade mark
used by UCL Press with the consent of the owner. UCL Press is an imprint
of the Taylor & Francis Group.

Library of Congress Cataloging-in-Publication Data

McDermid, Jane.
    Midwives of the Revolution : female Bolsheviks and women workers
in 1917 / Jane McDermid and Anna Hillyar.
        p.   cm.
    Includes bibliographical references.
    ISBN 0–8214–1289–2 (cloth). — ISBN 0–8214–1290–6 (pbk.)
    1. Soviet Union—History—Revolution, 1917–1921—Women.
2. Soviet Union—History—Revolution, 1917–1921—Participation,
Female. 3. Women—Soviet Union—History—20th century. I. Hillyar,
Anna, 1957–   . II. Title.
DK265.9.W57M38   1999
947.084′1—dc21   99–21962
                                                               CIP

Typeset by Graphicraft Limited, Hong Kong
Printed and bound by T.J. International Ltd., Padstow, Great Britain

Contents

Preface

We do not claim to be the first to consider women in the history of the revolutionary process, but we have shifted the focus to set the history of women within the context of the revolution, and to include "ordinary" women and rank and file female Bolsheviks, as participants in their own right, as well as the more well known individuals, such as Alexandra Kollontai. Hence the choice of "midwives" of the revolution: not only was midwifery a traditional occupation among village women, but pregnant peasants and workers preferred an experienced woman of their own class to deliver their child, to the professional physicians. "Midwives of the Revolution" indicates our belief that women were not only present at the birth of the new order, nor that they simply induced it before turning it over to the professional revolutionaries, but that they helped in the final stages of delivery. How the new order subsequently developed, and how the midwives fared, should not obscure the crucial role that they played both in gestation and parturition.

We did not set out to discover new sources which prove that women played a major role in the 1917 Revolution. Instead, we are convinced that there already exists evidence in published works which, if read from a perspective that puts women in the foreground, would show both that they were not passive spectators, and that we should think in terms not only of what impact the revolution had on them, but of what they contributed to it. All the works cited here are available in libraries and through the inter-library loan service. Taken separately, they reveal how compartmentalized the history of the 1917 Revolution is, and continues to be, as attention is focused on the outcomes of the Bolshevik seizure of power. For readers new to the subject, we hope that this will encourage them to view the revolutionary process from a range of perspectives, rather than reducing it to a narrowly political and essentially masculine enterprise.

There are specialist studies on Russian women in the nineteenth and early twentieth centuries on which we rely heavily, but most seek to explain the failure of feminism, or the lack of feminist consciousness among revolutionaries, which contributed to the persistence of patriarchy after the Bolsheviks took power. Such a perspective is valuable, but can result in a diminution of women's contribution to the making of the revolution itself. In this survey of the revolutionary process, we have attempted to merge women's history with the history of the revolution. That a male-dominated political party eventually came to power was at least partly attributable to women. By means of biographical details, anecdotes and narrative, we have attempted to show that women were not only on the scene, that they were not simply extras to the main action on stage, but that they helped set it. They were more than exclamation marks punctuating the beginning and end of the 1917 Revolution. As the Ul'ianov sisters, Anna and Mariia, proclaimed in *Pravda* on 5 March 1917:

> On Women's Day, February 23, a strike was declared at the majority of factories and plants. The women were in a very militant mood – not only the women workers, but the masses of women queuing for bread and kerosene. They held political meetings, they predominated in the streets, they moved to the city duma with a demand for bread, they stopped trams. "Comrades, come out!" they shouted enthusiastically. They went to the factories and plants and summoned workers to down tools. All in all, Women's Day was a tremendous success and gave rise to the revolutionary spirit.

The gestation period of this book has been a difficult one. While we did not always agree with the criticisms from anonymous readers, we benefited from them. We are grateful to our colleagues at University of Southampton New College for advice and support, intellectual, moral and technical.

CHAPTER ONE

Introduction

In his pioneering study *The Women's Liberation Movement in Russia: Feminism, Nihilism, and Bolshevism, 1860–1930*, Richard Stites noted that most accounts of 1917 feature women only twice: as an elemental force when they set in motion on 23 February (or 8 March according to the western calendar) the revolution that would topple tsarism, and as a conservative force on 25 October (7 November) when female soldiers defended the Provisional Government against the Bolshevik Red Guards who stormed the Winter Palace.[1] Stites believed that the absence of women from depictions of the revolutionary process was not surprising given the nature of writing on the Russian Revolution, which tended to stress political interpretations at the expense of social, with the implication not only that the latter was the feminine sphere, while politics was inherently masculine, but also that the social and political were always separate spheres. His own account viewed the period between the two revolutions as a clash between feminists and Bolsheviks. The victors were the latter, and Linda Edmondson's study of Russian feminism portrays the October Revolution as the "obliteration of the feminist movement" which the Bolshevik regime effectively declared "redundant".[2] Yet, while the Bolsheviks stressed the oppression of class over gender, they also recognized that women suffered a double oppression which they believed had its basis in peasant patriarchy as well as in capitalism. In addition, the Bolsheviks were forced to pay attention to the woman question, not only by the circumstances of greatly increased numbers of women entering the labour force, especially during the First World War, but also under pressure from some of the female members of their own party.

1

The fact that the Bolsheviks feared feminism as a divisive force, and sought to combat it, shows that there was a political facet to the role played by women in 1917. Bolsheviks feared that factory women were responding to feminist ideas, which might serve to divide the working class. The context in which the revolutionary process developed, that of war, gave women a prominence that they would otherwise not have had, and forced political parties, both radical and moderate, to pay attention to their demands. The following quotation from an eyewitness to the February Revolution (and opponent of the Bolsheviks) suggests that the women at first had no overtly political demands in mind:

> If future historians look for the group which began the Russian Revolution, let them not create any involved theory. The Russian Revolution was begun by hungry women and children demanding bread and herrings. They started by wrecking tram cars and looting a few small shops. Only later did they, together with workmen and politicians, become ambitious to wreck that mighty edifice, the Russian autocracy.[3]

While women's issues in 1917 were above all social, the separation of material from political concerns is too facile. Historians tend to see the protests on 23 February as spontaneous. That women were the instigators of the unrest is not seen as being of particular importance, except in emphasizing the notion of spontaneity, with the assumption that the female workers were too politically backward to be capable of the conscious expression of their criticisms not only of the deteriorating conditions, but against the war. Even Stites, who puts women in the foreground, believes that their actions in February proved to be the catalyst to revolution "almost by accident".[4]

Women workers were notoriously difficult to organize, but in a situation of the mass conscription of men no protest could succeed without drawing them into it. The Bolshevik Party, including the female members who had tried to organize women workers, had suffered severe repression since 1914 because of their opposition to the war, and many of them were either in gaol, exile or emigration. No one, it seems, was prepared for revolution; no one expected it. Superficially, this view is borne out by Eduard Nikolaevich Burdzhalov in *Russia's Second Revolution: The February 1917 Uprising in Petrograd*, the first serious Soviet study of the February Revolution, which was published in

Moscow on the fiftieth anniversary of the Revolution. Under Stalin, the February Revolution had tended to be ignored by Soviet scholars since the Bolsheviks had not played a leading role. The genesis of Burdzhalov's work lay in articles which he had published in the late 1950s, in which he had argued that the February Revolution had not been directed by the Bolsheviks, but that, like all other political parties, they had been left hesitating while the people took decisive action.[5] Burdzhalov's thesis seemed to confirm what Nikolai N. Sukhanov, who joined the Mensheviks (the "moderate" wing of the Russian Social Democratic Labour Party) in May 1917, and who had been present in Petrograd at the time of the February Revolution, noted in his memoir which was published in 1922: "Not one party was preparing for the great upheaval."[6] "Spontaneity", then, may be taken to mean that the political parties had not organized, directed, led, or even foreseen the February Revolution. Yet from exile in Switzerland, Nadezhda Krupskaia had written to a comrade on 6 (19) February 1917:

> You'll have to get to Russia right away or else you won't get in on "the beginning". In all seriousness, the letters from Russia are filled with good news. Just yesterday one came from an old friend, a highly experienced person, who wrote: "The difficult period apparently is passing, a turn for the better can be seen in the mood of the workers and educated young people. Organisation is poor because all the adults are either at the front or subject to call-up. The influx of women and adolescents into the workforce is lowering organisational capacity but not the mood. Even so the organisations are growing.[7]

Moreover, a close reading of Burdzhalov's account of the February Days reveals that not only was there evidence of organization at the grassroots level, but that women played a significant part. Despite harassment by the authorities since the war began, the Bolsheviks and the Inter-District Committee (a group which sought to unify the Russian Social Democratic Labour Party (RSDLP), which in 1903 had split into two main factions, the Bolsheviks and Mensheviks) had continued agitating among the women workers. On the eve of the revolution, Bolshevik women had set up a city-wide women's circle which co-operated with the women's circle of the Inter-District Committee. These female activists decided to commemorate International Women's Day

3

with an anti-war demonstration. None of the revolutionaries expected that the outcome would be the fall of tsarism, but like Krupskaia in exile abroad, these women in Petrograd had realized that revolution was on the agenda, and no longer consigned to some indeterminate future when the parties were better prepared.

Thus, we should not simply equate spontaneity with lack of organization or political consciousness. Still, the debate around who took part and who, if anyone, led the February Revolution from International Women's Day does not throw any more light on the role played by women, and certainly does not see them as having been in the vanguard. Instead, it is an examination of which political group could claim to have offered a guiding hand to the demonstrators between 23 and 27 February. The arguments concerning who wrote which leaflet during that period are detailed, depending on a close reading of sources, but what is clear is that none of the revolutionary parties was preparing to overthrow tsarism in February. Even the Inter-District Committee which produced the leaflet for International Women's Day wanted to limit the women's actions to a few meetings and discussion of the role women should play in the labour movement.[8]

Certainly, since the 1870s revolutionaries had found women workers extremely difficult to organize, largely because the latter had domestic responsibilities that men did not share, had a lower level of literacy than men, were given little chance to develop skills at work, and earned considerably less than the average male wage. At the same time, women were seen as a threat by male workers, partly because of the increasing division of labour in factories which allowed employers to dilute skills, and partly because the image of the docile, abstemious and politically unconscious woman worker was attractive to employers, particularly after the 1905 Revolution, as a possible replacement for militant men. Factors that help explain the lack of interest of most working women in the labour movement, as well as the latter's concentration on men, include the difficulties of conducting revolutionary propaganda and organization when political parties and trade unions were illegal until the 1905 Revolution, where the secret police was effective in harassing activists, and where there were few public places in which to meet apart from the tavern, which was a masculine environment with the exception of waitresses, prostitutes and a few female proprietors. While revolutionaries generally are criticized for failing to pay particular attention to the needs of women, in practice there had been special efforts, notably by Marxist groups, to organize women since the late 1880s. The low level of female literacy meant that much of those efforts had to be educational, which in turn meant that they could reach only a minority of women, and then those who had already shown some interest.

Of course, lack of organization did not mean that women workers simply accepted their lot. Strikes in the textile industry in the mid 1890s and the revolution of 1905 both revealed that women workers were capable of self organization, though they seldom felt confident enough to sustain their actions. Again, the traditional ways in which women were expected to protest – through noisy crowd actions, riots and attacks on people as well as property – were taken as a sign of their lack of political consciousness. Thus women workers could be both subservient and militant, quiescent and spontaneous. Any actions initiated and executed by women workers were assumed merely to reflect popular unrest in an elemental way, and not expected either to persist or to succeed.

Hence the surprise of the revolutionaries as well as the government in February 1917 when the women workers and soldiers' wives who went on to the streets sustained their protests and pulled in male workers and soldiers. Precisely because the protest began on International Women's Day, which had been introduced to Russia by the Bolshevik Konkordia Samoilova only in 1913 and had been a small affair, no one expected that the end of tsarism was so close. In his study of the Russian people and "their revolution", Christopher Read conflates the women's protest with the men's and sees the revolutionaries as overwhelmed rather than unprepared:

> Tens of thousands of working people, men and women, poured into the streets. The members of the main socialist parties were busy printing leaflets, sending out speakers and doing whatever they could to articulate the workers' demands and make known their protests but the numbers on the streets were far beyond their capabilities to organise in the real sense. At most, they were midwives of worker protest.[9]

The women went far beyond what the professional revolutionaries, including the skilled male workers, envisaged, or indeed considered sensible. It was the women who took the lead in approaching the troops, and trying to persuade them not to fire on or charge the demonstrators.

Ironically, the fact that the thousands of troops stationed in and near the capital quickly sided with the demonstrators has tended to take the spotlight off the women, since the soldiers consolidated what the women had started. "In February 1917, as women in the bread queues were joined by demonstrating workers, the soldiers held their fire and joined them."[10] The decisive point, then, is seen as the soldiers taking the side of the crowds against the police. Too often the mutiny of the Petrograd garrison is allowed not simply to eclipse the working women, but to push them out of the picture completely, as if having done their job they could leave the real politics to the men.

This study seeks to lift the curtain on women's actions during 1917, not to claim an inflated role for them but to show that they were an integral part of the way in which the revolution developed, in political as well as social terms, and to challenge the easy distinction that tends to be made between the social and the political, always with the inference that the latter is the more important. The reason for this leaning towards the political explanation is that the history of the revolution has been seen in the light of what came after, and the search for causes of the one-party state. In his revision of "the old story" of 1917, Ronald Suny argues that "for too long Russian history has been written not only from the top down, but with the bottom left out completely".[11] Yet he too ignores women's particular role, seeing them as just part of the mass of desperate people who took spontaneous action in February.

Not all works on 1917 are narrowly party political. There have been a number of social histories that look at factory workers as political actors in their own right and who were not simply manipulated by the Bolsheviks.[12] Though such works pay attention to women and the influence of gender on the workforce, their focus remains the male, especially skilled, worker. Such studies are valuable for widening our understanding of the revolutionary process, but in practice factory workers were in a minority. There were more employees in the service sector in Petrograd in 1917 than in the metal industry.[13] Women predominated in the former and men in the latter. After nearly three years of combat, moreover, women were moving into those areas previously exclusive to men. On the eve of the war, women made up three per cent of the labour force in the metal industry; by the eve of the revolution, that percentage had risen to 18.[14]

Even social histories of 1917 concentrate on the relationship between the political parties, and in particular the Bolsheviks, and the workers.

Efforts to understand the significance of popular participation in the revolution generally relegate women to a secondary role: "women, who formed a significant minority of the working class, tended to be involved in the revolutionary struggles to a lesser extent than their male co-workers."[15] Generally, they were seen as part of the mass of unskilled, inarticulate and militant labour force that the revolutionary groups appeared to try to lead from behind for much of 1917. While the influence of gender divisions on the labour movement has been recognized, the general picture of the revolutionary crowd in 1917 is that it was above all male. Yet it is the image of an elemental force of women workers and their contribution to the social chaos of 1917 that underwrites the mirror image of the Bolsheviks as arch manipulators and usurpers of the popular movement. This study of women in 1917 reveals that it was only after sustained effort that the Bolsheviks were able to build a base among the most militant sectors in the working class. It also shows that the women workers were not simply duped by the Bolsheviks. They made conscious choices, just as men did.

Nor has the opening up of the Russian archives since the late 1980s led to any radical reinterpretation of the revolution. Indeed, women have retreated further into the background, while there has been a return to the focus on political elites and on the personality of Lenin. Thus in his 1990 publication, *The Russian Revolution 1899–1919*, Richard Pipes asserted that: "The Russian revolution was made neither by the forces of nature nor by anonymous masses but by identifiable men pursuing their own advantages. Although it had spontaneous aspects, in the main it was the result of deliberate action."[16] Even what has been regarded as women's main contribution, as instigators or catalysts of the revolution, has been diminished. Two recent major biographies of Lenin – *Lenin: His Life and Legacy*, by Dmitri Volkogonov (1994) and *Lenin: A Political Life: volume 3: The Iron Ring*, by Robert Service (1995) – narrow the focus even further, to the Bolshevik leader, whom both portray as a ruthless fanatic. Biographers obviously tend to insist on the centrality of their subject, often at the expense of neglecting the wider context in which he or she acted. This is especially the case with Lenin, and Suny has warned that:

Clearly, to isolate Lenin or his party from the rich and contradictory social context in which they operated not only distorts an understanding of the events in 1917 but may lead to unwarranted conclusions about the artificial, unorganic, manipulated nature of October, and to the more general view that great revolutions, like more modest acts of political protest, are the creations of outside agitators.[17]

We would go further and specify that this "rich and contradictory social context" must include women as an integral component and not simply as incidental interlopers or passive bystanders. Another weakness of the two biographies mentioned above is that their portrait of Lenin leaves little room for the women in his life, who are seen very much in his shadow, essentially filling the roles of housekeeper and secretary. Yet these women, his wife Nadezhda Krupskaia and sisters Anna Elizarova and Mariia Ul'ianova, were all committed revolutionaries in their own right and played an important part not only in maintaining the Bolshevik organization in the difficult years of emigration, but in building the party during 1917, with a particular concentration on women and youth workers.

The focus of this study will thus be not only the relationship between women workers and the revolution of 1917, but Bolshevik women who, with the exception of Alexandra Kollontai, are often dismissed, if considered at all, as simply the handmaidens of their male comrades. Kollontai is generally portrayed almost as a voice crying in the wilderness for special efforts to be made in organizing women workers and soldiers' wives, with other Bolshevik women either disagreeing with Kollontai's proposals or following in her wake.[18] Interestingly, Lenin is shown as siding with Kollontai. Kollontai's memoirs certainly give the impression that she felt very much isolated on this issue, and a glance at the Bolshevik press during 1917 confirms that she played a significant role in publicizing the activities of women workers, notably the efforts by soldiers' wives in April to improve their position and press for the return of their husbands from the front, and the lengthy strike of laundresses in May. As this study will show, Bolshevik women had been agitating and organizing in these two areas before Kollontai's return to Russia. It would seem that her main role in terms of work among women was continually to prod the Bolshevik Party into addressing the issue, as propagandist for working women's struggles and, ironically, as the party's leading theoretical and political opponent of the feminist movement. Rather than put Kollontai on a pedestal as *the* "Bolshevik feminist", we seek to place her in the context of her female comrades, albeit a minority, who were committed both to the labour movement and to the particular grievances of women workers within it.

It is interesting that so many studies of the 1917 revolution focus on personalities. The towering figure is, of course, Lenin, while feminist accounts that concentrate on the Bolsheviks emphasize Kollontai. Both, however, were absent for the duration of the war and both missed the February Revolution; Lenin was in hiding from early July until the eve of the October Revolution, and Kollontai was in prison in August. Placing the spotlight on individuals has been at the expense of underestimating the role played by ordinary people, men and women, as well as rank and file revolutionaries. Moreover, when the focus has shifted to the workers, women are rarely centre stage. This might be because the main point of interest is in establishing the development of class consciousness and class organization, so that the areas under study are mainly factories and their committees and trade unions, where skilled male workers predominated.[19]

Although the revolution had been begun by women workers, the initial concessions made by employers tended to favour skilled men. Just when the moderate revolutionaries had entered the Provisional Government in May, the economic situation deteriorated and the employers were less willing to meet workers' demands. The coalition government of socialists and liberals saw workers' protests as undermining the war effort and creating social instability from which the Bolsheviks would gain. Once again, it was women workers who were to the forefront of the upsurge in strike activity. Moreover, they were unskilled and service sector workers, among whom the Bolsheviks were building a base. It was a Bolshevik woman, Sof'ia Goncharskaia, who headed the union of laundry workers.

Thus, the voices calling for moderation in the labour movement were precisely those who had made some gains from the February Revolution: skilled workers and the socialists who were now members of the government. The latter, along with the liberals and the feminists, endeavoured to maintain the 1914 spirit of national unity, but while the moderate socialists sought class compromise, the liberals seemed to move further to the right, insisting on the continuation of the war effort, and looking to the officer corps for protection from the lower classes.[20] Feminists believed that women had to prove themselves responsible citizens, worthy of full sexual equality, and that the way to achieve this was by wholehearted support for the war effort. They assumed a unity of interests between women, and failed to see the deepening class divisions reflected in the women workers' protests against their low pay and poor conditions. What the Bolsheviks realized was that by 1917 national unity was impossible under the strains of a seemingly endless war. They took power because they alone had voiced the demands of the workers, women as well as men.

The fall of communism and break-up of the Soviet Union in 1991 has directed attention back to 1917, and the question of whether the victory of the Bolsheviks was inevitable. In the west, there have been reassessments or revisions of the revolution in which women scarcely appear, giving the impression that the revolution was something that happened to them, rather than something in which they participated and which they helped shape.[21] Such works tend to focus on key events in 1917 in order to trace the Bolshevik path to power, still assuming that political history will provide the explanations. Histories "from below" have demonstrated that at each stage of the revolutionary process, the fortunes of the Bolsheviks, and of their rivals, depended on the mass of unskilled workers among whom were the majority of working women. Yet even in the latter, women are considered for the impact they had on the workforce rather than the role they played in political events.[22] Again, this may stem from a narrow definition of what constitutes politics.

To understand what role women played in 1917, and why they tend to be identified with social rather than political studies of the revolution, we need to consider the "woman question" in nineteenth century Russia, which is the subject of the first chapter. In a patriarchal and economically under-developed society and an absolutist political system, the inequality to which women were subjected in the former seemed balanced in the latter by their equality with men in the general lack of civil and political rights. One result was that the women's movement concentrated on social and economic issues, and did not take up the demand for female suffrage until the 1905 Revolution. In a country which was predominantly agricultural, a minority of politically and socially conscious upper-class women felt that their privileged position came at the expense of the peasantry and struggled to be accepted into higher education and the professions so that they could be of service to the mass of the poor. They did not neglect relations between the sexes. As Chapter 2 will show, literary as well as political writings took the position of women in the patriarchal family as a symbol of the general political tyranny.

Individual women who rebelled against the tsarist regime had a significant impact on political developments from the 1870s, with some revered as heroines; but again they saw themselves as dedicated to the good of the whole, instead of acting in their own interests; or rather, they equated the two. The second chapter looks at the factors and forces since the 1870s that shaped female revolutionaries in Russia by examining the lives of some who were drawn to terrorism and others to Marxism, concluding with a consideration of female members of the Bolshevik Party in 1917.

Most female revolutionaries did not specifically address themselves to women, while peasant and urban lower-class women proved difficult to reach because of their particular conditions and responsibilities at home and work. It was easier for radical upper-class women to make contact with working-class men who had basic literacy, though some of the latter put the former in touch with women workers, helping establish female study circles. These, however, constituted a tiny minority of working-class women. The third chapter outlines the situation of working women on the eve of the First World War, showing the variety of work that was open to women, especially those with more than a basic education. Nevertheless, whatever the opportunities a developing economy opened to women from the late nineteenth century, equality with men was not one of them. Only the small feminist movement insisted that sexual equality was a priority, though it still put more emphasis on education and employment than on the vote. For revolutionaries, female as much as male, the scale of poverty and illiteracy took precedence over everything. Even before the outbreak of war in 1914 there had been growing social polarization, reflected in the widespread labour unrest of the mid 1890s and the revolution of 1905, though again the part women played in both is generally overlooked.[23]

It was the impact of the First World War that ultimately drove more people into outright opposition to the state, and so the fourth chapter traces the changes in female responses to the conflict between the declaration of war in 1914 until the eve of revolution in 1917. The conscription, and deaths, of millions of men meant that women were forced to play a major part in maintaining the home front, while a minority volunteered to serve at the front, not only in support roles but in combat. The reactions of women to the war differed considerably between individuals and social classes, and also over time, ranging from widespread patriotism to profound disillusionment. The impact of war on living and working conditions blurred the distinction between political and material grievances, while the fact that by 1916 women made up a third of the labour force ensured that any protests could be successful only if women were involved. The assumption was still that women were not interested in politics, but their traditional concern with the cost of living and food and fuel supplies in the context of this war meant that when they finally took to the streets on 23 February 1917, their demands were for justice as well, and as much, as bread.

The fifth chapter begins with a detailed examination of the role women played in the overthrow of tsarism, and from there traces their actions and reactions to events until the Bolshevik seizure of power. For some, notably the feminists, the revolution was over in February, and the task was to build the new constitutional order, ensuring that women were accorded equal rights with men. For some revolutionaries, too, the task in hand was to consolidate the political situation, bring the war to a speedy, successful conclusion, and dissuade the workers from taking further militant actions that might endanger the Provisional Government. Women workers in particular found that their situation had changed little after February, reflected in the increasing incidence of strikes by the summer among which that in May by predominantly female laundry workers seemed particularly notable. What is remarkable about the protests by workers after the February Revolution is the prominence of the service sector, including domestic servants, shop assistants and waitresses. The Bolsheviks alone seem to have recognized the political significance of such protests by women who until then were considered not only dormant but unreachable. Bolshevik women expended considerable effort in organizing female workers, soldiers' wives, and young women. Moreover, the women's strike action served to pull them into the general labour movement, strengthening their consciousness of class interests.

As the war dragged on, and after an attempted right-wing military coup in August that the Bolsheviks helped defeat, increasing numbers of women turned against the Provisional Government which seemed incapable of meeting, and even hostile towards, popular demands. By then, the question of subsistence, which had sparked the February Revolution, had become deeply political. Hence, as the revolutionary process developed conflict between women grew, with the feminists and some revolutionaries persisting in their support for the war effort which the majority of women workers came to see as the main cause of their

12

misfortunes. Women's strikes in 1917 had some success, but the collapse of the economy undermined their material gains. Wage rises were quickly overtaken by price increases. As the revolutionary process deepened, strikes seemed less and less effective. To improve workers' conditions would involve a massive redistribution of wealth which the Provisional Government resisted. Hence women workers, as well as men, took direct political action. When women turned to the Bolsheviks in October – and there were more women who stormed the Winter Palace (which housed the Provisional Government) than defended it – it was not simply a negative choice. The Bolsheviks called for the immediate end of the war, and also were in the forefront of efforts to organize women.

Our consideration of women's role in the revolutionary process of 1917 centres on Petrograd, the capital city (with war in 1914, "Petersburg" had been dropped because it sounded too German). It was an urban revolution that brought an urban party to power. Nevertheless, it would not have succeeded without a parallel revolution in the countryside, in which the peasantry imposed their own solution on the land question, which the Bolsheviks simply accepted. While this study shows the prominence of women in the overthrow first of the tsar and then of his self-appointed successor, the Provisional Government, peasant women generally did not vote in the local elections of May, and were in a minority in the village assemblies that in 1917 were opened up to villagers who were not members of peasant households (such as skilled workers, landless labourers, returning soldiers keen to set up their own, separate household, and local professionals).[24] The conclusion puts the Petrograd case study into the wider context, which reveals that elsewhere, in cities as well as in the countryside, women played a less prominent, yet not insignificant, role. Perhaps, then, the fact that women faded from the historical stage was due not only to the preference for political interpretations of the Bolshevik victory, but also to the civil war that followed so soon after they took power, resulting in the militarization of the revolution, and the subsequent need to placate the peasantry. The removal of the seat of power from Petrograd to the older, more traditional and patriarchal Moscow in 1918 ensured that women's contribution to the making of the revolution would not only be downgraded, it could be forgotten.

This was also owing to the fact that women did not shape the communist state, as their absence from the political elite throughout the soviet period confirms. Hence, it has been assumed, they must have been losers in 1917. Yet they had played a significant part both in the downfall of the old tsarist regime and the victory of the communists. The backlash against sexual equality (associated with the communists, though never achieved under them) and the transition to a market economy at the end of the twentieth century has also made women the particular victims of the collapse of communism.[25]

This book is an attempt to merge the history of women and the history of the Russian Revolution to show that women were an integral part of the revolutionary process, challenging assumptions that they served merely to ignite an essentially masculine revolt. Focusing on women in 1917 not only forces us to consider the revolutionary process from aspects that have rarely been taken into account, but also deepens our understanding of that process. As Dominique Godineau has observed of the French Revolution, too often "women are presented apart from the Revolution or beside it; they are not included in the revolutionary process, conceptualized as it is without reference to their involvement". Alternatively, the revolution exists only as a backdrop to the history of women whose actions "play more importance in the history of women than in the history of the Revolution. It is as if," she concludes, "women constructed their stories alongside the 'big story' which remains masculine and in which they are merely the eternal victims."[26]

Two recent works have examined in detail and depth women who joined the Social Democratic movement, and in particular the Bolshevik Party. Both attempt to construct a "collective" biography of female Marxists. In *Bolshevik Women*, Barbara Evans Clements presents a history of women who joined the RSDLP and its factions, the Bolsheviks and Mensheviks, before 1921. Working from a database of over 500 individuals, Clements provides a detailed examination of six women whom she sees as fairly representative of all the "founding" Bolshevik women, in terms of social origins, revolutionary motivation, and political careers before and after the 1917 Revolution. Her intentions were "not only to fit the Bolshevik women into their times but also to explain, whenever possible, the choices they made" and to question their reasons for rejecting feminism, despite being concerned with the woman question.[27] Clements shows that before the Revolution, female Social Democrats were about as likely as males to hold party office, particularly at the level of city committees, and especially in St Petersburg and Moscow. Only a few women, however, achieved top leadership positions.

Like us, Clements disagrees with the suggestion made by Beate Fieseler, among others, that women joined the RSDLP on the basis of their emotions, morality or ethics rather than intellect.[28] Certainly, the lives detailed by Clements and our own findings do not support such a gender stereotype, but Fieseler's study, *Frauen auf dem Weg in die russische Sozialdemokratie, 1890–1917* has much more to offer.[29] She too has a database of more than 500 women, though she covers a more limited timescale (1890–1917). Whereas Clements interweaves biography with narrative, Fieseler has adopted a more thematic approach, providing a collective portrait, rather than Clements' representational lives, of female members of the RSDLP. Fieseler draws on quantitative analysis, type of work performed and position in the party hierarchy, age, political experience, social origins, education, profession and nationality. She then considers the process of and motivation behind the radicalization of female Social Democrats. She agrees with Clements that these women's party careers generally ended at local level, notably when the Bolshevik Party grew substantially after the February Revolution, but especially in the soviet era when female membership fell back in numbers and status.

Nevertheless, both Clements and Fieseler have constructed a portrait of strong, determined Bolshevik women, activists in their own right, who made a positive contribution to the revolution. It is not enough, however, to examine party political women or the writings and actions of key individuals to comprehend women's relationship to the 1917 Revolution, it is necessary also to consider the actions of the crowds, made up of thousands of individual women as well as men, and on occasions, of more women than men. Ordinary women were part of the revolutionary process from the beginning, and did not retreat into the background after the overthrow of tsarism. Nor did they revolt simply over "bread and herrings". We need to address as issues of political importance in certain circumstances, what are too often categorized and dismissed as domestic and implicitly female concerns. Certainly, few women in 1917 challenged the traditionally female role; instead they entered into the political movement on the basis of that role, sometimes by themselves, often together with men. Only a minority would be deemed feminist today, but the women of 1917 nevertheless asserted women's rights to intervene in politics by refusing to separate the economic and social from the political, revealing how much their lives diverged from the notion of separate spheres for the sexes.

Certainly, the gendered division of labour constrained women's lives, and continued to do so after the revolution, but as their actions in 1917 show, women did not passively accept their situation. Some used the ideology to justify entering the public sphere of politics; others entered the public sphere of paid employment to support the domestic sphere; and though very few rejected the notion of female domesticity, women's actions served further to blur the distinctions between public and private.

In fact, women did not "take to the streets" in 1917, they already spent much of their time there, travelling, working, socializing, on errands, queuing, scouring for provisions, looting, rioting, and "gossiping". As recognized by revolutionaries and tsarist police alike, women's gossip provided not only a snapshot of public opinion, but a means for the gossipers to articulate and develop their ideas and beliefs, as well as prejudices. Too often working women are described as "silent", as voiceless because they did not speak out at political or trade union meetings, afraid of their ignorance and of men's hostility and condescension. After the February Revolution, some developed the courage to speak and address meetings, but most educated themselves by listening. When women spoke together, it was still seen as gossip, especially because the women did not express their ideas conceptually, but still talked of "bread and herrings". Yet that talk was itself a devastating critique of the Provisional Government which had replaced tsarism and of the revolutionaries who supported it.

At each stage of the revolution, women's actions seem to have been based on material concerns, intimately linked to the price and availability of food. That should not lead us to dismiss them as apolitical, as uninterested in the "bigger" issues of principle. Both feminists and Marxists pointed out and explained the nature of patriarchy and sexual inequality; but while peasant and urban women protested against the ill-treatment they suffered from men, those same women did not demand equal pay, let alone sexual equality. Why should we expect them to do so? Too often we examine women's lives to find out not so much who they were or what they did, but why they "failed" to act as we think they should have.

This is not to deny the importance of individuals such as Kollontai, but to seek to understand her role by setting her within the wider context of ordinary women in 1917. That Kollontai's ideas on women's role and sexual morality remain interesting at the end of the twentieth century may tell us more about our contemporary concerns than about the women of 1917, to whom Kollontai's calls for a "new morality" and the "new woman" were alien. Moreover, during the revolution and the ensuing civil war, Kollontai did not rouse the women to the cause by addressing issues of sex and gender inequality so much as by focusing on questions of everyday life, pointing out the crucial role women's domestic skills could play in the public sphere. In a recent study, *The Baba and the Comrade. Gender and Politics in Revolutionary Russia*, Elizabeth Wood argues that after the revolution, in contrast to most other female Bolsheviks, Kollontai tried to give women workers a voice, to organize them for their own sakes, but she might also be seen to be determined to liberate women by forcing them to be free.[30] In 1917, Kollontai was concerned to draw women workers into the revolutionary movement, and to preserve them from the divisive influence of feminism.

The dismissal of the communist regime as anti-feminist, despite its rhetoric of sexual equality, has led to the roles that women actually played in 1917 being undervalued. Women did not simply instigate the revolution but contributed significantly to maintaining its momentum. True, the division of labour between women and men remained, but rather than conclude that women had failed to challenge male domination, we might consider how they manoeuvred within their traditional sphere and what that meant for the revolutionary process. The expectations and protests of ordinary women, as well as men, help us to appreciate their thought. We too easily accept the view of the mass of women in 1917 as uneducated, motivated solely by hunger and irrational anger, and lacking in political consciousness, as if they existed only through their material lives, and ideas were the prerogative of the politically aware minority. Of course, there is much truth to the stereotype of the ignorant, abused woman concerned above all with feeding her family, but that should not lead us to ignore her. Such women participated in the upheavals of 1917, as part of the revolution, not outside of it. We may still conclude that they were victims, but history is not only about winners. By examining the forces and circumstances that shaped women in later nineteenth and early twentieth century Russia, we can see why women acted as they did in 1917, and by focusing on their participation in the revolution we should gain greater understanding of their role in shaping that process, rather than limiting our quest to the effects the revolution had on women.

As we hope to show, considerable numbers of ordinary women, and not only prominent individuals such as Kollontai, engaged in politics in a variety of ways. Of those who supported the revolution, only a few would be recognized as leaders; some were moderates in the sense of being satisfied to build reforms on the abolition of tsarism, resisting what they saw as the extremism of the Bolsheviks and the irrationalism of the masses' demands for more radical measures. Whichever standpoint they took, and women were as politically divided as men, women as well as men made history in 1917 and were not just shaped by it. Women entered the political sphere through their domestic role in 1917; we should at least permit their entry into the history of the revolution that they helped to make.

CHAPTER TWO

The woman question before 1917: what was to be done?

Until 1861, political, social and economic relations in the tsarist empire were determined by the institution of serfdom, in which the vast majority of the peasant population were tied to the land and the ruler, the tsar, had absolute power. The society was patriarchal, with the woman owing complete obedience in law to her husband or father. Despite widespread illiteracy, especially among women, literature played an important role in developing ideas on the woman question among the upper classes in Russia and portraying the ideal woman. Some have detected a "strong woman" motif.[1] In her study of women in nineteenth-century Russian literature, Barbara Heldt sees this as an essentially male image of women, an image of "terrible perfection": terrible to the women expected to incarnate it, and to the men who could not match it. She claims that heroines such as Vera Pavlovna of the radical Nikolai Chernyshevskii's novel *What is to be done?* were not the literary equals of male characters, but rather were the foil for the larger preoccupations of men.[2] This novel was published in 1863, and had been written while the author was in prison during the political reaction that had followed the tsarist reforms associated with the abolition of serfdom in 1861. Chernyshevskii not only put Vera Pavlovna at the centre of his novel, he wrote to his wife that men were obliged to end the subordinate, servile relationships between the sexes from which they benefited, even if it meant that for a time women would be the superior sex, and man "a slave".[3] Both women and men of the upper classes were to dedicate themselves to the "people", who were then overwhelmingly from the peasantry.

Service to the people

From memoirs of female revolutionaries in particular, Chernyshevskii's novel seems to have had a profound effect on young upper-class Russians from the 1860s and 1870s, and especially those who saw the traditional patriarchal family as a major obstacle to their self-development and, above all, to their desire to be socially useful. *What is to be done?* was being read in Sunday schools and circles aimed at workers by the 1880s and into the twentieth century.[4] Why did this particular novel prove so appealing to radicals? It seemed to be providing rational and practical solutions to the problems of family tyranny, divorce, jobs and education for women, and even of prostitution, in a period of economic and social upheaval. The story outlines the development of Vera Pavlovna, a sensitive woman trapped in an obscurantist family, who is given the chance of escape by means of a fictitious marriage. She later discovers that marriage, even one based on mutual love and respect, is not enough for a woman to lead a full life, and that economic independence is essential for a woman to enjoy sexual equality. While Chernyshevskii did not ignore the erotic or the sensual nature of sexual relations, he held that work was the central force in life, of women as much as of men. Self-confident and socially conscious, Vera Pavlovna seemed to embody all the characteristics of the "new woman" of the 1860s. The "new man" was embodied in the ascetic, scrupulously honest revolutionary, Rakhmetov. Between them, there was freedom and equality, though interestingly, no sexual relationship. Elizabeth Wood reads the attitude of Chernyshevskii towards his heroine as one of authorly condescension, pointing out that later revolutionaries, including Lenin, focused on Rakhmetov who rejected relationships with women.[5] While Lenin certainly did not follow his hero's example in this respect, it is also interesting that whereas Marxist women seem to have been attracted by the character of Vera Pavlovna, female terrorists were more impressed by Rakhmetov, who abandoned all personal life for the cause of the people.[6]

Chernyshevskii's ideas were not original. Fictitious marriage, freedom in sexual relations (though still monogamy), rational egoism, socialist communes (or *artels*) for living and working, and medicine as a career for women had all been discussed and tried before the publication of his novel and the abolition of serfdom. For the first time, all these elements were woven together in a coherent, if didactic, whole.

20

Vera Pavlovna's life was taken as a realistic programme for the future. This literary character seemed to be more than just a reflection of the unattainable ideal of passive, saintly womanhood. Rather, she appeared to represent a positive, practical example that could be followed.[7]

In her study of female members of the Russian intelligentsia, Barbara Alpern Engel sees a tension, perhaps even a contradiction, between the woman's desire for self-realization and the goal of service to the people.[8] There was, however, a belief in the late nineteenth century that any conflict between the two would be overcome, or reconciled, through rational egoism: in the pursuit of self-interest, women and men would inevitably pursue the best interests of society as well. This notion of rational egoism can be traced back to the "father" of Russian socialism, Alexander Herzen. In the middle of the nineteenth century, before the abolition of serfdom, he had written that in Russia "the individual has always been crushed, absorbed, . . . engulfed in the state, dissolved in the community".[9] He recognized the importance of the individualistic ethic, but did not advocate simply abandoning the Russian tradition of communitarianism for a western stress on the individual. For Herzen the future lay with the peasantry, freed from serfdom, whose commune had "preserved the Russian people from Mongol barbarism, from Imperial civilisation, from the Europeanised landowners, and from German bureaucracy".[10]

Though he wrote about the commune in a rather romantic way, Herzen did not idealize the peasantry. He acknowledged that peasant women for the most part led an oppressed life, and that patriarchy as well as serfdom held back the development of socialism. In his view, the future harmonious community demanded change in the position of women if Russia was to be liberated not only from the dead-weight of tsarist bureaucracy and serfdom, but also preserved from the horrors of industrial capitalism as experienced by the west. He was also impressed by western thought on the woman question, notably the German Romantics, who idealized woman's moral qualities, and the early French socialists. Of the latter, he wrote:

Firstly, they proclaim the emancipation of women – summoning them to a common task, giving them control of their own destiny, and making an alliance with them on terms of equality.

Their second dogma was the restoration of the body to credit – la réhabilitation de la char [rehabilitation of the flesh].

These mighty watchwords comprise a whole world of new relations between human beings, a world of natural and therefore pure morality.

Herzen conceded that the idea of freedom for women and the recognition of "the rights of the flesh" were mocked by many "for our minds, corrupted by monasticism, fear the flesh and fear women".[11] He sympathized with the early focus on personal life, but believed that there had to be a parallel concern with general social issues. He believed that the upbringing of upper-class women ill-prepared them for life and love, but warned against simply replacing parental tyranny with romantic love:

> Surely woman has not sought to be free from the yoke of the family, and from perpetual tutelage and the tyranny of father, husband, or brother, has not striven for her right to independent work, to learning and the standing of a citizen, only to begin all over again, cooing like a turtle-dove all her life?[12]

In his novel *Who is to blame?* (1847), Herzen portrayed the marriage bond as symbolizing antiquated notions of authority and property, which could be directly traced to the despotism of autocracy and the abasement of serfdom.[13] Yet while he championed the personal and the individual, and warned against simply substituting one set of convictions for another, Herzen's novel may have contributed to a blurring of the boundaries between the individual and society, through the identification of personal problems with the social and political system. The woman question was thus part of the general movement against authoritarianism. While the 1860s saw a stress on personal liberation among upper-class women, by the 1870s the woman question had been subsumed into the larger social question.

Given their own privileged, if politically powerless, position, caught between a hostile autocratic system and an uncomprehending mass of peasantry, the radical intelligentsia sought both purpose and identity by means of service to society. From the beginning of the woman question in Russia, a contrast (indeed, an opposition) was drawn between the individual and the social aspects of the question, between the supposed selfishness of the former and altruism of the latter. Herzen's novel had asserted the moral superiority of women, but there was still no clear idea of what woman's role in society should be, nor of how to achieve change in what it was. What was clear was that gentry women, no less than the men, owed a debt of service to the people. Moreover, from the 1840s and even more so from the 1860s, radical writers such as Herzen and Chernyshevskii tied the emancipation of women to the liberation of society as a whole.[14]

What did upper-class women think? Ekaterina Zhukovskaia described the ideas and fantasies of many young gentry women like herself in the middle of the century:

> I shall establish a school, teach the children myself, talk with the peasants and try to raise their consciousness. My husband and I will read the best works on agriculture, and buy machinery for the peasants. And how I shall love my husband for helping me do all this![15]

More realistic was Mariia Vernadskaia, who took up the issue of economic independence for women in the late 1850s. She linked economic and job opportunities to the need to improve women's education. She stressed the liberating aspects of employment for upper-class women, whose subservience, she felt, stemmed from the fact that the economic responsibility for the family fell solely on the man. To be independent and socially useful, a woman had to have a job, which meant that she would also have to fight against the deeply engrained prejudices that condemned such a public role for women. Vernadskaia refused to accept the usual justification – in her view, excuse – that the mother had to stay at home to care for her children. She maintained that, in practice, a great deal of the upper-class woman's time was devoted to trivia, and she exhorted women to study, think, work and stand on their own two feet, just as men did. Useful work would command respect, and lead to the emancipation of women from the yoke of sexual prejudice.[16]

Vernadskaia's writings anticipated the economic dislocation that the 1861 emancipation of the serfs would entail for gentry women (which will be discussed in Chapter 4). She linked sexual equality to economic progress, and insisted that besides a better education, upper-class women needed the will to work. She was also responding to the debate on female education that had been prompted by the recent Crimean war, and the article "Questions of Life" written by N.I. Pirogov, a noted surgeon and pedagogue who had organized women nurses during the conflict.[17] As part of his consideration of the relationship between education and the condition of Russian society, Pirogov insisted that upper-class women had to be educated for the realities of life, and taught to think for themselves. He argued that Russian society could no longer afford to place these women on a pedestal, and though he still saw their main role in life as that of wife and mother, he believed that the scope of their education had to be broadened to include the natural sciences and pedagogical training.[18] His article was widely read among the literate minority, and held to be deeply influential.[19] Along with Vernadskaia's writings, Pirogov certainly struck a chord with upper-class women in the 1860s. The student Elizaveta Yunge derided the "empty" lives, the endless social round of frivolous pleasure, which was expected of young ladies, and lamented how difficult it was to break away from all previous conditioning and view the world critically. Yunge saw those women like herself who struggled to get a serious education as idealists, striving to acquire useful skills, especially medical, so that they could devote themselves to the people.[20]

Thus in the mid nineteenth century, there was a coming together of three major themes of the woman question in Russia: the idealization of unselfish devotion, of self-sacrifice, by women for the good of others; the proposition that, to be independent, women must work outside the home; and the implication that these privileged women could not just work for themselves, but owed service to the people. These ideas were developed by the radical writer M.L. Mikhailov in the early 1860s, who argued that the superficial education of upper-class women actually undermined whatever talents they might have had, and rendered them unfit even to carry out those domestic tasks consigned to them by conservatives. Mikhailov believed that equal education with men, and not just the limited reforms suggested by Pirogov, would make women capable of many things, within both the family and society at large.[21]

The intellectual, social and political turmoil of the 1860s stimulated the campaign for the entry of women into higher education. The need for inexpensive personnel to carry through the tsar's reforms provided a responsive context for the campaign.[22] Given the disillusionment with the 1861 emancipation settlement, purely feminist goals were considered selfish, even by those gentry in difficult financial straits. Personal fulfilment would be found through public service. Nevertheless, radical women realized that they suffered specific disadvantages. Thus in the early 1870s, the Russian female students in Zurich formed a women's circle (the Fritsche) because they recognized that as a result

24

of women's lack of experience in public debate, men tended to dominate in study groups. The Fritsche felt that women had to develop confidence and skills through study and discussion among themselves, away from male competition and authority.[23] They still insisted that the emancipation of women could be achieved only through social revolution.

Women and social revolution

This absence of concern with women's political rights in a period when female suffrage was being demanded, albeit by a minority, in western Europe and north America, was partly owing to the Russian situation in which the lack of political rights was shared by women and men. It was also because critics of tsarism, reformist and revolutionary alike, thought in social rather than political terms. The 1861 statute outlining the details of the emancipation of the serfs had tried to cater for the development of an industrial economy (necessary if Russia was to remain a great power) while maintaining the great landed estates and ensuring social stability. Not only had the peasant commune been preserved, it had been strengthened: after 1861, ownership of land was vested not in the individual peasant or even in the family, but in the commune, which was given many responsibilities of local government, including collection of taxes and provision of military conscripts. To avoid the problems of a massive dislocation of over 20 million ex-serfs from farming, the peasants were liberated with land; but what they were given was deliberately insufficient in most cases to support a family and meet the communal responsibilities. In addition, the former serfs had to pay their former masters for their plots which, together with the weight of government taxation, meant a huge and growing burden of peasant debt. Hence the peasants had a continuing stake in the land, but were under pressure to send at least some of their numbers to work outside the commune. Many millions migrated for work in the late nineteenth and early twentieth centuries, especially from the less fertile region of the northern provinces, providing a pool of cheap labour for rural and urban employers alike.

Thus, industrial capitalism developed in late nineteenth-century Russia alongside the pre-capitalist commune. Peasants devised ways and means to maintain their ties to the land and the commune. It was the family household and the community that counted. A common strategy, as we shall see in Chapter 4, was for the husband or eldest sons to migrate in search of work, and the wife and marriageable daughters to remain in the village. If that still provided insufficient income, then the women too were expected to contribute cash earned from the sale of farm produce and rural crafts, or by hiring out as field hands on the large estates. Women who migrated to the cities for work were those who were in some ways a drain on the peasant household: they were generally single (including widows and wives of soldiers), and either childless or with children too young to contribute labour to the farm. The plight of these women convinced critics of capitalism, both conservative and revolutionary, that it could lead to the disintegration of the peasant commune and repeat, though on a much larger scale, the evils of western industrialization and urbanization. Women, therefore, came to represent both the hope for the preservation of the commune, and the threat of its disintegration. For radicals such as Chernyshevskii, the commune had to be not so much preserved as improved if Russia was to avoid social misery on a vast scale. Sexual equality was integral to that improvement.

Progress was seen in moral terms. By the late nineteenth century the general assumption among the Russian intelligentsia was that women had special moral qualities that society needed but could benefit from only through a revolution in the position of women. The woman question was seen as part of the whole, essential but not so pressing as other problems. Chernyshevskii's question, "what is to be done?", stimulated thousands of young upper-class women and men a decade later to "go to the people" (v narod) by living and working among the peasants. One of these was Vera Figner, a member of the Fritsche circle who saw the goal of her personal development as the good of the society.[24] The failure of that movement of students to the people, partly a result of police harassment, but also partly due to the refusal of the peasants to accept the radical intelligentsia whom they distrusted as outsiders, did not diminish Figner's belief in the need for a transformation of society. If anything, it gave it a greater sense of urgency. Moving on from piecemeal reform, she recorded that those women who developed a revolutionary consciousness turned away from personal concerns for education and a profession towards dedication to social revolution. The former, for Figner, was merely a palliative, "a small patch on a dress which should not be mended, but rather should be discarded and replaced with a new one".[25] Hence she renounced personal ambitions for the cause of the masses.

Figner and her contemporaries, such as Sof'ia Perovskaia, had begun by seeing the way to transform society as starting from the bottom, eschewing politics for medicine and teaching. With their male comrades, their focus remained social rather than political change, in which they would assist the common people (*narod*) to realize their goals. The hostility or indifference of the peasantry to this idealism of their social superiors, and the frustration of the latters' efforts by the tsarist authorities, intensified the radical intelligentsia's sense of alienation. After that initial setback, they tried to reach the peasants indirectly, through those migrants who left the village for work in the factories. Ironically, however, this meant that members of the intelligentsia abandoned their recently acquired professional skills, and disguised themselves as workers. Ironically, too, they found that women migrant workers were the most resistant tó their revolutionary message, which the infiltrators put down to the low level of female culture and literacy as well as the material conditions under which they laboured. In practice, it was the female revolutionaries who had gone into the factories in the mid 1870s who found those conditions too difficult to endure for more than a few months at most.[26]

It was the failure to bridge the gulf between themselves and the masses which convinced Figner and her comrades that the people were simply suffering too much to be able to respond positively to their propaganda. Government repression, with the arrest and exile of thousands of young students, forced the revolutionaries to pay attention to the question of organization, resulting in the establishment in 1878 of a society called "Land and Liberty" (*Zemlia i volia*). The revolutionaries worried about the developing industrial system, fearing that unless it was interrupted by a social revolution, Russia would go the way of the west, with the destruction of the peasant commune through industrialization and urbanization, and all the attendant problems. Hence, Figner reasoned, they had to act quickly by striking at the heart of the political system through acts of terrorism.[27] This turn to terrorism led to a split in Land and Liberty, and the establishment of a terrorist wing (People's Will, or *Narodnaia Volia*) of the revolutionary movement.

While terrorism was a political weapon, their goal remained social revolution. Figner's comrade, Sof'ia Perovskaia, was one of the five terrorists executed in 1881 for the assassination of the tsar, Alexander II. That act did not precipitate the revolution which they had expected, while their organization, People's Will, was severely weakened as the authorities moved against it in defence of the established order. Figner concentrated on reviving the People's Will, but was soon arrested and spent many years in tsarist prisons, 13 of them in solitary confinement (from 1883 until 1904 when she was sent into exile). The influence of such women on the revolutionary movement is often held to be profound.[28] That influence must have stemmed from the example of their personal self-sacrifice and high moral standards, rather than any political achievement.

Often held out as the model for the female terrorists in the 1880s was Vera Zasulich who in 1878 had attempted to assassinate the governor of St Petersburg, General Trepov, in outrage at the savage flogging of a political prisoner simply for not removing his cap in the General's presence. What was startling about the case was that Zasulich was lauded as a heroine in Russia, and the governor a cruel monster. Moreover, the previous repression (1869–72) which she had suffered through imprisonment and solitary confinement, merely on suspicion, was accepted as partial explanation, and in mitigation, of her action. To widespread astonishment, Zasulich was found innocent by the jury. Her act of violence was seen as symbolizing society's indignation at the brutalities of arbitrary rule, personified in General Trepov. She quickly had to emigrate to escape re-arrest. Once abroad, her political studies led her away from terrorism to Marxism, but at the time, she had seen no alternative to the assassination attempt: "I decided, even at the cost of my own life, to prove that one cannot be sure of going unpunished in thus violating the human personality".[29] Her one act of terrorism had not been meant as a catalyst for the overthrow of tsarism, but rather to bring into the open the mistreatment of political prisoners. The shooting of the governor-general had been meant as a moral act, to publicize state brutality. Zasulich saw terrorism as an isolated, individualistic action, no alternative to sustained work building a mass movement; possibly even an obstacle to that end, since it provided the government with justification for repression and the means to widen the gulf between the revolutionaries and the people.

Nevertheless, she still supported the People's Will in 1881. By this time, Russian revolutionaries who hoped that the peasant commune would preserve Russia from the horrors of western-style capitalism were influenced by the writings of Karl Marx. It was a reciprocal relationship, explored recently by James D. White in his study of Marx and the Russians. White records correspondence between Zasulich in Geneva and Marx in London in 1881, in which Zasulich asked Marx's opinion on the commune. He replied that it could serve as the basis for a socialist society, but only if the economic, and especially the tax, pressures on it were removed.[30] Few in Russia were aware of Marx's thought on the commune, while the revolutionary movement fragmented between those who considered themselves Marxists and assumed that the peasant commune would, indeed must, disintegrate as capitalism developed, and those whom they dismissed as "populists" (Narodniks), that is socialists who continued to put their faith above all in the peasantry.

Among the latter were the terrorists, who included a small minority of upper-class women. Besides sharing a determination to be of service to society with their non-terrorist peers, both Narodnik and Marxist, the terrorists seem to have felt a greater sense of urgency. The question facing the radical and reforming intelligentsia as a whole remained: what are we to do? It was taken as the title of an article written by the famous and revered novelist, Lev Tolstoy, published in 1886, in which he criticized the ruling class for its parasitic existence and called on the intelligentsia to share its knowledge with the masses. Five years earlier, Tolstoy had appealed to Alexander III to commute the death sentences on the revolutionaries who had assassinated his father, Alexander II. Also in the early 1880s, Tolstoy had gained first hand knowledge of the conditions of the poor in Moscow when he ran a school for peasant children on his estate, and then when he organized aid to the peasantry after the disastrous harvest of 1891. He condemned individualism, believing it an evil that only dedication to the people would transcend. Ironically, while he rejected the established order, Tolstoy did not embrace the revolutionary cause. He opposed violence, and in "What are we to do?", he criticized the capitalist system, in particular the division of labour, while idealizing the traditional peasant way of life, including patriarchy. Despite inveighing against "progress" and women's liberation, Tolstoy's writings held a strong appeal because of their passionate denunciation of the existing system.

The article "What are we to do?" was in the form of a reply to a group of young female students in Tiflis who had written to the great writer for advice. He reminded them of their duty to educate the people, and suggested that in the meantime they could do some immediate practical work by assisting in correcting and proof-reading inexpensive literature which was very popular among the literate working class. This literature consisted of both Russian and translated foreign works.

Eighteen years of age in 1887 and not yet a Marxist, Nadezhda Krupskaia was moved to respond to Tolstoy:

> Recently I began to feel more and more acutely how much effort and energy was used up by so many people for me to benefit from the fruits of their labour. I used them partially to accumulate knowledge which I thought I could later pass on to help others. But now I see that others may not need the knowledge which I have acquired, and that anyway I do not know how to use it to redress the wrong I have committed by doing nothing. I don't even know where to start. . . . When I read your letter to the young women of Tiflis I was so glad. I realise that proof-reading books which will be read by so many people is an important task.[31]

Proof-reading was hardly a guaranteed means of either reaching the masses directly or raising their consciousness, especially since much of the literature which was popular was for entertainment rather than enlightenment. Krupskaia's request for some books on which to begin work elicited a copy of Alexander Dumas' *The Count of Monte Cristo*. Krupskaia went on to study Marxist literature and joined the RSDLP. Not known as a feminist, and probably best known as Lenin's wife, Krupskaia seemed typical of so many socialist women who insisted on working-class solidarity while acknowledging the need for special efforts to be made both to include women in the political struggle and to improve their position in society. Such women were not fighting for the rights of women only, but for rights which neither men nor women in Russia possessed. For Krupskaia, as for Zasulich, participation in the revolutionary movement would bring sexual equality. As Zasulich wrote in 1892:

> In the 1870s women revolutionaries ceased to be exceptional phenomena. In their persons, ordinary women – a whole network of such women – achieved a good fortune seldom attained in history: the possibility of acting in the capacity not of inspirers, wives and mothers of men, but in complete independence, as equals with men in all social and political activities.[32]

Zasulich lamented that so few working-class women were involved in the labour movement. She believed that the female intelligentsia – not

only revolutionaries, but students, doctors, and teachers – would undermine the patriarchal prejudices held by the majority, women as well as
men, through their example of economic independence and political
activity. In her view, the prejudice that "considers a woman by nature
more foolish, weaker, and more cowardly than a man must disappear,
as well as the view that a woman by nature is incapable of public
activity and that, because of this, only domestic obligations, not public
ones, must be her lot".[33] In contrast to Krupskaia, whose first publication was *The Woman Worker* (1901), Zasulich did not believe there
was a need for special work among women; but in common with
other socialist women, Zasulich held that only when economic equality
between the sexes was achieved could women be considered the true
equals of men.

Organizing women workers

By the 1880s, those economic changes that the radicals of the People's
Will had feared and which Marx had identified as undermining the
commune were underway, accelerating in the 1890s. Under Sergei Witte,
Minister of Finance from 1893, industrialization "took off" concentrating on expanding railways and heavy industry, predominantly male
areas of work. Within the revolutionary movement by this time there
was an ongoing, and sometimes bitter debate, between those socialists
who looked to the peasants, and those influenced by the growth of
industry and by the ideas of Marx on the development of capitalism in
the west. Ironically, as noted above, Marx's sympathies with the former
were not widely known. Those Russian followers who understood from
his work that capitalism was inevitable tended to dismiss the peasantry
as a backward class which would become obsolete as industrialization
progressed. Yet since the peasantry remained by far the largest single
social group in Russia into the twentieth century, and peasant culture
proved so tenacious and helped shape the attitudes of urban workers,
Marxists could not in practice simply ignore the village. The problem
for all socialists remained: how to raise the consciousness of the lower
orders, workers as much as peasants? At least among the former, there
was a minority of educated, skilled workers who might prove receptive
to revolutionary ideas. That meant that Marxists tended to focus the
bulk of their attention on skilled male factory workers. As we shall see

in Chapter 4, there were few skilled women workers. Nevertheless, both the legacy of Russian radical thought and the influence of Marxism on the woman question led revolutionaries from the 1880s to pay some attention at least to women workers. While some revolutionaries associated the separate organization of women with feminism, and generally saw feminism as divisive, the growing numbers of women workers, especially during periods of economic and political crisis, forced them to consider ways of drawing women into the struggles of their class. Marxism identified the living peasant inheritance of patriarchy as a barrier to progress.

Like the female peasantry, women workers were considered by government, employers, liberals, feminists and revolutionaries alike, to be the most backward and passive of their class. Like the peasantry, too, they were not completely passive, but at times were prepared to take action, usually spontaneous and direct, notably in the textile strikes of the mid 1890s and the revolution of 1905. Nevertheless, they were also seen by employers as docile enough to be used to replace male workers where feasible (for example, through a process of mechanization and dilution of skills), which encouraged the latter to feel under threat from the perceived incursion of women into what had been considered masculine territory. Social Democrats, then, had a double-sided concern: that women would act to hold back working-class men's political consciousness, and that women would divide the labour movement. Hence, despite a persistent resistance to the idea of special work among women, from the early 1890s Social Democratic revolutionaries had been doing precisely that – though on a small scale, and often against the wishes of their comrades, female as well as male.

In the late 1880s, Social Democratic circles had been established in various cities of Russia which were organized by the student M.I. Brusnev, and survived for three years (1889–92). Though Brusnev was from the intelligentsia, his main aim was the development of a working-class movement led by workers themselves. The job of the intelligentsia, in his view, was to provide whatever educational and organizational assistance was necessary to equip workers to lead their own movement. The stress was on unity, between unskilled and skilled, women and men. The women were considered to be starting from a lower cultural base than the men, requiring special efforts to reach them.[34]

At first, these circles had been attended by men only, but by the end of 1890 a few female workers had joined. These women were then helped by the male workers and the intelligentsia to set up women-only circles in an effort to attract those who would not otherwise have attended a mixed-sex group. It was in St Petersburg that the first significant effort to win over women was made, with the establishment of circles directed mainly at female textile workers, but open to women in other industries as well as the service sector. Among the works studied in these circles was Chernyshevskii's *What is to be done?* and the poetry of Nekrasov, as well as political and economic texts.[35] Besides textile workers, women drawn into the Brusnev circles included seamstresses, women from dye works, housemaids and women who had been brought up in foundling homes as illegitimate children. Young women in particular took a full part in building the circles: "young, healthy and lively, we attracted male workers. Our meetings took on a social character. With many young girls, love matches occurred".[36] The Brusnev circles did not last long, having been crushed by 1892, while the attitudes towards women displayed by the male members was not representative of the working-class as a whole. Nevertheless, it set a precedent for special organizational efforts directed at women, with the aim of integrating them within the wider revolutionary movement. Women who went on strike in the mid 1890s, including tobacco and textile workers, were encouraged by revolutionaries to join study circles once their protest was over.[37]

Although accounting for a tiny minority of the female workforce, the circles by the twentieth century had attracted a number of women workers who would play an important role in drawing more women into the labour movement. One of them, Anna Boldyreva, was among the very few women elected to the Petersburg soviet, the council for workers that developed from the 1905 Revolution. Another, Vera Karelina, was instrumental in organizing at least a thousand women in support of the Petersburg Assembly of Factory and Mill Operatives in 1904, whose demonstration in January 1905 provided the catalyst for the revolution. As a textile worker, Karelina understood the fears of working-class women whose husbands seemed to move away from the family as their education improved and their political interests grew through attendance at Sunday schools and study circles. Few were married to men who encouraged and supported their wives to follow their examples, in contrast to Karelina and Boldyreva. Though critical of male workers' attitudes towards female comrades, Karelina still believed that the interests of both were fundamentally the same.[38]

Herself a worker, wife of a worker and a mother, Karelina did not suffer from the same outsider status associated with the upper-class revolutionaries, although the fact that she had sought a political education and was dedicated to the labour movement put some distance between herself and the other women workers. Their immediate concern was their families, and they feared the impact of strikes and demonstrations. They tended to be critical of any action which their husbands might take that would lead to the loss of pay, or of job. That conservatism convinced some Marxists at least that they had to try to reach the women, if only to neutralize their influence on their men. How was that to be done, when so much propaganda and agitational work was carried out in that male haven, the tavern? Some took jobs as teachers in Sunday schools and evening classes.

As for circle work, teaching in Sunday schools required a great deal of effort in order to reach a few workers. More men than women attended, owing to the latters' domestic commitments and lower levels of literacy. Again, as for the study circles, some of those propagandists who infiltrated Sunday schools recognized the need to make special efforts to attract women, who were keenly aware of their ignorance, and afraid to speak out in public. Starting from a base of illiteracy, it took some time before they could be introduced to political pamphlets. The women who attended Sunday schools began to spread the ideas to which they were being introduced among their co-workers. By the mid 1890s, the focus of propaganda was on the conditions in which the workers found themselves, making the revolutionary ideas directly relevant: the long hours at work, the low pay, the lack of concern on the part of the owner and managers for health and safety, the job insecurity, and the abuse and insults from foremen. The latter included sexual exploitation of women workers, while their conditions of work and living made coping with pregnancy and motherhood extremely difficult.

Sunday schools offered direct contact between the intelligentsia and the workers. In the light of the very low educational level of workers, especially women, the numbers reached in this way had to be small if they were to achieve both literacy and political consciousness. Since female experience of schooling was generally inferior to that of men, women were usually taught separately. Generally, it was younger women, with few domestic responsibilities, who went to the literacy classes and the study circles, already with a desire to widen their horizons. The young intelligentsia who wanted to teach in study circles and Sunday schools, however, did not always have the appropriate skills or personal attributes. Krupskaia, who as we have seen was a Marxist revolutionary by the end of the century, had become involved in the Brusnev group in 1889, but had had her request to lead one of the circles refused. She explained that:

> Such illegal circles were few and far between. In fact there were more people wishing to lead a circle than there were circles available. Thus I, a quiet, shy young woman who had only just begun to understand Marxism, could hardly hope to get one.[39]

Krupskaia realized that she had to find other ways of reaching the workers, and began to teach in Sunday schools devoted to the education of the latter. From 1891 to 1896, she taught in a number of such schools located in working-class districts of Petersburg. Other revolutionary women set up circles among particular groups of workers, both male and female; but their experiences were not always as positive as Krupskaia's. Their youth, their inexperience and their sex as well as their social class background made them stand out among the workers, who did not always take them seriously. Moreover, police surveillance and repression meant that any contacts the intelligentsia made with the workers tended to be of a brief duration.

These various efforts to reach and educate workers received a boost in 1896 with the wave of textile strikes, which encouraged revolutionaries to turn from such small deeds of propaganda, to mass agitation. The labour movement attracted even unskilled workers, including women, particularly in the tobacco and confectionary industries. The response of the tsarist authorities included an attempt by the secret police chief in Moscow, Sergei Zubatov, to control the workers' movement under his jurisdiction by establishing unions. This experiment was ended in 1902 when it was clear that the police had lost control.[40] The secret police was much more successful at infiltrating and suppressing than initiating organizations. What is interesting here is that Zubatov's unions attracted women (though in a minority) as well as men.

Economic depression at the end of the century and the swift repression of any attempt by workers to organize, whether in trade unions or study circles, resulted in a downturn in the labour movement that lasted until the 1905 Revolution. Economic problems continued until around 1910, while the tsar sought to strengthen his hold on power by stepping up political repression from around 1907, frustrating hopes for the development of a constitutional order. In any case, the majority of women workers still tended to stay aloof from the labour movement, which they considered as mainly concerned with the situation of male workers, who in turn looked down on them as incapable of organization, or even seeing beyond the machine in the factory and the stove at home.

There had also been a few efforts to raise the consciousness of male workers regarding their female counterparts. Memoirs of skilled male workers reveal a strong degree of condescension, and even hostility, towards women workers whom they considered a drag on their political and cultural development.[41] To counteract this attitude, a pamphlet devoted to the position of women workers under capitalism was written for study in the workers' circles of the mid 1890s. It described the particularly harsh conditions of labour and life for women who were given such low pay (between a third and a half of the average male wage, though there was no call for equal pay) that for many prostitution was a necessary supplement to ensure them basic subsistence. In the workplace, they were vulnerable to sexual abuse, while the heavy physical labour, unsanitary and unsafe working conditions, lack of maternity benefits and prevalence of venereal disease contributed to a high rate of infant mortality. The pamphlet noted that few women workers had any hope of regular marriage, since so many of the men had families back in the village.

The pamphlet tried to link the oppression of women as a sex to that as a class, arguing that capitalism used machinery not to improve conditions for workers, but to force wages down, increase competition for jobs, and divide the workers between women and men, skilled and unskilled. The only way out was to struggle against the employers as a united class, with women joining and being active in trade unions.[42] There were few such pamphlets published in Russia devoted to the situation of women workers (and this one was written by a man). Then in 1901 Krupskaia's pamphlet, *The Woman Worker*, was published in the west. Though mainly concerned with urban women, it also considered the position of female peasants. In addition, the writings on the woman question by the leading German Social Democrat, Clara Zetkin, founder of International Women's Day, were studied in the Russian workers' circles of the 1890s. Another key text circulating among those who attended workers' circles in the early twentieth century was still Chernyshevskii's *What is to be done?* Alexandra Artiukhina, a worker who attended Social Democratic clubs for women workers in 1907, later joined the Bolshevik Party and participated in the 1917 revolution, wrote that:

> When we started to attend the Sunday and evening schools, we began to make use of books from the library and we learned of the great Russian democrat, Chernyshevskii. We read his book, *What is to be done?*, secretly, and found the image of Vera Pavlovna, the woman of the future, very attractive.[43]

That novel seems to have had a seminal influence on Russian revolutionaries, with Lenin even taking it as the title for the work of 1902 which outlined his vision of an organization of professional revolutionaries, the party that eventually attracted Artiukhina. Hence, thinking on the woman question among revolutionaries was influenced by both western and Russian writings.

Of the former, the German Social Democrat August Bebel's *Women under Socialism* (1879) seems to have been particularly influential for the later ideas of Alexandra Kollontai on the woman question. An active revolutionary from the late 1890s, she joined the Bolshevik Party in 1915, and played a significant role in the organization of women workers during the revolution. She wrote a laudatory preface to the 1918 Russian edition of Bebel's work, which she termed the woman's "bible", laying a solid foundation of knowledge for the socialist women's movement.[44] Kollontai claimed that before the publication of Bebel's work, women had tended to take what amounted to a bourgeois position. She believed that Bebel's contribution was a clear exposition of the class basis of the woman question, showing that the position of women was historically and not naturally determined, and that only through a socialist revolution would women be liberated. While the women's movement should, in Bebel's opinion, always be part of the general socialist movement, he stressed that the latter must recognize that women suffered a double-edged oppression, being sexually as well as economically exploited. To Kollontai's frustration, it tended to be the first part of his argument that most Russian Marxists accepted, at the expense of the second.

The new woman

By the turn of the century, socialist efforts were increasingly concentrated on arguing over whether or not Russia was a capitalist society. Kollontai appeared to accept that capitalism already existed in Russia. She developed the Marxist view of the impact of industrialization on women: despite the disadvantages, it offered them the only way to raise their consciousness and make them independent of the family. Kollontai believed that working-class women grew aware of their needs only when they became an integral part of the labour force. Kollontai's "new woman" was conscious of herself as a social being, as a member of a community based on trust and solidarity. Previously, woman had been chained to the home and the husband through her economic dependency. With the development of capitalism, the "weaker" sex was unceremoniously thrown onto an extremely arduous, thorny path for which she had had no preparation, an unknown road leading her into new forms of subjection through the system of wage-slavery.[45]

The developing economy in the late nineteenth century had needed women to provide additional labour power, and serve as a cheap and reserve, indeed alternative, pool of labour to male workers. Besides the hostility of the latter to what they perceived as female competition for their jobs, Kollontai pointed to the contradictions women faced in their triple burden of worker, housewife and mother. While demands for women's rights could be traced back to the French Revolution of 1789, Kollontai believed that it was the tremendous upsurge of industrialization and urbanization in Russia since the 1890s that revealed the essential role of women in the economy, and which was then confirmed by the impact of the First World War.

Hence, Kollontai claimed that the new woman was essentially the "child of the large-scale capitalist system". She was compelled by the "scourge of hunger" to adjust rapidly to the changing economic conditions of developing industry, experiencing at first hand the struggle of her class. Her prime duty lay with the collective and not the individual family. She saw the sexual division of labour, in the sense of men being associated with productive work and women with work in the family home, as the root cause of female inferiority, and one that predated capitalism. She did not challenge that division of labour in the home, assuming that mechanization of housework and the replacement of the isolated labour of housewives by public services and collective living would suffice to ensure female equality.

Kollontai admitted that the new woman attempted to cling to the past, but saw her as being torn from it by the "dark satanic mills" that forced the development in her of a new consciousness, of an independent personality. Expelled from the womb of the old family, deprived of its customary protection and authority over her, and catapulted into the class struggle, the new woman would refuse to be submissive.[46] She would not wait for the transformation of her position by the revolution, but instead would struggle alongside men for the good of her class, and not just herself. The harsh reality of capitalism demanded entirely different characteristics from passivity and gentleness, such as determination, toughness and activity, previously seen as masculine traits. Before capitalism, Kollontai held, the main axis of a woman's life had revolved around marriage. The growth of industry made imperative a break from the traditional dominance of the family. Kollontai associated romantic love with progress and the development of the economy, but like Herzen regretted that it led women to focus increasingly on their emotions, especially those who remained within the home, clinging to the male breadwinner. Material dependence on men rendered women helpless, forcing them to structure their relations with men in such a way as to ensure security. The new woman would experience marriage as a form of imprisonment.[47] Rather than submit to the "tyranny" of emotion, the new woman must demand respect from men, and consideration as their equal.

Kollontai acknowledged the power of the past over the new woman. It was an extremely difficult task to throw off the education of centuries that taught women to see men as their masters, to renounce dependence, emotional as well as material, on men.[48] Nor would the ideal of independence and equality be achieved under capitalism, though it was essential to begin the struggle now. In Kollontai's view, revolution alone was not enough to attain the desired "harmony and spiritual closeness, a union of love with freedom, and a union of comradeship with material independence". What was also necessary was that women and men should transform their ways of thinking, and create a new psyche, as part of the revolutionary struggle. Women should learn not to be submissive, and men not to insist on female subservience. Work and not emotion should be the driving force of the woman's life, as of the man's.[49] Hence, while the class struggle took precedence, Kollontai insisted that women's oppression was sexual as well as economic, and that the emancipation of women had to be a vital facet of the class struggle, and could not simply wait for the overthrow of capitalism.

Kollontai claimed that not only was the working-class woman's struggle to assert herself coincident with her class interests, but that it was seen to be so by her class. She saw sexual equality within the working class as based on an instinctive principle of solidarity. Inequality between women and men undermined the labour movement, helping capital to exploit workers by playing off the former against the latter, giving men a spurious sense of superiority and thus a vested interest in the established order that oppressed them.[50] Yet in practice, Kollontai did not pay as much attention to the need for a change in male attitudes to women, as if she saw the inferiority of the woman as more of an obstacle to overcome than the superiority of the man.

According to Kollontai, the woman of the middle class had a more difficult time than the working-class woman, because the former came up against the hostile ideology of her own class, which insisted that the woman's place was in the home. The middle-class woman's struggle, therefore, was against her class, whereas the struggle of the working-class woman was the same as that of her class. Kollontai did not romanticize the lives of working-class women. She wrote of the terrible working conditions, the abysmal poverty, below subsistence pay, and the domination of men. She regarded the sometimes brutal attitude of working-class men towards women as a legacy of their recent peasant past. She firmly believed that the increasing numbers of women earning a living outside the home was contributing to the creation of a new psyche, by giving them confidence and independence.[51] Her idealization of working-class solidarity led her to underestimate the strength both of the peasant culture that shaped the development of urban society, and of the traditional family, however much urban conditions may have modified both. Kollontai saw the peasant woman as a possible agent for revolution in the countryside, while her new woman was the creature of an industrialized society. In practice, peasant women sought to preserve their traditional way of life, while the harsh urban reality was that working-class women often earned barely enough to survive, as we shall see in Chapter 4. It was more often among the privileged classes, from which Kollontai sprang, that the new woman was to be found.

Kollontai's ideas on the woman question were presented to the first feminist congress in St Petersburg in 1908. Because Kollontai had to go abroad to escape arrest, her speech was delivered by a member of the women workers' club she had set up in Petersburg the previous year. Until the 1905 Revolution, Russian feminists had concentrated on providing charitable and educational works for needy gentry women in particular, with a view to finding them respectable employment. While there was considerable development in the provision of higher education for women from the 1870s, only a minority of women were affected. Moreover, radical women such as Vera Figner quickly concluded that the feminist campaigns excluded the majority of women, and that only the overthrow of tsarism could solve the widespread social problems.[52] Ironically, once tsarism was overthrown in February 1917, Figner sided with the feminists in supporting the new government's decision to remain in the war against Germany, which Kollontai and her Bolshevik comrades denounced.

Even the feminists in the late nineteenth century were not interested in political rights. They were aware of developments in the feminist movement in the west, and in contact with a number of leading advocates of women's rights, including Josephine Butler, the English suffragist and campaigner against legalized prostitution.[53] Like feminists elsewhere, the Russians campaigned to change the established order from within. They organized on a variety of social and cultural issues, including the improvement of education at all levels, widening job opportunities, "rescuing" women deemed to be in moral danger, rehabilitating prostitutes, raising the age of consent to sex as well as the age at which a woman could register as a prostitute (with the ultimate aim of ending the system of registration). Feminists not only lobbied government ministers and influential people, they supported many practical philanthropic activities aimed at helping girls and women, such as providing cheap accommodation for female workers, helping to establish schools, work co-operatives (such as for book-binding and translating) and crèches for workers' children, and supporting Sunday schools. However, all these efforts depended on the tsar's approval, which could be withdrawn at any time. Slowly, feminists, notably Anna Shabanova in the Mutual Philanthropic Society (set up in 1895), began to see the need for political rights; indeed, as the male liberals called for a constitution, feminists worried that women would be excluded. If a constitution were granted, women would move from a certain position of equality within a patriarchal system, in which they shared with men a lack of political and civil rights, to one of inequality, in which men but not women had the vote.

It took the 1905 Revolution to provoke a small number of women (around 30) in Moscow to establish a women's union for equal rights. By 1906, the union's membership stood at 8,000. It called for universal suffrage, but was not a single-issue organization. Among its other demands were the admission of women to all areas of state service, protective legislation for women workers and equality for peasant women in any agrarian reforms.[54] Kollontai saw the union as an opportunity for promoting socialist ideas on the women question, but found herself distrusted by the feminists and criticized by the Marxists, including Vera Zasulich.[55]

Both feminists and socialists concentrated on working-class women, seeing the female peasantry as too ground down by patriarchy to respond positively. The revolution of 1905 provided opportunities to reach the former, notably in the activity around the Shidlovskii Commission, set up by the tsar in January to investigate the causes of workers' discontent. Although it sat for less than a month, before the tsar dissolved it on 20 February, the workers, female as well as male, had taken the election of representatives to the commission seriously. Women had been allowed to vote, but not to stand, which they deeply resented. Indeed, despite the bar on women representatives, a few had been selected in the first round of voting.

Women and the 1905 Revolution

Women workers' participation in the revolution of 1905 had precedents in their involvement in the widespread labour unrest of the mid 1890s. The textile industry had been the key industry experiencing militancy. Strike action did not reflect strength of trade unionism among women workers. The textile industry depended on huge numbers of mainly unskilled workers, and an extreme division of labour that prevented them both from improving their skills and developing a sense of unity, let alone a permanent organization. In any case, the secret police and the power of the mill-owners ensured the failure of the latter. Any women who showed organizational skill and leadership potential, such as Karelina, were, like their more numerous male counterparts, sacked, arrested, put under police supervision or exiled.[56] Such women proved persistent, moving from job to job and city to city, always trying to organize their sister workers, but unable to sustain their activities. Moreover, a minority of women workers, not only from the textile but also from the tobacco and confectionary industries, were drawn to the labour movement in the late nineteenth and early twentieth centuries. Karelina, after a six-month prison term in 1893, continued to pay special attention to drawing women into the class struggle and took part in the strikes of 1896–7. These were defeated, the workers' organizations crushed and the links between them and the intelligentsia severed. Economic depression in 1898 completed the rout of the labour movement. Women worker activists such as Karelina continued their efforts. As noted above, she played a key role in organizing at least a thousand lower-class women in Petersburg in 1904–5 and, with one of her Brusnev comrades, Anna Boldyreva, she was elected to the Soviet in 1905, along with five other Social Democratic women workers.[57] Karelina, however, had to withdraw because of ill-health.

Karelina seems to have been acutely aware of the need to exert special efforts to organize women workers, not only because of their backwardness but because of the patriarchal attitudes towards them held by many men, both workers and revolutionaries. Even as she stressed the necessity for class unity, she accepted that women had particular needs (related to childbearing), and grievances (notably sexual abuse in the workplace), which their male comrades either did not take seriously, or regarded as low on their list of priorities.[58] Karelina was not unique among women workers, but she was among a minority of those who sought education and pursued their own form of service to the people by committing themselves to concentrating on women workers, even as they insisted on class solidarity. The success of state repression of the strikes in the mid 1890s and the 1905 Revolution confirmed the need for the latter, while concerns for the effects of class divisions reinforced fears in the revolutionary movement of the consequences of the separate organization of women.

At the same time, assumptions about the conservatism of women workers were widespread, despite the militancy of predominantly female trades such as tailoring and dressmaking, tobacco and confectionary, thread and bindery. It was not only factory women who were involved in the 1905 Revolution, but service sector workers too, including domestic workers and most notably laundry workers, as was the case again in May 1917, which will be discussed in Chapter 6. Women in both sectors went on strike and tried to establish trade unions in 1905–6. Despite the isolated and varied nature of domestic service (including work for individual families, in restaurants, hotels, taverns and brothels), in 1906 servants' unions in various cities, such as Petersburg, Moscow and Ekaterinoslav, demanded protective legislation, not only setting limits to the hours they should work, but demanding state inspection of their employment conditions (along the lines of a factory inspectorate) and benefits (such as health and unemployment insurance, and maternity benefits).[59] Thus, during the 1905 Revolution, even those considered the most backward of workers, generally ignored by revolutionaries, showed an interest in and capacity for organization in defence of their interests. When tsarism reasserted itself in 1907 and began to claw back any concessions it had made to political and trade union activities, such initiatives were not sustained. Yet neither were they forgotten, as we shall see in Chapter 6.

Upper-class women, both feminists and revolutionaries, were also active in 1905. The former widened their scope from social issues to politics. They supported strikes by women workers, participated in activities of professional (especially teaching and medical) associations, and established organizations with political goals, including for the first time, suffrage. The feminists were divided not only over how to achieve suffrage, but over priorities. Many continued to concentrate their efforts on expanding women's opportunities in higher education and the professions. The demand for the vote was new, and was campaigned for by two feminist organizations that sprang up with the revolution, the All-Russian Union for Women's Equality and the Women's Progressive Party, as well as by the Mutual Philanthropic Society.[60] The Union for Women's Equality was set up in 1905. It was an urban organization, mainly of the liberal upper classes, such as Anna Miliukova and Ariadna Tyrkova. It admitted men.[61] Its demands included universal suffrage without discrimination (of nationality and religion, as well as sex), legal equality of the sexes, equality between peasant women and men in any land reforms, protective legislation for women workers and their inclusion in welfare legislation, and co-education at every level, from elementary to higher. Like the Marxists, the liberals insisted that the women question could only be resolved through fundamental change in the established order, which for the liberals would be when a constitution was adopted.[62] These female liberals found that their male counterparts would support the call for female suffrage in principle, but argue that in practice it was premature, and might be regarded as so extreme both by the established order and the peasantry, that it would undermine the case for a constitution. In fact, it seems that the male liberals were as afraid of the conservatism of women, especially peasant women, as of the reaction of peasant men and the ruling elite.[63] Such ambivalence led some feminists to lean towards the left, both the Socialist Revolutionaries (SRs, established in 1901, heirs to the "going to the people" movement of the early 1870s) and the Marxists.

The Mutual Philanthropic Society, established in 1895 and now under the leadership of Anna Shabanova, supported the demand for the vote, but avoided association with any particular political group and conducted its campaign in the usual way of lobbying and petitioning men in government, at all levels of administration, and in positions of influence.[64] Whereas the Union of Equal Rights at least won the support of male liberals for the principle of female suffrage, Shabanova failed to get any commitment from the governing class.

A third way, between the militancy of the liberals and the behind-the-scenes tactics of Shabanova, was tried by the feminist physician, Mariia Pokrovskaia, through her Women's Progressive Party, established at the end of 1905. This was a women-only organization, in contrast to the other two; it was liberal in its politics, but paid close attention to the situation of working-class women and advocated social reforms to improve their lot, including equal pay as well as the more usual demands for protective legislation, and provisions for maternity leave and childcare. Yet despite the interest in social reforms, Pokrovskaia refused to work with the parties of the left.

When the Duma, the new parliament, was established in 1906, women were not given the vote. All three feminist organizations continued to press for the franchise to be widened. Their campaign penetrated into the villages, and found some favourable response, especially from the female peasantry.[65] All their efforts failed, however. The tsarist authorities became more confident in resisting calls for further reform as the revolution retreated. In frustration, the feminists, liberals and socialists blamed each other. The tsar dismissed the first Duma in the summer of 1906; the feminists continued to gather signatures (including the names of a minority of peasant and working-class women) to present to the second Duma. Elected in February 1907, it had a similar fate to the first. By the third Duma (also 1907) the tsar seemed to have regained control, and with legislation that year which restricted the franchise, it was clear that female suffrage had no hope of being granted. From 1907, in the general atmosphere of political reaction, the female suffrage movement went into decline. It was also rent by divisions over tactics and priorities, co-operation with men, and political allegiances. It faced the hostility from Social Democratic women, such as Alexandra Kollontai, to any efforts to persuade working-class women to concentrate on suffrage at the possible expense of defence of the labour movement, now under threat from government repression of both trade unions and political parties.[66]

During the revolution, some Social Democratic women had tried to radicalize the suffrage movement, especially the Union for Equal Rights, from within; but most focused on party work (the production and distribution of agitational material, serving as messengers, keeping "safe" houses) and supporting strikes. The SRs did likewise, though its terrorist wing (descended from the People's Will) also responded violently to any brutal attacks on strikers or demonstrators. With their male comrades, female revolutionaries were subject to harsh physical repression, though it seems that attacks by troops and police on the latter had the additional ingredient of sexual violence.[67]

Upper-class women still participated in the terrorist movement, though it had changed since the 1880s, with an increase in the acts of terrorism and an apparent decrease in the ideological justification for such acts. By the time of the revolution, assassinations were directed not only against prominent representatives of the state, but also against a wide range of minor government officials as well as businessmen. The terrorists appear to have become effectively independent of the political party, the SRs, and even to act against the wishes of the latter. The women in particular seem to have had a very personal relationship to terrorism. One SR, Fruma Frumkina, admitted that: "I have always been strongly enticed by the idea of carrying out a terrorist act. I have thought, and still think, only of that, have longed and still long, only for that. I cannot control myself."[68] Such women were not interested in women's rights. Their terrorist acts were conceived either as revenge for a perceived injustice, or as an attempt to exploit the weakness of the established order.

While SRs such as Ekaterina Breshko-Breshkovskaia (whose revolutionary activities will be discussed in the next chapter) called for complete identification with the peasant movement, including violence, for the most part the activities of political women were peaceful and concentrated in the cities and towns. Some of the urban feminists had campaigned in the villages and attracted a few peasant women. Generally, the majority of peasant women who were active in 1905 did not call for women's rights. Even more than working-class women, they thought in terms of the family; their main preoccupation was the farm, though they showed interest in civil rights, and complained about non-payment of the allowances due to the wives of soldiers who had fought in the recent (1904) disastrous war against Japan. Nevertheless, the outcome of the revolution – limited male suffrage – angered peasant women who had seen a certain rough equality with men in their previous shared lack of civil and political rights, however patriarchal the system was: "We are able to discuss things no worse than the men. We have a common interest in all our affairs, so that the women should take part in deciding them". The women question was not a burning issue in 1905, but the revolution seems to have developed working-class and indeed peasant women's consciousness, so that, according to Kollontai, "there was no corner in which, in one way or another, the voice of a woman speaking about herself and demanding new rights was not heard."[69]

From political reaction to world war

After 1907, the revolutionary movement suffered intensified surveillance and repression, the labour movement was pushed on to the defensive, and the feminist movement retreated. Within two years, the Union for Equality had collapsed. It was the more conservative Mutual Philanthropic Society that provided an opportunity for the revival of the woman question by securing permission to hold a congress on women's issues in Petersburg in 1908. Since the defeat of hopes for the establishment of a constitutional monarchy, this was the first public forum for political discussion, and attracted men as well as women, Social Democrats as well as liberals. Though debate was limited by the presence of secret police agents, the issues tackled were varied, and there was debate and disagreement, especially between those who saw women as a single, oppressed group and those (both conservative and socialist feminists) who disputed the antagonism to men.[70]

Discussion ranged over the economic situation of women, including their access to higher and vocational education and training, and to the professions; protective legislation for factory women workers and child labour; and the legal position of married women. Fundamental disagreements between socialist and feminist women were highlighted by the speech of Kollontai, which as noted above was given on her behalf by a woman worker. In Kollontai's view, feminists were themselves part of the privileged elite, despite their lack of political rights, while by working to reform rather than destroy the system, feminists effectively acknowledged its legitimacy. She saw a huge gulf between the majority of women who were driven out of the home and into wage labour by poverty, and the minority who sought self-fulfilment through equal participation with men in the workforce and political arena.[71] Ironically, she was not fully trusted by either the feminists or her socialist comrades, with the former harbouring doubts about her sincerity, and the latter suspicions that she was advocating separatism for women workers. For her part, Kollontai saw the feminists, even when divided, as a threat to the labour movement. Despite opposition from her Social Democratic comrades, she tried to draw women workers into the class struggle by setting up separate clubs for them. The concentration in her organizational efforts and in her publications was on the material needs of women as both workers and mothers, rather than on more overtly feminist claims for equal rights. In *The Social Basis of the Woman Question*, intended for the 1908 feminist congress, but published only in 1909, Kollontai sought to draw a class line between feminists and factory workers:

> The feminists seek equality in the framework of the existing class society; in no way do they attack the basis of this society. They fight for prerogatives for themselves, without challenging the existing prerogatives and privileges . . .
>
> First of all we must ask ourselves whether a single united women's movement is possible in a society based on class contradictions . . .
>
> The women's world is divided, just as the world of men, into two camps: the interests and aspirations of one group of women bring it close to the bourgeois class, while the other group has close connections with the proletariat, and its claims for liberation encompass a full solution to the woman question . . .
>
> However apparently radical the demands of the feminists, one must not lose sight of the fact that the feminists cannot, on account

of their class position, fight for that fundamental transformation of the contemporary economic and social structure of society without which the liberation of women cannot be complete.[72]

Feminist struggles took the form of seeking change without transforming the system. Feminists often sought to prove their loyalty to the established order, notably during the First World War, to convince it that women's rights would strengthen, even purify it. For Social Democrats, although revolutionary struggle included the ideal of sexual equality, the latter could be achieved only through destroying the old order. For critics of tsarism such as Kollontai, reform was impossible because it would be at the whim of an arbitrary power: witness the disillusionment with Alexander II's reforms of the 1860s, the precarious existence of the reforms from the 1870s by which women could get higher education, and Nicholas II's retreat from constitutional reform after the 1905 Revolution. For revolutionaries, feminism was in a sense petty because it pleaded for amelioration rather than actively seeking to destroy the oppressive system. Women's emancipation was not ignored by revolutionaries; rather, it was seen as integral to the fulfilment of the whole personality to which the intelligentsia aspired, Chernyshevskii's "new women" and "new men".

Kollontai's methods in approaching and attracting women workers to the revolutionary movement were not new, though her reminiscences show that she felt like an isolated pioneer. As discussed above, literary works since the 1840s had shown awareness that women had special needs and were oppressed as women, and not simply as subjects to an absolutist state. At the time Kollontai was trying to organize women workers, they were still reading Chernyshevskii's *What is to be done?* in their study circles, and still finding inspiration in the character of Vera Pavlovna. Moreover, since the late 1880s revolutionaries had, on a limited scale, organized women workers on their own, though always with the intention of integrating them into the wider labour movement. Women workers themselves had actively participated in the strike movement of the mid 1890s and the revolution of 1905. The latter had seen the first serious efforts of women to organize themselves in trade unions. It seems that with the growth of a politicized feminist movement and the defeat of the 1905 Revolution, relations between feminists and revolutionaries had become increasingly tense. With tsarism recovering after 1907, hopes for reform faded, and co-operation with the authorities to achieve reform, favoured by the feminists, seemed increasingly futile. More than that, Social Democrats feared such collaboration might persuade women workers that revolution was unnecessary.

Ironically, while Social Democrats and feminists disputed with each other, the latter were less willing to criticize the Socialist Revolutionary Party, which was, like the RSDLP, an overwhelmingly male organization, but which, unlike the RSDLP, did not pay special attention to women workers. This was partly owing to the fact that the SR programme of 1904 called for universal suffrage, and their allies in the Duma, the Trudoviki, under the leadership of Alexander Kerensky (who was to become prime minister in the summer of 1917), were consistent supporters of calls for female suffrage. (Women finally gained the vote on equal terms with men in July 1917.) It was also because of the persistently heroic image of the terrorist women. From 1907, when the authorities cracked down on the revolutionaries, which included the execution of a considerable number of female terrorists, including Frumkina, liberal feminists, like the liberal movement in general, could not bring themselves to denounce acts of terrorism. Ariadna Tyrkova of the Union of Equal Rights and of the main liberal party, the Kadets (Constitutional Democrats), explained her implicit sympathy for terrorist actions by pointing to the intransigence of the government, the usefulness to the liberals of the threat of extremist violence against the authorities, and the liberal fear of losing electoral support.[73] It was the First World War that was to unite such terrorist heroines as Figner and Breshkovskaia with the feminists in support of the government's determination to continue the war after the fall of tsarism in February 1917, and in opposition to the Bolsheviks whose leader Lenin denounced the war and called for an immediate peace. In 1917, prominent female Bolsheviks such as Kollontai continued to make special efforts to pull women workers into the revolutionary struggle, while their attack on feminism was not only on the old grounds that it was potentially divisive to the working class, but also that its support for such a bloody conflict was destructive.

CHAPTER THREE

The making of a female revolutionary

Warning against idealizing them, Barbara Engel nevertheless concludes her study of radical female intellectuals of the nineteenth century with the assertion that they were "truly remarkable women, strong, determined and dedicated . . . [they] added a moral dimension to revolutionary politics seldom seen before or since".[1] For women as well as for men, the influences behind the choice of a career, or vocation, as a revolutionary were varied. Engel's focus was on women of the 1870s, such as Sof'ia Perovskaia, who were drawn to a kind of agrarian socialism. Others, from a later generation attracted to Social Democracy in the 1890s, such as Nadezhda Krupskaia, had been influenced in the 1880s by the ideas of the novelist and pacifist, Lev Tolstoy, rather than the People's Will. Still, while Krupskaia had not been attracted to terrorism, the examples of female terrorists had been influential in drawing women of her class into the revolutionary movement.

Mothers and daughters of the Revolution

In the person of Vera Zasulich there was a link between the terrorist and the Marxist strands of the movement. From an older generation, Zasulich (1849–1919), like Krupskaia, was born into an impoverished gentry family. One of five daughters, Zasulich's father died when she was three years old and, like Krupskaia's mother, Zasulich's future was to support herself by working as a governess (from 1867). It was the growth of a revolutionary movement which, Zasulich felt, made her the equal of any man: she, too, could dream of acting, of playing a part in the struggle.[2] Trotsky acknowledged the importance of Zasulich for the development of the Russian Marxist movement: "It was not only her heroic past that had placed Vera Zasulich in the front ranks: she had an exceedingly sharp mind, an extensive background, chiefly historical, and a rare psychological insight. It was through Zasulich that the "Group" in its day became connected with old Engels."[3]

Even before she could begin to play such a part in the struggle, she was arrested on suspicion and served two years in gaol (from 1869), followed by a period of administrative exile. That experience convinced her that Russia was one huge prison from which the only escape was to overthrow tsarism. She joined in the "going to the people" movement in the mid 1870s, but like so many of her comrades was distrusted by the peasants as a city lady who did not even have the basic domestic skills of cooking and housekeeping.[4] Her next step was a terrorist act in 1878: the attempted assassination of General Trepov, governor of St Petersburg. As noted in the previous chapter, after her unexpected acquittal and her flight to Geneva to escape further arrest, Zasulich turned to Marxism. She sought unity in the Social Democratic movement and within the working class, disapproving of the 1903 split between Bolsheviks and Mensheviks and of suggestions for the separate organization of women. She clung to the Brusnevite view of the role of the intelligentsia as the educators and assistants of the workers, who in time would take over the leadership of the revolutionary movement. She viewed feminism as divisive, and Lenin's notions of party organization as elitist. She considered the Bolshevik seizure of power in October 1917 to be premature.

While she had sympathized with the People's Will in the 1880s, Zasulich saw terrorism as politically mistaken: in her opinion, it could become an obsession, a substitute for hard work among the masses, and a convenient justification for intensified government repression. Her attack on the governor-general had been intended as a moral, rather than a political action. Ironically, it was taken by many for the latter. In general, female revolutionaries in the later nineteenth century seem to have felt a deep sense, on the one hand, of isolation from the very people they wanted to reach and, on the other, of urgency. Hence for Zasulich's contemporary, Vera Figner (1852–1942), terrorist acts were to serve as catalysts for shocking the masses into rising against their oppressors, while striking at the heart of the state.[5] When Zasulich, Perovskaia and Figner carried out their terrorist acts in the late 1870s there had seemed to be no alternative; but the next twenty years had seen economic and social changes with the spread of industrialization and urbanization, working-class militancy on a large, if not sustained, scale, the establishment of the Russian Social Democratic Labour Party (1898) with its stress on political organization, and the development of a liberal movement that pushed for reforms within the system. As pointed out in the previous chapter, there seems to have been a shift in the terrorist movement by the early twentieth century, from terrorism being seen as a prompt for a popular rising to becoming an end in itself. Acts of terrorism not only continued, they increased. Interestingly, while among the female members of the SRs (the early twentieth century successor to the Narodniks) there was still a preponderance from the upper classes, the social composition of the men who joined reflected the economic developments of the late nineteenth century, being increasingly from the urban working class, and especially recent migrants from the countryside.[6] Certainly, on the surface, women drawn to terrorism by the early twentieth century seem to have been roughly divided between the privileged and the lower orders, but those from the latter appear to have had an atypical experience of education, at secondary and even higher level, while the areas of employment of the former (including elementary school teaching, nursing and midwifery) brought them into direct contact with the widespread social misery, even as it alienated them from their own social group.[7]

Whereas the older generation of female terrorists from the 1870s seem to have become revolutionaries after studying political theories, the next generation appear to have been drawn first to action through the inspiration of their "elders". Their example of heroism was still potent enough to win women from the Social Democratic movement in the early twentieth century. Thus, for example, Irina Kokhovskaia had joined the Bolsheviks during the 1905 Revolution at the age of 17, but her admiration for the female terrorists, and especially Mariia Spiridonova, drew her to the SRs within a year. Spiridonova had been born in 1886 into an aristocratic family; in 1906, she assassinated the general who had been appointed by the tsar, Nicholas II, to lead a punitive expedition against the peasantry in Tambov. In revenge, Spiridonova had then been brutally beaten and sexually abused by soldiers, before being imprisoned. In Siberian exile for a decade from 1907, Kokhovskaia met her heroine.

Once imprisoned, some of the women turned to books, studying together literature, philosophy, theology, and the bible, rather than political theory. While early terrorists, such as Zasulich, had been influenced by Marxism, others, such as Breshkovskaia and Spiridonova, were repulsed by Marx's philosophy of materialism. Instead, they stressed morality. Some, such as Frumkina, continued to attack the state from within prison, either by assaulting its agents (in the figures of prison guards or police officers), or by trying to escape, as Spiridonova did, though without success. She was freed by the February Revolution.

In both the terrorist and Marxist movements, half the women activists were Russian, while there was a significant minority who were Jewish (by the 1905 Revolution, around 30 per cent of SR terrorist women, and almost half of Social Democrats).[8] Jewish men who were radicalized were more likely to be drawn to Marxism than terrorism, and in the context of widespread anti-semitism, the relatively high proportion of Jewish membership in the Social Democratic movement sometimes made it difficult to find acceptance among the workers. Thus, one female Bolshevik who stood for election to the executive committee of the textile workers' union after the revolution in February in 1917, was initially insulted by the male factory workers for her Jewish appearance, rather than her sex.[9]

The "grandmother" of the revolution, Ekaterina Breshko-Breshkovskaia (1844–1934), was a link between the People's Will and the Socialist Revolutionary Party.[10] She had taken part in the "going to the people" movement in the early 1870s. Although a member of the SRs by the early twentieth century, Breshkovskaia went against the leadership's policy of peaceful economic means of struggle in the countryside by advocating full support for, and participation in, peasant violence against the authorities. She won over a considerable number of younger SRs by her calls to take up arms against the state. While the debates between the Narodniks and the Social Democrats since the 1880s had centred around the question of the development of capitalism, Breshkovskaia and other SR women were repulsed by what they saw as the materialism of the Marxists. For Breshkovskaia her debt to the people, and the need to repay it immediately, took precedence over theory, programme and organization.

Although some see a spirit of equality between female and male terrorists, in which the latter greatly respected the former's total dedication to the cause of revolution, the women were seen in the traditionally reverential way of sacrificing themselves for the greater good. Moreover, among the younger generation of terrorists, that dedication has been seen as fanaticism.[11] Frumkina is one example: even when the SRs, of which she was a member, refused to condone her offer to assassinate someone, she went ahead on her own initiative. When in prison in Kiev, she tried unsuccessfully to kill the chief of police; incarcerated in Moscow four years later, in 1907, her attempt to kill a prison official led to her execution. For such women, the means seem to have become more important than the goal. On being sentenced to death for the assassination of that prominent general in 1906, Spiridonova wrote that her death would be of value to society, and that she saw it as infinitely preferable to a prison term. In the event, she was denied martyrdom through execution when the death sentence was commuted, and instead, as we have seen, spent the next decade in gaol, in Siberia.[12]

She emerged to play a key role in splitting the Socialist Revolutionaries in 1917, became leader of the Left SRs, was elected to the Petrograd Soviet and presided over the First Congress of Peasants' Soviets. In her short history of women in the soviet period (1917–91), Barbara Evans Clements points out that Spiridonova was the only woman to rise to a position of genuine leadership in a revolutionary organization, but suggests that "she may have owed her prominence to the fact that she was adored as a revolutionary martyr, a role women had played since Perovskaia's time".[13] Spiridonova's rejection of Marxist materialism did not prevent her from allying with the Bolsheviks in support of the October seizure of power. She seemed to think that it was the duty of the Left SRs to serve as the moral conscience of the revolution. Soon Spiridonova had broken with the Bolsheviks over the separate peace with the Germans in April 1918. However, another leading female Left SR, Anastasia Bitsenko, had represented her party during the negotiations with the Germans, and when the SRs rejected the peace of Brest–Litovsk, she joined the Communist Party (as the Bolsheviks had renamed themselves in 1918). Spiridonova returned to terrorism, organizing the assassination of the German ambassador to Russia, Count Mirbach, in July 1918. The Communists also denied her the supreme sacrifice of dying for her cause at the hands of the state at a time when her execution might have had a political impact. Instead, they silenced her through censorship and imprisonment more effectively than tsarist gaols had done. She is thought to have died in the years between 1937 and 1941.[14] One biographical note states that she was condemned to death by a military tribunal in 1941.[15]

Spiridonova claimed that the peasantry saw her as a mother figure, the only one to whom they could turn after the 1917 revolution.[16] In fact, she could do little, since terrorism, and in particular the attempt to assassinate Lenin in 1918 by a woman, Fanny Kaplan, who had been influenced and impressed by Spiridonova, led the Bolsheviks to crush the opposition. They suspected a plot against their government by the SRs, but like so many terrorist women Kaplan seems to have taken the initiative on her own after coming to the conclusion that "the longer Lenin lived the longer he would betray the ideals of socialism".[17] Though she is generally thought to have been the first woman executed by the Bolshevik regime, there is a suggestion that she may have survived in camps until after the Great Patriotic War.[18] Whatever her fate, Kaplan's individual act of terror precipitated the Red Terror, and the destruction of the SRs, both Left and Right.

The SR focus remained "land and freedom", but while their pre-decessors, the Narodniks, had regarded the working class as a conduit to the peasantry, the SRs increasingly appealed to the urban workers as well as the peasants, and by 1905 half the membership was working class.[19] An attempt by the Narodnik movement to reach female factory workers in the 1870s had proved short lived. Even before leaving the factories the female intelligentsia had given up on the unresponsive women and turned to agitation among the male workers.[20] In practice, the male working class was the focus of SR activity, since they were more likely than the women to have maintained ties with the villages. Moreover, the fact that the SR support among workers was in metal-working, engineering and the railways, rather than in textiles, meant that their appeal to factory women was limited. The few women workers who were drawn into the study circles of the late 1880s and early 1890s looked on the female intelligentsia in the People's Will as inspirational figures because of their selfless dedication to the cause, and not because of their political tactics. Whereas female terrorists generally eschewed personal lives, sacrificing themselves to the revolutionary cause, female Social Democrats often married and had families, and like women workers had to struggle with the demands of domestic life. In addition, while the terrorists disdained materialism, the main concerns of the workers revolved around basic material problems of subsistence. Those intellectuals who were attracted by the Marxist stress on economics thus seemed closer to the concerns of the workers. Certainly the image of the selfless female Social Democrat, quietly and doggedly busy in the background doing essential but support work for male dominated organizations whose constituents were also predominantly male, seems overshadowed by the heroines of the terrorist People's Will such as Vera Figner and Sof'ia Perovskaia, a pale reflection of the ideal of devotion to the people and abnegation of self which they so dramatically represented.

Brides of the Revolution

In *Bolshevik Women*, Barbara Evans Clements chronicles the history of the first two generations of women in the Soviet Communist Party, examining the lives of a number of "representative" women from childhood to old age. She focused particularly on Inessa Armand and Konkordia Samoilova (both of whom she describes as Marxist feminists), Elena Stasova and Evgeniia Bosh, all four of whom held important positions in the Bolshevik Party at least until the civil war; Rozaliia Zemliachka, the only woman to sit on the Council of People's Commissars under Stalin; Alexandra Artiukhina and Klavdiia Nikolaeva, two working-class women, both of whom became head of *zhenotdel*, the Communist Party's women's department, in the 1920s and whom Clements believes were more typical of the Bolshevik Party rank and file in their careers than leaders such as Armand and Stasova.[21] Clements includes, but does not provide much personal detail on, Kollontai, whose biography she had earlier published.[22] While it is difficult to disagree with her chosen representatives, it is nevertheless somewhat surprising that Krupskaia's biography was not included, of whom Clements acknowledges "no one was more important to the Bolsheviks", and even that no one "made a greater contribution to the creation and maintenance of the Bolshevik faction".[23]

In an earlier study of biographies of Bolshevik leaders, first published in French in 1969, Georges Haupt and Jean-Jaques Marie provided material on 56 party members, of whom only four were women: Nadezhda Krupskaia, Elena Stasova, Alexandra Kollontai and Larissa Reisner.[24] The main source of information had been the famous *Granat* encyclopedia, and in particular volume 41 which had been prepared for the tenth anniversary of the October Revolution.[25] The editors noted in the introduction that Lenin's life had been related by Anna Ul'ianova-Elizarova, who was not only his sister but also his close collaborator and confidante.[26] She was, as well, a revolutionary in her own right, participating for many years in the propagandistic and agitational work of the Social Democratic movement. She was arrested in July 1916, released in October, and rearrested in February 1917 on the eve of the revolution. In addition to this, and in contrast to her male comrades and family members, she had domestic responsibilities. During the First World War, she lived in Petrograd, taking care of her mother (who died in 1916), her husband and a lodger. She delivered hot meals to Lenin at Bolshevik headquarters during the October Revolution to ensure that he did not go hungry.[27] Her sister Mariia, another full-time revolutionary, took over the domestic responsibilities in Anna's absence.

Both women refused to allow either the demands of home or political repression to stop their work. After the February Revolution, Mariia and Anna participated in the production of the Bolshevik newspaper, *Pravda*, for which they also wrote. Both became members of the bureau of the Bolshevik central committee, and contributed to the special paper dedicated to women workers, *Rabotnits*a, whose publication was renewed in May, after a prolonged interruption (since 1914).[28] While their role in the revolutionary movement, compared to that of their brother, Lenin, was very much in the background, in support rather than leadership, nevertheless their political activities were crucial for the survival and effectiveness of a clandestine organization whose leader was in emigration from 1900, returning to Russia only for revolutions that had already broken out, in 1905, from which he had to retreat in 1906, and again in April 1917, from which he went into hiding in July until the eve of the Bolshevik seizure of power. In addition, even as Anna's life reveals the persistent division of labour between the sexes, in which the home was seen as the woman's domain, it also confirms the continuing importance of the family, undermining the general assumption that women who became revolutionaries were rebelling as much against their parents as they were against the state.

Haupt and Marie argued that the 246 biographies and autobiographies of the *Granat* encyclopedia revealed how diverse the Bolsheviks had been: some had been Bolsheviks from the outset (in 1903), some had been Bolshevik dissidents, and some were from other political parties.[29] The four women whom they included either belonged to the first category (Krupskaia and Stasova) or the last (Kollontai and Reisner). If anything, the women who joined the revolutionary movement were seen as having a more uniform background than the men, more likely to come from the upper classes and to have had a higher education, and least likely to perform a leadership role or participate in ideological debates. The recent specialist works by Clements and Fieseler, discussed in the introduction, bear out these conclusions.

Within the intelligentsia, there were considerable differences in wealth, though once in the RSDLP the women generally fulfilled similar administrative functions. Among the impoverished upper class was Krupskaia, whom Clements describes as "Lenin's administrative assistant", suggesting that Krupskaia's service to her husband "was also service to the cause of liberating Russia": rather than simply performing her wifely duty, Krupskaia saw herself as a revolutionary married to the man who would lead the revolution.[30] This is a more nuanced view than that provided by Robert McNeal, the title of whose biography of Krupskaia, *Bride of the Revolution: Krupskaia and Lenin*, confirms this stereotype of revolutionary helpmate.[31] Certainly, however much a pioneer of Social Democracy in Russia, Krupskaia seems to "fit" this general picture. Though born into a gentry family in St Petersburg in 1869, her parents were not well-off; before marriage her mother had had to take the usual job of an impecunious upper-class woman, that of governess. Both parents had become interested in revolutionary ideas, but her father, who had been an army officer, died when Krupskaia was 14, after which she and her mother lived on various sources of irregular income, including giving private lessons and taking in lodgers. In the first half of the 1890s she had taught workers in Petersburg at Sunday schools and evening classes. It was in this period that she became a Marxist. Arrested during the strike wave of 1896, she was imprisoned for six months and then exiled for three years. From 1901 she lived abroad and played a key role in developing the Bolshevik organization, serving as secretary, and contributing in various ways to the party's publications. She also studied and wrote about educational theories and practices. During the 1905 Revolution she returned to Russia, again doing important organizational work for the Bolsheviks. She went abroad in 1908 to escape arrest. After the next revolution in February 1917, she returned to Petrograd with Lenin in April, and concentrated much of her efforts on organizing women workers and youth, while he spent months away from the capital in hiding from the government.[32]

According to McNeal, "like the other Bolshevik women, she was content to allow the men to run the most important organs of power".[33] *Bride of the Revolution* gives the impression that Krupskaia came to her political position under the influence of her husband, which has since been reinforced by Lenin's numerous biographers. For example, in *Lenin: Life and Legacy*, published in 1994, the Russian historian, Dmitri Volkogonov described Krupskaia as Lenin's shadow, "her life having meaning only because she was linked to him". He acknowledged that she "played a part in her own right", as evident from the many editions of her writings on education, which he dismissed without examining: "all of her ideas on Communist education were based on her husband's comments". In Volkogonov's view, Krupskaia's main claim to a place in history were her notes entitled "The last six months of the life of V.I. Lenin".[34] In fact, she had already arrived at Marxism and was politically active in the revolutionary movement before they met, and her interest in education, both as a teacher and a theorist, was long-standing. Much of her work on education was published only after Lenin's death. She recalled that in 1905 she met many of her former Sunday-school "pupils", one of whom had been deported from Petersburg under escort to his native village in 1895 simply for arguing against the increased work norms that the manager at his textile factory was imposing. She recognized how great was his political development since she had taught him in the early 1890s, which reinforced her early belief in the necessity for popular education.[35] Certainly, since the general view of Lenin is that he was single-mindedly focused on revolution and power, the mirror image of his wife is indeed that of his personal assistant. Krupskaia herself contributed to this image which historians have accepted unquestioningly. In her *Memories of Lenin*, she described their life in exile in Munich, 1901–2:

> After my arrival we went to live with a German working-class family. It was a big family – six of them. They all lived in the kitchen and a small room. But everything was scrupulously clean. The kiddies were both clean and polite. But I decided to put Vladimir Ilyich on home-cooked food. So I organised the cookery. I used the landlady's kitchen for cooking in, but had to prepare everything in our own room. I tried to make as little noise as possible, as Vladimir Ilyich was then beginning to write *What is to be done?* When he wrote anything he generally paced briskly from one corner of the room to the other and whispered what he was about to write. By that time I had already become used to his manner of working. When he was writing I never spoke to him about anything, nor

asked him about anything. Afterwards, when we went out for a walk, he told me what he was writing, and what he was thinking. It seemed to become a necessity to whisper any article over to himself, before writing it. We used to go for rambles on the outskirts of Munich, choosing the most desolate spots where there were few people.[36]

By the time she wrote these recollections of life with Lenin, the cult of his personality, which she had initially opposed, and the dominance of Stalin, whose treatment of Krupskaia had outraged Lenin during his last illness, made any other representation of their marriage impossible. What is clear is that she left the role of leader, in theory and politics, to Lenin. What is also clear is that her contribution to building and maintaining the organization on which that role depended was considerable. Again, that is generally portrayed as a selfless act of service. Volkogonov's acknowledgement that she was "exceptionally intelligent and hard-working" was qualified by his assertion that as soon as she married Lenin in 1898, "she at once assumed her role as [his] assistant".[37] What did this position entail? In his memoirs, Trotksy describes Krupskaia's work for the Social Democratic group in exile in the early twentieth century. Secretary of the editorial board of *Iskra*, the group's journal:

> she was at the very centre of all the organisation work; she received comrades when they arrived, instructed them when they left, established connections, supplied secret addresses, wrote letters, and coded and decoded correspondence. In her room there was always a smell of burned paper from the secret letters she heated over the fire to read. She often complained, in her gently insistent way, that people did not write enough, or that they got the code all mixed up, or wrote in chemical ink in such a way that one line covered another, and so forth.[38]

Clements reinforces Trotsky's portrait of "an extraordinarily diligent, competent woman, who could write 300 letters a week (most in code), keep track of the addresses and aliases of people almost constantly on the run within Russia, and maintain financial accounts".[39]

Krupskaia's concluding sentence to the autobiographical sketch in the *Granat* encyclopedia – "All my life since 1894 I have devoted to helping Vladimir Ilyich Lenin as best I could" – convinced Haupt and Marie that the many years of collaboration between Krupskaia and Lenin robbed the former of her independence.[40] That should not necessarily be taken as proof that she possessed no initiative, or that she worked only as Lenin's administrative assistant, as her own description of her work during the 1905 Revolution in Petersburg reveals:

> At that time I was secretary of the Central Committee [C.C.] and immediately plunged headlong into the work. The other secretary was Mikhail Sergeievich Weinstein. My assistant was Vera Rudol'fovna Menzhinskaia. That was our secretariat. Mikhail Sergeievich was engaged more on the military organisation, and was always busy carrying out the instructions of Nikitin (L.B. Krassin). I was in charge of appointments and communication with committees and individuals. It would be difficult to picture what a simplified technique the C.C. secretariat made shift with. I remember that we never attended C.C. meetings, no one was "in charge" of us, no minutes were taken, ciphered addresses were kept in matchboxes, inside bookbindings, and in similar places.
>
> We had to trust our memories. A whole crowd of people besieged us, and we had to look after them in every way, supplying them with whatever they needed: literature, passports, instructions, advice. It is difficult to imagine how we ever managed to cope with it all, and how we kept things in order, being controlled by nobody, and living "of our own free will".[41]

Having just outlined the central, responsible role she played in the Bolshevik organization, Krupskaia added the usual incantation of devotion to and reliance on Lenin: "Usually on meeting with Ilyich I told him in detail about everything". Even here there are glimpses that, however unequal, their relationship was a partnership: "The most interesting comrades on the most interesting business we sent straight to the Central Committee members".[42] Moreover, Lenin appears to have depended heavily on the women in his family, his sisters as well as his wife, and not merely for domestic care. As a family, the Ul'ianovs relied on each other a great deal, politically as well as personally. Lenin's older sister, Anna (1864–1935), had been arrested in 1887 in connection with her younger brother, Alexander (1866–87), whose execution (for his part in an attempt on the life of Alexander III) seems to have had a tremendous political as well as personal impact on all the members of his family, and not only Lenin, who was four years younger than Alexander and six years younger than Anna. Alexander had been a Narodnik, in the tradition of the People's Will. He was influenced by Marx, and already looked more to the urban working class than to the peasantry.[43] Alexander's execution seems to have drawn the family closer together. Anna worked as a teacher, and wrote revolutionary leaflets in the early 1890s. She joined the Social Democratic Party when it was set up in 1898, spent two years abroad working for the party newspaper, *Iskra*, and on her return to Russia in 1902 continued clandestine work, moving to avoid arrest, from Tomsk, to Samara, Kiev and then Petrograd. She had participated in the 1905 Revolution. In 1910, Anna was arrested in Saratov for her role in publishing the Volga region's Bolshevik newspaper, while the local police considered her younger sister, Mariia, central to the Saratov party organization.[44]

Anna maintained communications with Lenin and Krupskaia throughout the years of their political exile and emigration, a crucial task during the First World War when Bolsheviks were harassed because of their stance against the war. Anna proof-read all of his books before the 1917 Revolution. She also worked for the Bolshevik press, including the newspaper *Pravda*, and the journal *Rabotnitsa*. She did not blindly follow instructions from abroad, resisting Inessa Armand's efforts to make *Rabotnitsa* more theoretical. In 1917, Anna played a significant part in keeping the party's presses going, especially in July after they were raided by the government. On top of all this work, she kept home for her mother, as well as for her husband, Mark Timofeievich Elizarov, who was also a Bolshevik.

Lenin's younger sister, Mariia, also remained in Russia. In 1914, she had been active organizing circles of railway workers in Vologda, but the war brought a stop to her activity because so many of the men were conscripted. In October, she went to live in Moscow where the Bolshevik organization had effectively collapsed. In January 1915 she joined a medical course training nurses for the front, reasoning that she could propagandize among the troops. In the meantime, she kept in contact with Lenin and Krupskaia, and supported herself by teaching French and doing translations of French and German short fiction for publication. She also kept safe flats, and organized meetings of comrades coming from outside of the city. All the time, she was followed by police agents. She had a relationship with a married comrade, who when conscripted told Mariia that he had to go to the front to prove himself to the troops: otherwise, they would consider Bolshevik anti-war propaganda the words of a coward. In 1916, she went to Petrograd, joining her mother (who died that year) and sister, and taking over the latter's domestic responsibilities when she was imprisoned between July and October, and again in February 1917.

Together, the Ul'ianov sisters participated in producing the first post-revolutionary edition of *Pravda*, contributing their own impressions of the revolution. As noted above, both became members of the secretariat of the central committee, and of the editorial staff of *Pravda*.[45] When Krupskaia and Lenin returned to Russia in April 1917, they were met, before they arrived in Petrograd, by his sister Mariia, as well as by the prominent female Bolshevik Liudmila Stal' and some women workers. It was Krupskaia to whom Stal' turned to address the female workers. Krupskaia, who was used to working behind the scenes and was rather shy, admitted that she was speechless, both excited and worried about their reception in the capital.[46] Once in Petrograd, Krupskaia and Lenin went to live with Mariia, Anna and her husband, Mark.

The women in Lenin's life seem to have accepted supportive roles, both politically and domestically; but that did not prevent them either from making vital contributions to the revolutionary movement or indeed from taking the initiative. Robert McNeal has suggested that Krupskaia did not meekly follow Lenin's line on their return to Russia in April 1917, and that Lenin reacted by withdrawing his support for her career in the Party secretariat. For McNeal, Krupskaia turned to work in the educational and youth sectors in a working-class district of Petrograd (Vyborg) because she doubted that socialist revolution which Lenin called for would occur soon. Even though she was elected in June as a Bolshevik representative to the Vyborg district duma, her work in the cultural and education section, and on the Committee for the Relief of Soldiers' Wives, is dismissed as "reformist", not part of "the real business of the Bolshevik Party in 1917: the seizure of power".[47]

Such an assessment of Krupskaia's work rests on a very narrow conception of how the Bolsheviks were to win power, while implicit is the assumption that organizational work always took second place to theoretical. Yet throughout 1917, as we shall see in Chapter 6, the revolutionaries seemed to be straining to catch up with the increasingly militant masses. To manipulate the workers, the Bolsheviks first had to establish a strong base among them. Hence the necessity for systematic work at local level. We, therefore, suggest an alternative reading to Krupskaia's work from the summer of 1917. Rather than simply continue as a central committee secretary in 1917, she insisted that she serve the party in the way she thought most suited her talents and which also reflected her interests in education, women workers and young people. Thus, while at first she had been expected to serve in the secretariat of the party's central committee on her return, Krupskaia had requested that she be based in the working-class district of Vyborg which had seen the start of the revolution. She recognized that working at the secretariat in 1917 could not compare to the work she had done abroad, or to her experience of revolutionary activity in 1905–7, when she had "had to carry out rather important work independently under Il'ich's directions".[48] Soon bored by the work for the secretariat and reluctant to take a lesser role than years earlier, she spent some time observing what was happening and listening to what was being said on the streets, paying especially close attention to what women, youth and teachers (whose conference she attended soon after her arrival) had to say. She also wrote extensively for the party press, and from May was on the editorial staff of *Rabotnitsa*. Besides organizing working women, Krupskaia took a particular interest in youth work, seeing both as important constituencies that the Bolsheviks had to reach. In June, she was elected to the Vyborg district duma. Her main area of responsibility was education, and she concentrated on setting up literacy classes and libraries for workers.[49] Employers were asked by the Bolsheviks to provide rooms in the factories where classes could be held for instructing the illiterate. When one of them refused, Krupskaia noted that it was the women workers who raised a tremendous outcry, and forced the employer to rent premises outside the factory for the school.[50] Yet she is still seen as Lenin's helpmate above all. This image of Social Democratic women is tenacious, mirroring their views of working-class and peasant women as subservient to men, in the home and the workplace.

Bolshevik feminists

The exception among the Bolsheviks is usually, and uniquely, seen to be Alexandra Kollontai. Born in 1872 into a landowning gentry family, she later recorded that, although impressed by the Narodnik movement and terrorism, it was a visit in 1896 to a textile works, where she witnessed "the enslavement of the 12,000 weavers", that led her to Marxism.[51] Kollontai was a prolific writer on sexual morality and relations between women and men. As seen in the previous chapter, her ideas were in line not only with Marxist writings but also with the development of Russian thought since the 1840s. In particular, she put forward the view that had been propagated in Russia since at least the 1860s, that paid employment outside the home would make women independent and personally fulfilled. Having received a liberal education at home (her parents were afraid of the possible influence of revolutionary ideas had she attended university), Kollontai refused an arranged marriage and instead wed her second cousin against her parents' wishes in 1894. The marriage lasted three years, during which time she had a son. She became a socialist in 1896, the year of the big textile strikes in Petersburg. She then broke with what she experienced as a restrictive family situation and in 1898 went to Zurich to study political economy and statistics at the university. She returned to the tsarist empire in 1903 when she made a study of Finland. In 1904, she taught in workers' circles; in 1905, she participated in the revolution; in 1906 she joined the Mensheviks; in 1907 she set up a women workers' club in Petersburg to combat what she saw as a growing feminist influence; and in 1908, she organized a group of female workers to attend the first feminist congress, from which she had to flee abroad to escape arrest. It was the outbreak of war in 1914 that brought her to Bolshevism. Although her position was initially pacifist, Kollontai committed herself to Lenin's theory that the imperialist war would turn into civil (class) war in 1915, when she joined the Bolsheviks.

Thereafter, she was a consistent supporter of Lenin until the October Revolution, after which she opposed the peace with Germany in April 1918 (calling instead for a revolutionary war), became a leader of the Workers' Opposition, writing its manifesto in 1920, which criticized the growth of bureaucratic, centralized power. She was the first woman to be elected to the Bolshevik central committee after the revolution, and headed the party's bureau for women (*zhenotdel*) in 1920.[52] The reasons for her dismissal in 1922 are unclear, though her biographers believe that her removal from the leadership was a blow to the *zhenotdel*, and to hopes for a real change in the position of women in general.[53] Kollontai then became the first woman ambassador, principally in Scandinavia, a post which is generally seen as a form of political exile.

As a "Bolshevik feminist", Kollontai has eclipsed her contemporary, Inessa Armand (1874–1920). Moreover, the latter's biographer, R.C. Elwood, sees Armand as not only marginalized by soviet historians, but patronized by western historians as Lenin's assumed mistress.[54] What is interesting about Armand in terms of her membership of the Bolshevik Party is that she came to it from an early concern for women's rights. Frustrated by the slow progress of feminist philanthropy and lobbying, Armand turned to Marxism. Elwood sees her as leading the fight to convince the Bolshevik male leadership that special efforts should be made to organize women workers. Armand was instrumental in setting up the journal, *Rabotnitsa*, in 1914, as well as special commissions for work among women in 1918 and *zhenotdel* in 1919, of which she became director, succeeded on her death by Kollontai.

While Elwood disputes the rumour that Armand and Lenin were lovers, he confirms that there was a close friendship between them, and that Lenin depended on her considerable linguistic skills. Elwood believes that by 1915 Armand had grown reluctant to fill the role Lenin assigned her as his "Girl Friday", and differed with him on a number of issues.[55] While she appears to have had a warm friendship with Krupskaia, as far as Armand's relations with Kollontai were concerned, Elwood portrays them as rivals, judging Kollontai the more charismatic, Armand the better politician. Yet Armand seems to have lacked understanding of the problems of everyday life that faced women workers, and to have been more concerned with raising their consciousness than defending their interests. Criticisms from Bolshevik women that *Rabotnitsa* was out of touch with its audience may well have been aimed at Armand. She seemed to lose interest in the journal when she found that the editors based in Russia (including Lenin's sister, Anna) preferred accounts of events of interest to women workers, as well as correspondence from and poetry and fiction written by them, to the theoretical and propaganda pieces written by herself and other emigré women. Thus, while Armand championed special efforts to organize women workers, she seemed unable to bridge the gap between them and her upper-class, intellectual concerns. She spent much of 1917 in Moscow, but played only a small part in the revolution, owing to the serious illness of her son, one of her five children.

Another Bolshevik champion of women's rights was Konkordia Samoilova, who was born in 1876 and came from a humbler background than either Armand or Kollontai. Samoilova, whose father was a priest, attended higher education courses for women in St Petersburg in 1896, quickly becoming acquainted with Chernyshevskii's *What is to be done?* and Marxist theory, and involved in student protests.[56] In exile abroad in 1902, she became a Social Democrat. In 1903, when conducting agitational work in Baku among railwaymen, she was accosted by some of the workers' wives, who accused her of trying to "steal" their husbands, an incident which helped convince her of the need to focus attention on working-class women.[57] Ten years later, she was instrumental in organizing the first celebration of International Women's Day in Russia. Though she had difficulty persuading her comrades in St Petersburg to support her action, the day was successful in attracting women workers.[58] When publication of *Rabotnitsa* (of which she had been a founding member in 1914) was renewed in May 1917, Samoilova was on the editorial board. She put her efforts into the political education of women workers, through courses held in factories and in planning conferences for women, the first of which was held in November 1917 just after the Bolsheviks took power. She then concentrated on attracting women to the *zhenotdel*. Like Armand who predeceased her by a few months in 1920, Samoilova died (in 1921) of cholera.

Another Bolshevik woman who concentrated on women workers was Vera Slutskaia. Daughter of a skilled worker, Slutskaia had trained as a dentist. Like Krupskaia in 1917, Slutskaia was based in the militant Vyborg district of Petrograd. Although in 1908 she had been resistant to the separate organization of women, by the February Revolution she had shifted her position considerably. Slutskaia was already organizing women workers from March, in order to maintain their revolutionary momentum. She participated in rallies of Vyborg women, and proposed to the Bolshevik Party that a special bureau to co-ordinate such work be established. This was resisted by comrades who feared that such feminist tactics would divide the labour movement, and so *Rabotnitsa* had to serve as both journal and organizational centre for women workers. Slutskaia played a leading role at local level which she combined with special work among women, and despite opposition from comrades to the latter, she did not see them as incompatible.[59] She was killed defending the October Revolution soon after the Bolsheviks took power.

Hence there was considerable work specifically directed at women workers from May 1917 by these Bolshevik feminists. Though in a minority, and within a few years of the October Revolution either dead or politically marginalized, these leading female Bolsheviks seem to have had considerable influence on their party in 1917, even if they had to compromise on the proposal for a bureau dedicated to work among women.[60] Women's importance in the labour movement in Petrograd during this year of political upheaval and economic collapse, their militancy as well as their backwardness, persuaded at least some of the predominantly male Bolshevik leadership, including, crucially, Lenin, that such efforts should be made, whatever the perceived dangers of setting male against female workers.

This is an aspect of the revolutionary process in 1917 that had a significant impact on Bolshevik fortunes. In practice, there was little difference between Bolshevik and Menshevik thinking on the woman question, while the SRs made no special efforts to recruit women workers. Lidiia Dan and Eva Broido of the Mensheviks, for example, also accepted that special efforts needed to be made to raise women's consciousness and to challenge male prejudices and discrimination against women.[61] The former was shocked by the low cultural level of woman workers in the 1890s and felt that "it was easy to understand that cigarette-makers and weavers cannot readily be made into activists, whereas metal workers and typographers were ready-made revolutionaries". She worried that the women workers lacked a "sense of organisation", explaining that when the female cigarette-makers were on strike:

> it immediately took on explosive proportions, despite our most energetic warnings, and, in 1896, they threw thousands and tens of thousands of cigarettes into the street. Afterwards I never heard, in Petersburg at any rate, of workers trying to destroy machinery (probably this would have been difficult for women), but the sight of huge boxes of cigarettes being thrown into the street – it was frightful.[62]

Broido, like Kollontai, was interested in the women question and had translated August Bebel's *Women and Socialism* from German into Russian in the winter of 1899–1900; and though it was banned, the ten copies that were smuggled out of the printing house were used in the underground study circles of the Social Democratic movement.[63] Broido's memoirs show that, while she recognized the importance of clubs for women workers (such as those organized in 1907 in St Petersburg), she was not one of the organizers; and though she participated in some of the discussions, she simply recorded, without comment, the indignation of female as well as male Mensheviks at what they saw as unequal rather than special treatment of women.[64] The impression from her memoirs is that, despite her interest in the position of women workers, there was no particularly strong commitment to making special organizational efforts. Perhaps, then, it should not be surprising that, in the circumstances of 1917, women workers' frustration with the failure of the Provisional Government to improve their position made Broido's suggested reforms (such as a female factory inspectorate, whose remit would include the service sector), however sensible, seem out of touch with their deteriorating situation, especially as employers were becoming increasingly intransigent in resisting workers' demands, which will be discussed in Chapter 6.

While most of the Social Democratic women who advocated special work among female workers did so for tactical reasons, based on their assessment of the women's needs, consciousness and importance to the class struggle, both Armand and Kollontai were particularly interested in theory and the woman question. Both were well educated and from early in their membership of the Social Democratic Party were close to the leadership. Biographers of both reveal the tensions they experienced between the pressures of politics and family, and the difficulties of establishing themselves as individuals in their own right, of getting themselves and their ideas taken seriously by their comrades, both female and male. Both women undermine the generalization that personal life and romance were luxuries that radical women did not allow themselves, which would seem to apply more to terrorist than to Marxist women.[65]

Women in the Bolshevik Party in 1917

Both Kollontai and Armand spent much of their time abroad, returning to Russia after the February Revolution. Neither seems to have been typical of the Bolshevik women who remained in Russia. A soviet publication on Bolsheviks who played a role in the October Revolution, published on its tenth anniversary, focused more on those women who remained behind, working underground. It revealed that, whether from the intelligentsia or the working class, female party members became professional revolutionaries through a combination of factors, just like men: personal experience of oppression, influence of family members, and study (whether in a workers' circle or evening class, or through higher education). The women included in this collection played a relatively important but unremarkable role in the revolution, generally at a local level and rarely in a prominent leadership position.[66]

One example was Nina Agadzhanova, born in the Caucasus in 1889, who had been a student in Moscow, and joined the Bolsheviks in 1907.[67] In 1914 she was a member of both the Vyborg and City district party committees in Petrograd, and had been recommended by Anna Elizarova to be executive secretary for *Rabotnitsa*, which appeared seven times before being suppressed. A year later Agadzhanova was arrested and exiled to Irkutsk, from where she escaped in the autumn of 1916. Returning to the capital, under an assumed name, she found a job as a machine operator in a metal factory, and again went to work for the Vyborg and City district committees of the party. With a friend, Mariia Vydrina, she organized mass meetings of both male and female workers. In February 1917, they helped organize strikes and demonstrations of metal and tram workers, and together with soldiers who had joined the revolution freed political prisoners from gaols and barracks. At the beginning of March, Agadzhanova was involved in setting up first-aid units to treat those injured in clashes with government forces. She was one of the Vyborg representatives who met Lenin on his return to Russia, at the Finland station. Elected by the Vyborg district to the Petrograd Soviet, Agadzhanova continued to organize and participate in demonstrations from the fall of the first Provisional Government in April until the collapse of the last in October, when the Bolsheviks took power.

Agadzhanova's political life seems typical of those female members of the intelligentsia who joined the Bolsheviks and remained in Russia. They became interested in Marxism while students, either at grammar school or at university, and by virtue of their education they often served as secretaries to local party branches, which in the conditions of clandestine activity was a dangerous and highly political role, vital to the survival of the organization. As a result of police harassment, they frequently had to move throughout Russia. For example, E.N. Adamovich (1872–1938), who joined a Marxist circle as a student in Estonia in 1893, and became a Bolshevik in 1903, was in Khar'kov in 1896 after a short term of imprisonment, moved to Moscow in 1898, then was in Petersburg during the 1905 Revolution until 1910. She was back in Khar'kov in 1912, where she was secretary to the local Bolsheviks; was exiled to the north near the Ural mountains in 1913 and then further away, to Iakutsk province. Released after the February Revolution, Adamovich worked as a party secretary in the Vasil'evskii Island district of Petrograd, and in the cultural section of the city duma. During the October Revolution, she served the Military Revolutionary Committee, and was based at Bolshevik Party headquarters in Smol'ny.[68]

The experience of the First World War also seems to have been a factor that pushed women towards the Bolsheviks by 1917. Thus Elena Giliarova, who was born into a teacher's family in Riazan in 1896, became involved with the Bolsheviks in 1915. She went as a nurse to the Russian–Turkish front, where she also acted as a propagandist for the Bolsheviks among the troops, although she was not yet a member of the party. After the February Revolution, she was elected by the soldiers to represent them at the Petrograd Soviet. In May 1917, she formally joined the Bolshevik Party. On the eve of the October Revolution, Giliarova was running courses in first-aid for female Bolsheviks and sympathizers, and preparing young women workers to join the Red Guards. During the seizure of power, she ran a medical station on the outskirts of the city.[69] In fact, during the October Revolution, a major activity of Bolshevik women had been to serve in the Red Cross and many then went to the front during the civil war (1918–20), as medical workers or political commissars. Some even entered the secret police, the Cheka (the Extraordinary Commission for Combating Counter-Revolution and Sabotage, established soon after the October Revolution), such as Elza Grundman (1891–1931), who went on to become an administrator in its successors.[70]

After the 1905 Revolution, increasing numbers of working-class women had turned to the Bolshevik Party. Petronelia Zinchenko came from a very different social background from the female intelligentsia such as Giliarova or Agadzhanova. Zinchenko had been born into a poor peasant family in the Lithuanian–Polish area of the tsarist empire. She entered the labour market at the age of eight, first as a nanny and then as a dock worker, loading ships. Her employment history before the 1917 Revolution reveals a high rate of job turnover, and a breadth of work experience, from field labourer to button-maker, from tobacco factory to printing house. At the time of the February Revolution, she was employed at the naval base of Kronstadt, near Petrograd, making sailors' uniforms. After the revolution, she was elected to the Kronstadt soviet, and joined the Bolshevik Party in August. Her ability to speak

Lithuanian and Polish, as well as Russian, made her an effective propagandist, among Kronstadt women workers as well as the sailors at the base. In October, she organized sailors to be sent to the capital, and was responsible for keeping order in the fortress and maintaining communications between Kronstadt and Petrograd. In 1918, she married a Bolshevik, and went with him on party business to Kursk, Ukraine and the Donbass.[71] Once again, Zinchenko seems typical of many Bolshevik women in this period, combining domestic and political life, and eventually working full-time for the party.

The work undertaken by Bolshevik women was often dangerous. E. Alekseeva (1895–1965) came from a family of textile workers in Petersburg, and began work at the age of ten. In 1909, she joined the Bolsheviks. Her political tasks consisted of distributing illegal party literature, participating in strikes, and collecting money for the party press and to support those comrades in exile. Sacked in 1912 for her political activities from the textile factory in which she worked, she found a job in a metal factory, which had poor health and safety conditions. Despite her varied revolutionary activities, and the fact that she played a full part at the grassroots level, organizing and participating in working-class actions throughout 1917, the 1967 soviet biography records the highpoint of Alekseeva's revolutionary activity to have been at the meeting that discussed the October Revolution, at which her responsibilities were to make the tea and serve as lookout. After October, she worked as an administrator in the Petrograd district duma.[72] This was a typical post-revolutionary career for Bolshevik women, becoming part of the state administration.

Mariia Vydrina-Sveshnikova was a working-class woman who joined the Bolshevik Party in Moscow in 1915 at the age of twenty, after having served a similar apprenticeship to Alekseeva (distributing Marxist literature, collecting funds). She went to Petrograd in 1916 and found work in a machine-tool factory, as a driller. Her party work during 1917 concentrated on organizing women workers. She participated in the overthrow of the Provisional Government, partly by setting up a first-aid brigade. She was one of the organizers of the first post-revolutionary national women workers' conference in Petrograd in November 1917, at which she also spoke. Thereafter, she worked in party and economic administration.

Thus, whether from the intelligentsia or the working class, after the October Revolution female Bolsheviks tended to be absorbed into the administration, of party, state, economy or education. A few of the former, such as Armand and Reisner (both of whom died in the 1920s), tried to carry on revolutionary activity abroad (in France and Germany) by virtue of their language skills, while Kollontai, also an accomplished linguist, embarked on a career as a diplomat from 1922, mostly in Scandinavia. In general, female Bolsheviks either became part of the soviet establishment or withdrew from political life.

While increasing numbers of working-class women joined the Bolshevik Party during and after 1917, their proportion of the female membership rose only marginally in 1917, by two per cent.[73] Most of these women had begun work at an early age, some, such as Alekseeva, as young as ten, others, such as Anastasia Deviatkina (1874–1929) around the age of 12. Alekseeva had, like the majority of female factory workers, become a textile worker, while Deviatkina had started work in a military factory, which may explain her political work among soldiers' wives during the First World War and in 1917. She had joined the Bolsheviks in 1904, and suffered various terms of imprisonment and internal exile. She participated in the February Revolution from the start, organizing and leading a demonstration of women workers and soldiers' wives on International Women's Day. Deviatkina was then elected a deputy to her local district soviet, and head of a union of soldiers' wives that she had helped set up in 1917. In the October seizure of power, she was at Smol'ny, ensuring that Bolshevik head-quarters maintained contact with the various revolutionary positions throughout the capital.[74] Deviatkina's role in the February Revolution challenges the notion, which will be discussed in Chapter 6, that it was spontaneous and leaderless. It also undermines the stereotype of the passive woman worker who, even if politically aware, would be unable to articulate her ideas or transform her grievances into political actions.

Another working-class woman who, at the time of the February Revolution, had been a member of the Bolshevik Party for over a decade (having joined in 1905) was Arishina Kruglova, whose parents had been employed in a tobacco factory. During the First World War, she had found a job in a munitions factory and carried out propaganda work among the reservist soldiers in the capital. Indeed, she sometimes combined the two jobs, packing boxes of grenades with Bolshevik leaflets. During the February demonstrations, Kruglova concentrated on freeing political prisoners. She was elected a member of two local soviets, for the Okhta and City districts. She also organized the Red

Guard in her areas, and during the October Revolution, she raided wealthier districts of the city in the search of weapons to arm the Guards, and disarm opponents. Kruglova also helped in the local medical and sanitation work. After the October Revolution, she worked for the party and the soviet.[75]

Of course women such as Deviatkina and Kruglova were in a minority, not only within the Bolshevik Party but also, and even more so, within their own class. The more educated and politically conscious they became through contact with the revolutionary movement, the more they stood out from the mass of their co-workers. Unlike many women from the intelligentsia, female workers did not see their political commitment as incompatible with family life. The seamstress Zhenia Egorova certainly appreciated being single and childless while she was active in the underground struggle and during the revolution, but she always expected that she would marry, which she did in 1918, and have children (she had two in the 1920s).[76] Thus, the need of working-class party members to earn a living, the fact that most of them married and had children, and their persistent efforts to agitate and organize in their places of work ensured that during the revolution the gap that grew between themselves and their workmates was not unbridgeable. Ironically, with the success of the Bolshevik seizure of power, and the absorption of so many party women into the organs of the Communist state, that gulf widened.

Two types of Bolshevik women, then, have been identified as working for the revolution in 1917: women from the intelligentsia, and from around 1904–5 especially, increasing numbers from the working class. Barbara Clements and other historians have seen the woman of the intelligentsia as personified by Elena Stasova (1873–1967), who came from a wealthy family with a father in the legal profession. Stasova recorded in the 1927 *Granat* encyclopedia that her father had had progressive ideas. Her education had been at home until the age of thirteen, by which time she was fluent in French and German. In the spring of 1887 she had begun attending a private grammar school for girls, from which she graduated with a gold medal. Stasova dated her political development as beginning in 1892–3, when she began to study political economy. She became more aware of a feeling of great debt to the people for her privileged position. Stasova began to teach in evening classes and at Sunday schools for adolescents and women workers. Through such work she met radical upper-class women such as Krupskaia who introduced her to revolutionary circles. Stasova had joined the Social Democratic Party in 1898, and so had nearly two decades of political experience behind her by the time of the 1917 Revolution. Besides her teaching, Stasova soon revealed her administrative and organizational talents by becoming the archivist for the Petersburg branch of the Social Democrats:

> Little by little the work grew, and my province came to include not only the caches of literature but everything connected with the technical side of the St. Petersburg Committee, that is finding rooms for meetings, secret addresses and beds for a night, receiving and distributing literature, equipping duplicating machines and printing-presses, as well as maintaining correspondence with abroad.[77]

She was described as "keeper of the party traditions".[78] During the long years of clandestine activity, information on Bolshevik Party members and organization was stored only in her memory, so that the secretarial work she performed was extremely important in political as well as administrative terms. Government repression in 1904 and again in 1906, as well as the needs of the party, led to Stasova constantly moving throughout the tsarist empire and working abroad. She returned to Petrograd from exile in Siberia in the autumn of 1916, where she remained, unable to work for the Bolshevik Party because of a serious illness. Nevertheless, she was still seen as dangerous by the authorities, and was arrested on 25 February 1917, two days after the outbreak of unrest on International Women's Day. She was released only two days later, once it was clear that tsarism had been toppled by the popular revolution. Stasova then served as secretary to the Bolshevik Party's central committee, again playing a crucial role in July, when many of the leading Bolsheviks were either in hiding or in gaol.

As Clements has shown, the new, young recruits coming from the working class were exemplified by Klavdiia Nikolaeva (1893–1944), a bookbinder and party member since 1909.[79] A factory worker since the age of eleven, Nikolaeva had soon become interested in politics, and participated in the women's club set up in Petersburg by Alexandra Kollontai in 1907. Nikolaeva's interest in organizing women workers and her links to Kollontai continued: in 1908, Nikolaeva spoke for the Social Democrats at the feminist congress in Petersburg, from which Kollontai had had to flee abroad; in 1914, Nikolaeva worked for the short-lived publication aimed at women workers, *Rabotnitsa*, to which she returned when it was revived in May 1917. After the October Revolution, she dissociated herself from Kollontai's radical ideas on the woman question. Nikolaeva became the first working-class woman to lead the women's section (*zhenotdel*) of the Communist Party in 1924.

What of the women who joined the Bolshevik Party in 1917? Writing on female communists in 1929, William Chamberlin related the story of a woman born into a poor peasant family, in the province of Tver', who had received little formal education. She had been sent by her father to work in a textile factory, and then married off by him when she was eighteen years of age. She went to St Petersburg with her husband, and both of them found factory jobs. Her husband died at the front in the First World War, and she became radicalized when the commission for the relief of soldiers' wives refused to help her. After the February Revolution, she joined the Bolsheviks, and left the factory to work for the Party.[80]

That woman had been radicalized by the war. A younger, single woman, Liza Pylaeva, found her way into the party under the influence of her family circumstances and her elder brother, who was a skilled worker.[81] Born north of Moscow, her father had worked at an inn in Petersburg, but he died in the autumn of 1914. While she moved with her mother back to the Moscow region, her brother (four years her senior) and her younger sister remained in the capital. As she and her mother struggled to survive, Pylaeva began to pay attention to the political exiles in her region. She also noticed the impact of the war, reflected in the hardships of her neighbour, a mother of five who had been widowed early in the conflict, and in the tears of young brides whose husbands were conscripted. In 1914, her brother was exiled to Irkutsk in Siberia because of his activities distributing anti-war literature among workers in the capital. With his wage lost, Pylaeva had to help support her mother and younger sister. She went to Petrograd and found work as a cashier in a shop selling china and crystal. Her year there acquainted her with the city, and her dealings with the upper-class customers made her more politically conscious. She had not been aware until then of her brother's membership of the Bolshevik Party. In the late autumn of 1916, he returned to Petrograd illegally from exile, and resumed his revolutionary activities. He set up a printing press for the Bolshevik newspaper, *Pravda*. Though not a member, Pylaeva helped him. She distributed leaflets for the party, collected money and acted as a courier. In her workplace, she sometimes stored large packages of party literature for safe keeping, reasoning that the authorities would not think to search a shop which sold luxury goods. On the eve of the February Revolution, and having effectively served her political apprenticeship, Pylaeva was recommended for membership of the Bolshevik Party by Mariia Ul'ianova.

After the February Revolution, and especially with the arrival of Krupskaia in April, Pylaeva was entrusted with building a youth movement for the party, in which she worked closely with Krupskaia, as will be discussed in Chapter 6. Pylaeva's soviet biographers saw her as a typical Russian woman of the lower classes who joined the Bolsheviks: kind and unsophisticated, she became politically conscious and able to articulate her ideas, partly through circumstances of deprivation and anger at social injustice, partly under the influence of her brother. Pylaeva, however, was not so typical of the urban working-class woman in that she had considerable experience of education, including some time in grammar school, which allowed her to get work as a cashier.

Nor were working-class women the only recruits to the Bolshevik Party in 1917. Female students were already turning to social democracy in the late nineteenth century. A Jewish student at the Institute of Psychiatry and Neurology in Petrograd in 1916, Rachel Kovnator was active in the February demonstrations. In July, when the Provisional Government had suppressed an armed demonstration of Bolshevik sympathizers, she participated in a strike of students who protested against the trials of some of the sailors from Kronstadt. She joined the Bolshevik Party that month, and worked with Kollontai and other Bolshevik women to organize the first women workers' conference to be held after the October Revolution. She went on to work for *zhenotdel* and for the journal *Rabotnitsa*, later becoming an editor of *Kommunistka*, the post-revolutionary theoretical journal aimed at women activists.[82]

As these case studies show, some of the women who were members of the Bolshevik Party in 1917 had already been working with it, while others had recently joined during the war. Thus, Alexandra Singer had attended meetings held by a Bolshevik woman while a student at the higher courses for women in Leskov, in 1912. Her flat was used for party meetings, and she also distributed illegal literature and took parcels to political prisoners. In 1916, she formally joined the Bolsheviks, and took a job in a factory in Petrograd. Singer participated in the protests on International Women's Day in 1917. She was among the Bolsheviks who took over the telephone exchange. When the terrified female telephonists fled, the soldiers and sailors had looked at the machinery in bewilderment. Singer stepped forward and quickly established the necessary lines of communication. She remained there for several days and nights, showing others how to work the exchange. After the October Revolution, she worked for a district party committee, and then spent 30 years in publishing.[83]

Such logistical work was necessary for the success of the revolution. Mariia Kotikova came from a civil servant's family, and after grammar school had served an apprenticeship (to 1915) at the post office. By 1916, she was active in protesting against deteriorating working conditions for the white-collar employees at the post office. She did not take part in the February demonstrations that resulted in the overthrow of tsarism but, by April, Kotikova had joined the Bolsheviks. She became a leading member of the executive committee of the soviet for a central district of the city (Admiralty), representing mainly white-collar workers. She sent the telegram in October to various parts of the country, including Moscow, to inform them that the seizure of power in the capital was underway. She organized a group of Bolshevik sympathizers at the post office, including her sister and four other female telegraphists, to keep the lines of communication open, and foil any attempt at sabotage. After the revolution, Kotikova worked for the government.[84]

The fourth woman included in *Makers of the Russian Revolution*, Larissa Reisner (1895–1926) had been born in Lublin, Poland, into a family of the intelligentsia (her father was a university professor), and spent her early years in Germany, often in the company of Russian exiles. Educated in Russia from 1905, she showed an early interest in the arts, especially literature. Like Kollontai, she opposed the war from its outset in 1914, and became associated with Social Democratic circles. From the February Revolution, Reisner opposed the Provisional Government. She spent a great deal of time working in the radical sailors' circles in the naval base of Kronstadt, near to the capital. Reisner, however, is better known for her contribution to the revolution after the Bolsheviks took power, notably at the front in the civil war, and also in Germany in 1923. A dashing figure, she seems to have been unable to accept the retreat from revolution at the end of the civil war, signified in the adoption of the New Economic Policy in March 1921, which was a form of mixed economy.[85]

While Reisner was not slow in picking up a gun to defend the revolution, it seems that more women Bolsheviks from the working class than from the intelligentsia transported weapons and fought in the Red Guard. Serafima Zaitseva, who, in 1915, had become a member of the party at the age of 20 when she had been employed in a metal works, joined the Red Guard in her factory, was in a contingent that stormed the post office in October 1917, and fought counter revolutionaries on the outskirts of the city. She joined the Red Cross and went to the front during the civil war, where she suffered from shell-shock. She was also wounded twice, and was twice imprisoned by the counter revolutionaries, each time escaping the death sentence.[86] However, although women joined the Red Guards and took part in the storming of key buildings in the city, including the Winter Palace, they were more likely to serve in support roles: as first aiders, transporters of weapons and information, as spies, scouts and messengers, maintaining communication with the centre of operations and, of course, making sure that the men were fed.

In 1917, the urban nature of the female membership of the Bolshevik Party, as indeed of the Mensheviks and the SRs, was overwhelming. If education was taken as a key factor in determining social status, then women from the aristocracy and intelligentsia, and a considerable proportion of the white-collar workers would roughly equal, if not outnumber working-class women in the Bolshevik Party. The social origins of female Bolsheviks before the revolution and in 1917 were recorded as:

	Pre-1917	1917
Aristocratic	20%	12.2%
Intelligentsia	16%	25.1%
White-Collar	4%	15.3%
Working-Class	43%	45.6%
Peasant	5%	1.8%
Other	12%	—

Source: *Kommunistka*, 1924, No. 4, pp. 8–10.

Nevertheless, the percentage of the working-class women, both before and during 1917, is remarkable, given their low levels of literacy, the demands the Bolsheviks made in terms of political education, and their concentration on skilled, and therefore male, workers. Krupskaia was impressed by the level of political awareness among the Vyborg women workers in 1917:

> The women workers of the Vyborg district did not resemble those I knew in the nineties or even in the 1905 Revolution. They were well dressed, active at meetings and politically intelligent. One woman said to me: "My husband is at the front. We lived well together, but I do not know how it will be when he returns. I am for the Bolsheviks now and I will go with them, but I don't know about him there at the front . . . Does he understand, does he realise that we must follow the Bolsheviks? Often I think at night – perhaps he does not understand yet. Only I don't know whether I shall see him again, perhaps he will be killed. Yes, and I spit blood, I am going to the hospital." [87]

Though worried that her husband might disagree with her, this woman was intent on supporting the Bolsheviks whatever he thought. Her poor health gives some indication of the conditions under which women worked, which shall be discussed in the next chapter. Whatever their social background, Bolshevik women remained in a minority, however, representing only about ten per cent of the party's membership.

An analysis of Bolshevik Party members in Moscow has shown that the women tended to be older (on average by four years) than the men, and that the women joined the party at a slightly older age (perhaps by two years), though a working-class female was more likely to join at a younger age than a female intellectual.[88] This is supported by the findings of Clements and Fieseler. By far the majority of women who joined the Bolsheviks in 1917 were from towns and cities, while there were more from the educated and professional classes than from the working class. Clements has suggested that the better educated and higher social class composition of female Bolsheviks than their male comrades may have indicated that rebellion was more difficult for women than for men, because the former had to challenge not only the state, but the patriarchal family structure and traditional notions of femininity and women's role.[89] It may be that women postponed joining the party because of the difficulties in combining domestic responsibilities with the commitment demanded by membership. Thus P. Sleptsova, whose husband joined the Communist Party in 1918, continued to work in a textile factory while rearing her eight children. She showed some interest in politics, becoming in 1920 a women's delegate and a member of the Moscow Soviet. She joined the Communist Party only in 1930.[90]

Fieseler has also shown that while female membership of the Bolshevik Party had increased after the 1905 Revolution, and while there were significantly more women Social Democrats (Mensheviks as well as Bolsheviks) than Socialist Revolutionaries, the female proportion of Bolshevik Party membership actually fell in the context of a massive influx of men in 1917. This discussion, and Clements' more detailed biographical research, challenge Fieseler's suggestion that female Social Democrats between 1890 and 1917 may have embraced the cause more for personal reasons than for abstract political ones.[91] It is unlikely that the latter lay behind the surge in female, anymore than male, working-class membership. Like their male counterparts, unskilled female workers who turned to the Bolsheviks were spurred into action by perceived injustice as well as by disappointment that the overthrow of the tsar in February had done little to improve their situation, either at work or at home. As for the intelligentsia, Galina Flakserman, a Bolshevik of long standing, hosted the meeting that decided to go ahead with the October Revolution, to which her husband, the Menshevik Sukhanov, was opposed.[92] There is also the case of Ekaterina Kuskova whose attraction to Marxism in the 1890s had been based on ideological conviction, elements of which she retained when she split from the Social Democrats at the end of the century. In the 1905 Revolution, Kuskova worked with the liberal Union of Liberation, and in 1917 she supported the Provisional Government and collaborated with the feminists.[93]

Fieseler has concluded that unlike other socialist parties in western Europe, "the RSDLP could have been proud (had this been due to a purposeful and deliberate policy) of its numbers of women on the eve of the 1905 Revolution" and that "as long as both men and women were deprived of the basic democratic rights, it was easier for women to carry out a common struggle alongside men".[94] Despite coming to the conclusion that there was no female Social Democrat in Russia who held such a prominent position of leadership as Spiridonova did among the Socialist Revolutionaries, Barbara Clements also acknowledges that:

> Some female SDs [Social Democrats] led local party committees, and a few were important members of the circles of expatriate radicals living abroad to stay out of the clutches of the police. The best known of this latter group was Nadezhda Krupskaia [whose]

job was to manage communications between Party leaders in Western Europe and underground workers in Russia. Yet despite the fact that women did not figure prominently among SR or SD leaders, the world of the revolutionaries was, by comparison with the larger Russian society, unusual as a place where women routinely experienced respect, creativity, even freedom.[95]

What is overlooked is that after her return to Russia in April 1917, Krupskaia's revolutionary work changed and that she developed politically through her contact with working-class women and youth:

> I learned a great deal from the work in the Vyborg district. It was a good school for Party and Soviet work. During the many years that I had lived abroad as a political exile, I never dared to make a speech even at a small meeting, and until that time I had never written a single line in *Pravda*. I needed such a school very much.[96]

It was not, therefore, a one-way process, with women workers learning from and following the lead of female Bolsheviks. As Krupskaia realized, not only did she have to strive to earn the trust and respect of women workers, they were not simply a drag on the labour movement but had much to offer it.

Besides looking more closely at the role of women in the 1917 Revolution, it is necessary also to re-evaluate the role of organizer and administrator, of manager of communications in a situation of underground political activity – not leadership positions, certainly, but also not simply servicing and following orders from a male leadership. Krupskaia's biographer, McNeal, has been rather dismissive of such "female" work, describing it as "humdrum secretarial functions" while Roger Pethybridge, in a review of *Bride of the Revolution*, complained that Krupskaia concentrated too much on "petty administrative detail" and that in 1917 she "dabbled in the municipal government of Petrograd, setting up children's playgrounds, etc., while Lenin put through the revolution".[97] Such work is not always so easily dismissed, as Ralph Carter Elwood observed in his study of the Russian Social Democratic movement in Ukraine before 1914:

> The fact that so many of these women fulfilled secretarial functions might indicate a degree of early twentieth-century male chauvinism;

i.e., a feeling that women were ill-suited for more important agitational and organisational roles among the proletariat. On the other hand, Lenin put great stress on maintaining accurate and consistent communication between his emigré headquarters and the leading party bodies in Russia. He was far happier with Samoilova's systematic work as secretary of *Pravda*'s educational board [in Ukraine] than he ever was with the activities of her male predecessors, F.F. Raskolnikov and V.M. Molotov. Secretarial functions included more than just correspondence and book-keeping. Samoilova and [Elena] Rozmirovich were also responsible for the coding of messages, the arranging of secret addresses, and serving as a liaison between the illegal and the new legal outlets in Russia. These well-educated women had the additional advantage of respectability, which was often useful in conspiratorial circumstances.[98]

Of course, there was not the same prestige attached to administrative work as to theoretical in the Social Democratic movement, but that should not obscure the fact that women were able to play important and even crucial roles during the revolutionary struggle. We need to stop condescending to these "daughters" and "brides" of the revolution, who possessed courage as well as dedication, initiative as well as selfless-ness. The achievements of Marxist women in Russia have to be set within the context of a very limited range of options open to women in such a patriarchal society.[99] That the type of posts which women had filled before the Bolsheviks took power lost their revolutionary signi-ficance after 1918, and that women were generally consigned to lower levels of work within the Communist Party should not be allowed to detract from their contribution to the revolutionary process.

CHAPTER FOUR

The lives of working women on the eve of the First World War

Before the 1917 Revolution, Russia was a predominantly peasant society headed by a ruler with absolute power, whose authority was mirrored in the institution of the family and vested in the eldest male. In general, the position of women, in law and in practice, was subordinate and the impression given by memoirs, ethnographic studies, travellers' accounts, and accepted by most historians, is of female passivity within a sometimes brutal patriarchy. There had, however, been female rulers, notably in the eighteenth century, and a wife could become head of household if her husband was dead, incapacitated or absent and there was no other suitable adult male replacement. Patriarchy was not static, and from the later nineteenth century was subject to huge pressures of growing peasant impoverishment, the terrible famine of 1891, industrialization and urbanization. That famine radicalized many in the upper classes who had previously been politically passive. The extent of peasant suffering, and the failure of the government to deal with the emergency, led to a growth in criticism of tsarist policies and priorities, but as reformers and revolutionaries alike found, there was a huge gulf between them and the peasantry. Peasant women in particular were resistant to change. Whatever their political views, the intelligentsia were caught between an autocracy that persistently refused to compromise or concede even the most moderate reforms, and a peasantry who remained suspicious of these self-appointed champions' motives, and impervious to their arguments.

Autocracy and the position of women

Most studies of Russian society acknowledge the importance not only of the peasant legacy but of serfdom, which was not abolished until 1861. A leading soviet scholar of the peasant commune before 1861, V.A. Aleksandrov, observed that serfs and state peasants spent their lives relatively isolated in their villages.[1] Theirs was an environment populated almost entirely by other peasants. In a very real sense, though the majority of Russians lived in the countryside, the village was a world apart from the rest of Russia. Landowners had such enormous power over the serfs that serfdom appeared in many respects akin to slavery. Aleksandrov has shown that in practice landowners had also had a strong interest in the cohesion of peasant families and hence in their economic viability. He recorded that the norm was for the landlord to set certain standards, or regulations, for the marriage of his serfs. Thus, for example, while it was a common requirement that female serfs marry by the age of seventeen, and males by the age of twenty, many peasants paid fines rather than marry off their teenage daughters who were valuable contributors to the household labour force.[2] It seems that after the abolition of serfdom, when early marriage remained the norm, a peasant girl might make herself useful in every way to her parental household in order to postpone marriage.[3]

Aleksandrov's study shows how much the reality of rural Russia differed from the simple assumption of "rule from above", and that in practice the omnipotent serf-owner could seldom impose demands without some kind of negotiation, or compromise with the peasant commune. Patterns of communal authority varied, but the communes displayed a fundamental similarity, playing a major role in peasant life that persisted after the end of serfdom, and even survived the 1917 Revolution.[4] Integral to that authority was a gender hierarchy, and a particularly heavy workload for peasant women, as is discussed below.

The abolition of serfdom did not entail the end of patriarchy. The Russian woman owed complete obedience in law to her parents; she could not, for example, leave home or receive a passport without their permission. On marriage, that obedience was owed by the wife to her husband. She could not legally leave him without a pass from him, while he had the right to require his wife to live with him.[5] Yet his power was not absolute. There were reciprocal rights and duties of husband and wife. Women had property and inheritance rights, which though not on an equal basis with men could not be changed by marriage. Certainly, men had the right to chastise their women with corporal punishment, as reflected in the peasant sayings: "Beat your fur coat, and it will be warmer; beat your wife and she will be sweeter"; "a wife isn't a jug – she won't crack if you hit her a few times".[6] However, there were also aphorisms that cautioned against the use of force: "who beats the *baba* will soon become poor".[7] Moreover, by the late nineteenth century, peasant women were increasingly resorting to the courts if they considered their punishment had been too severe.[8]

Within the village, the peasant family was like a public institution. The authority of the male head of household was considered to mirror that of the tsar, and was also considered to be in the best interests of the community. It was not simply a case of the man wanting power; peasant society traditionally gave him authority, expected him to wield it and criticized him if he did not. One peasant saying declared that "a man is not a man if his wife rules".[9] Women, as that adage might imply, were not simply passive beasts of burden, but had a crucial role to play in the village community in which social solidarity and moral consensus mattered a great deal. Another example of village wisdom described the husband whose wife had died as an orphan, as if he could not survive without a marriage partner.[10] There was general approval at his quick remarriage, especially if he had children.

In pre-industrial society biology had a tremendous impact on the place of women. With the practice of early marriage, pregnancy was frequent. A female physician who studied 160 women murderers, and a further 150 "normal" peasant women at the turn of the century found that women in the village often married before they had begun menstruation. She established that the average age for menstruation for urban girls was 14, but for village girls it was between 16 and 17. In her view, the latter were not sexually mature enough for marriage and motherhood.[11] Certainly rural physicians came up against a host of gynaecological problems, and found women aged quickly from continual childbearing. Mikhail Bulgakov, who on graduation from Kiev University served his first medical post in a village in the province of Smolensk in western Russia in 1916, found that pregnant women came to the surgery for help only in extreme circumstances, preferring to rely on a village healer, or on customs that he found alarming. One of the two midwives working with him told the story of finding sugar in a woman's birth canal. The woman had been taught by the local wisewoman:

She was having a difficult birth, she said, which meant that the baby didn't want to come out into the light of day. She would have to entice it out, so the way to do it was to lure it out with something sweet!

Another method that peasants believed would ease the birth was to chew hair. One of the more drastic ways that the midwife recounted for dealing with a breech birth was to hang the woman upside down from the ceiling of the peasant hut to make the baby turn round.[12] Bulgakov's stories also revealed the strong bonds of affection between parents and their children, which serves as a useful balance to the image of widespread violence in peasant households, against both women and children.

Reproduction was clearly vital for a farming system in which the size of a plot depended on the number of male labourers. Since the household was the basis for the village economy, the peasant women's role was also social. The peasant was seldom left alone or regarded as an individual, while the division of labour between women and men (which is discussed below) was the traditional guarantee of social cohesion. In practice, for peasant women, work and home were not separate. Like their men, women inhabited both, but it was the women who were the pivot of the household. Though their skills were considered of less value than men's, the tasks women fulfilled were recognized to be vital for the continuation of the household. Thus peasant women had an essential, pre-determined role in a small world, which was sustained while the community remained relatively isolated. Change in the world at large in the last decades of the nineteenth century, most notably industrialization and urbanization, affected their position, but though some, especially among the younger generation, sought to modify traditional expectations of women, most were determined to preserve village culture.

Upper-class women also owed complete obedience to the male head of their household, although before 1861 these women had power over serfs. From the 1830s, the impact of romanticism on Russian thought was to question the position of women whom the Romantics saw as the moral guardians of society. In terms of marriage, the stress was on romantic love rather than family advantage, and on the need for a woman to have a serious education to enable her to fulfil the roles of companion to her husband and first educator of her children. Especially from the 1840s, radical critics of tsarism saw the emancipation of women as a symbol for the general liberty of individuals. Yet for those critics, equality between women and men remained a minor issue, given the overwhelming importance of the peasant question.

The abolition of serfdom in 1861 had a profound effect on single impoverished gentry women, many of whom now had to look for respectable paid employment, while they were influenced by the exalted image of female selflessness, endurance, and a feeling of guilt over the possession of privileges, especially in view of the growing impoverishment of the peasantry in the late nineteenth century. Many upper-class women had an ethical vision of devoting themselves to society, from which they derived great personal satisfaction. That self-sacrifice was not always understood or accepted by the common people, while some upper-class women even saw their position as inferior to that of lower-class women and would have agreed with Helene Lange who wrote in 1871:

> Now, as far as the lower strata of society are concerned, a part of them find occupation quite easily, partly in positions as servants occupied with purely female work, partly competing with men, with whom they stand in perfect equality, if not in wages, at least in regard to intellectual culture. Many of these have to toil inexpressibly, but they at least have the satisfaction that men have no better lot than theirs. In these walks of life there are no arbitrarily made differences between man and woman . . . But in the middle and higher classes we meet most unmarried women. Here man has privileges . . . has all the opportunities for education.[13]

Education was increasingly seen as a solution to the problems of the upper-class woman in Russia. Individual women petitioned for admission to the various institutions of higher education, with little success at first. Some attended lectures unofficially. Others went to foreign universities, notably Zurich. Whatever their personal needs, observers claimed that the concern of these noblewomen was not so much for social fulfilment, as the desire to be socially useful.[14] For most, however, study abroad was impossible. In 1872, the government approved, on an experimental basis, courses run by Professor Guerrier (Gere) of the University of Moscow, which would train women as teachers for the higher level of girls' secondary schools. The professor believed that women required a different, limited and specifically feminine education.[15]

Why had the government changed tack? It seems that a major reason was the state's need for more teachers. In addition, the government was concerned that if the demands of women for higher education were continually denied, they might be affected by the growing politicization of Russian students abroad. In 1873, the tsar decreed that Russian women who continued to study in Zurich would be ineligible for jobs controlled by the state, which meant virtual exclusion from the professions in Russia. While the decree attacked the sexual morality of the students in Zurich, it also promised educational opportunities for women in Russia. Thus, besides fear of radicalism, the government had also come to recognize, within limits, the social utility of women. Hence, the government also restricted the employment of women to the lower levels of teaching and medicine, and to clerical work. A statute of 1876 provided pedagogical courses at all secondary schools and the establishment of women's technical and industrial schools, and advocated higher education courses for women in all university towns. The most famous of the latter were the Bestuzhev courses in St Petersburg, which survived until 1918. Many of the Bestuzhev women utilized their learning by teaching in remote provinces of Russia. Others continued their studies and research. By 1881, female students represented 20 per cent of the total enrolment in higher education institutions in Russia.[16] Female students believed that the solution to the inferiority of women lay in higher education and professional employment that would equip them for their social role on an equal basis with men.[17]

The struggle for higher education was the most successful activity of Russian feminists and philanthropists in the late nineteenth century.[18] Philanthropy was generally left to wealthy individuals, women as well as men, though it was increasingly seen as a natural concern for women, allowing them to contribute to society without straying far from the domestic sphere. Part of the response to the economic dislocation experienced by upper-class women after the 1861 abolition of serfdom and the increasing industrialization in the 1880s and 1890s, was an increase in charitable enterprises directed at women, notably for education, training, employment and accommodation. Such efforts could ameliorate the lot of only a few, given the scale of demand, and were dependent on the arbitrary will of the tsar. In addition, the often patronizing regime of the charitable institutions alienated many of the needy women from their aristocratic benefactors.[19]

Upper-class women and work

Many of the politically active women whom radical male workers met were from the upper classes. There is, of course, the enduring image of the Russian revolutionary woman as a refined lady appalled by the living and working conditions of the masses, ashamed that the aristocracy or gentry from which she sprung lived at the expense of the peasantry and workers, and determined to atone for that exploitation, partly by adopting a frugal lifestyle, partly by devoting that life to the service of the people. A minority became revolutionaries, convinced that the task was too urgent to wait for the cumulative impact of their individual efforts which they despaired of as a drop of ineffectual penance in an ocean of misery, and which they feared might even shore up the hated regime. The majority of upper-class working women, however, sought employment that would enable them to support themselves and perhaps their families, and give them a sense of purpose in life. Most of them also hoped to perform some service to the people, especially in medicine or teaching (both professions were held in relatively low esteem in late nineteenth-century Russia, partly because women were accepted into them), and derived job satisfaction from a sense of social utility. Ironically, while peasant women who needed to earn their own living migrated to the cities, upper-class professional women often left the urban environment behind for jobs in the villages.

The latter increasingly looked to education to provide them with the skills necessary to enter the few professions open to them. Hence the late nineteenth-century campaign for the entry of women into higher education, alongside the setting up of those special higher education courses for women taught by sympathetic male professors in the major cities of the tsarist empire.[20] For the most part, such women sought education and work out of necessity, and while gender was a factor in limiting what they could do within a patriarchal system, their social position also distinguished what they did from their social inferiors. Moreover, while the former could dedicate themselves to improving the conditions of the latter, the cultural differences between the two ensured a gulf of understanding that proved almost impossible to bridge. The low educational and cultural levels of the majority of working women, both rural and urban, led many politically conscious male workers to consider a wife from their own class as a hindrance, too ground down by material deprivation and the responsibilities of family to become capable of understanding, let alone struggling for, ideals.[21] Rather than give up on them, upper-class women sought to raise their lower-class sisters' consciousness as well as improve their position, by moving to the villages to work among them in a professional capacity. A few, briefly in the early 1870s, disguised themselves as workers and took jobs in a factory. More took professional posts based in industry.

In both cases, they found acceptance difficult. Women who went to work among the peasants remained only a few years (generally up to three) before being physically drained by the heavy demands of the work and emotionally anguished by the personal isolation. Those upper-class women who disguised themselves as factory workers lasted a few months at most, demoralized by their failure to break down the barriers between themselves and their co-workers, and exhausted beyond endurance by the long hours and heavy labour to which they were so abruptly introduced.[22] To the workers, such women seemed like tourists to an unknown and unknowable world.

Professional women certainly did not have an easy time in their own world. The government was always grudging in its attitude towards higher education and job opportunities for women, while there was often parental disapproval of daughters who sought to work for a living. Not all women, however, had to struggle against their families; instead, many were given both emotional and financial support from their parents, notably their mothers.[23] One aristocratic woman received a serious education at home, along with her 14 sisters and brothers, and had the support of her family when training to be a physician. She qualified in 1886, becoming a respected eye surgeon before the end of the century and throughout her long working life (she died in 1936), during which she travelled widely, she had frequent visits from her mother.[24] From the 1870s women were granted further and higher education, but were for the most part restricted to certain areas (education, medicine, and administration) and to the lower reaches of the career ladder. By the eve of the First World War, partly through feminist campaigns and partly through government recognition of women as a cheap pool of labour for underfunded state services, the opportunities for female professionals, both in terms of posts and promotion, had widened considerably. It had also become clear that the best chances of advancement lay in the towns and cities, rather than in the villages. The general experience of female professionals in the countryside was of poor conditions of life, heavy demands of work with limited resources, the arrogance of local government bureaucrats, and the suspicion of the peasantry.[25]

Peasant resistance to female professionals coming into their villages and attempting to make changes in traditional practices was not simply a reaction from either a knee-jerk patriarchy, or a deep-seated social antagonism towards upper-class outsiders. In practice, the services of these women were often welcomed, since at last peasant women could openly discuss their illnesses, especially gynaecological, with another of their sex. Moreover, in general these female physicians were not replacing men or the traditional rural healers, but adding their skills and medicines to previously neglected areas, while the city-bred women often depended on a local, generally male, paramedic, and a nurse/ midwife to help with their large practices.[26] Rather, the residual resistance to the urban intelligentsia also reflected a preference for home-grown village "professionals", such as peasant healers and midwives, who were generally women, and teachers who were men from their own community and more likely to marry a peasant and establish a family in the village in which they worked.[27] In contrast, the urban women who found employment in the countryside were seen as, and seem to have regarded themselves as, temporary guests. Career advancement, better living and working conditions, higher pay, and the opportunity to associate with one's peers lay in the city.

In addition, in town and countryside female professionals, who tended to remain single, depended on servants to run their homes, partly because of the determination of the former to devote themselves to service of the people from which servants came, and partly because upper-class women did not regard domesticity as part of their sphere. The impression from memoirs of such women is that the demands of running a home were a distraction from what they considered their "real" work. One female physician had the hiring of servants for her rural practice as part of her duties, along with renting the accommodation for clinics and seeing to their upkeep. She had had no experience in such organizational tasks and had never had occasion to learn domestic skills, having lived with her family while a student when all such work was taken care of by the hired help. She looked on such duties as not only onerous and distasteful, but as interfering with her professional work. Hence she hired a servant to clean and to cook for her. Like other professional women, she was also very critical of the standards of housekeeping of these employees. Such complaints were often understandable. For example, the servant at one of her dispensaries used to shut the chimney in order to heat up the consulting room, but the result was the build-up of carbon monoxide, so much so that on one occasion the doctor collapsed and remained unconscious for half an hour, until found by a patient who took her out of the room, and sent her home once she regained consciousness.[28]

Such female physicians, though themselves lacking in experience of childrearing, were also intent on educating peasant women to improve their skills in this area. It was the view of the former that traditional methods of care were harmful to children, while the demands of farm work, especially in the summer months, resulted in neglect of babies and children too young to help in the fields. One method of combating the latter was to set up crèches in the village, as a female physician did in the summer of 1900. Infants of twelve months and over and children up to five years of age were brought to the crèche as early as 5am, and picked up by 7pm. The two crèches for which she was responsible lasted for three years and cared for up to 60 children. She judged them a success, not simply in freeing the mothers to work in the fields and improving the children's health, but indirectly as educating the mothers in modern methods of care and hygiene. Later, in the three years before war broke out in 1914, this doctor carried out bi-annual inspections of children in the 12 schools in her district.[29] Such efforts were commendable, but depended on the determination of an individual who often remained in a district for three years at most, before moving, or being moved on, somewhere else, and starting again, with nothing in place to ensure that the work done in the previous posting would be continued.

The merchant class in tsarist Russia, which largely originated in the peasantry, was also very conservative, but whereas the peasantry had the sympathy of the intelligentsia, merchants were often held in contempt, not least because the intelligentsia disapproved of merchant attitudes towards women and the family. Even more than among the peasantry, merchant family life was patriarchal: for example, the seclusion of women was practised to a degree even at the end of the nineteenth century. One foreign visitor in the early 1890s recorded that merchants' wives and daughters were still kept out of sight when male friends visited the male head of the household, that the wives did not manage the housekeeping finances, and that when shopping women were accompanied by a male relative.[30]

In a pioneering study of Russian merchant women between 1850 and 1917, Catriona Kelly noted the demeaning representations of these women, generally caricatured as completely submissive to their husbands and fathers, expected to mirror their men's wealth in their gaudy dress and jewellery, ostentatious domestic surroundings and idle frivolity.[31] Merchants' wives were portrayed as the embodiment of commercialism, exploiting rather than serving the people, with parents prepared to "sell" their own daughters for the sake of the family business or entry into high society. There were many female hawkers who worked for themselves, trading throughout the streets of the cities, indicating that there was considerable variety, and a hierarchy, among the merchants no less than among other social groups. Even among the richer merchantry, a few of the wives supported their husbands' enterprises, and in a minority of cases ran inherited businesses, though generally commerce on this scale was a masculine domain. Trading women were found in much greater numbers in small businesses (wholesale as well as retail, goods as well as services).[32] Female employers were not known to be any more generous than males in terms of the payment and conditions that they provided for their workers, but women running businesses were certainly in a minority compared to the men.

Certainly, at least until the mid nineteenth century, the great fair at Nizhnii Novgorod, whose commercial importance had peaked by the 1890s, had been a masculine affair, as far as the merchants were concerned. Peasant women, however, and female prostitutes traded there in great numbers. Interestingly, at the fair in 1896 there was a congress of white-collar workers at which the acceptance of women into mutual benefit societies was discussed. Previously, only a few women had been admitted as exceptional cases. Although some men objected, seeing women as a baleful influence (quarrelsome, for example, and even sexually threatening), a majority voted in favour of extending membership to women.[33]

Women in white-collar occupations reflected the late nineteenth-century improvements in female education. By the turn of the century, as the educational and cultural level of the merchant class rose and as travel (especially by railway) improved, they began to take their families to that great fair. Still, with the exception of wealthy merchant families, the way of life of this social group remained, like that of the peasantry, profoundly patriarchal and deeply religious. The merchants maintained their traditions by isolating their home life from the outside world, and educating both sons and daughters in the home. Moreover, the number of merchants grew through the addition of successful peasant traders, rather than from the development of an urban middle class. Hence the continuing political and social conservatism of the merchantry.[34] Still, there were at least a few businesswomen (both in their own right and in place of an incapacitated husband), while other women held positions and shares in family businesses. A minority of the merchantry became so rich that, over the generations, the education of their children, daughters as well as sons, resembled that of the aristocracy, while their wives became philanthropists and patrons of the arts.[35]

Still, it seems that women of the merchant community, like the female peasantry, were more likely to remain committed to the established order than their social superiors, though it was nevertheless a minority of the latter who dedicated themselves to the people through their professional, philanthropical, revolutionary, or feminist activities. As the economy developed in the late nineteenth and especially the early twentieth centuries, women of the upper classes who sought paid employment found an increasing variety of opportunities, though still restricted in scope by employers' assumptions about gender. There were growing numbers of white-collar jobs open to women, to which some from the lower classes who had benefited from a sustained period of education could also aspire. Women with good handwriting found work as scribes. Those with a wider education than the basics were taken on as translators, proof-readers, telegraphists and telephonists, bookkeepers and accountants. While these jobs were seen as appropriate for women, the place of work was still seen as essentially in the male sphere, such as shipyards and railways.[36]

Above all, it seems, it was the spread of literacy, the growth of the press and publishing, and of popular entertainments, notably the theatre, that allowed educated women to find a niche. Russian women's participation, and sometimes prominent role, in the theatre has often been overlooked. Catherine Schuler's study of the latter charts significant changes in the status of actresses between 1870 and 1910, including great increases in their numbers, the prominence of a few female stars, and the predominance of "women's themes" in their plays.[37] In contrast to Britain and the USA, there was no avowedly feminist theatre, but the issues raised both in the work produced and the situation of women in the theatre heightened the profile of the woman question at a time when the autocratic and patriarchal political and social system was under growing pressure. The increase in numbers reflected the growth in the female labour force at the end of the nineteenth century. While stars could command high salaries, at least until they began to show signs of ageing, most earned very little and always less than men in comparable positions. Theatre work was very insecure, while women were vulnerable to sexual harassment from their bosses as well as patrons, faced public condemnation of, as well as fascination in, their morals, and endured a peripatetic existence that made marriage and motherhood problematic, to say the least.

Fierce competition between women in the theatre was encouraged by critics and fans alike. Stars were few, and were, in Schuler's view, eclipsed by modernism, when the cult of the starring actress was replaced by the cult of the starring director.[38] Schuler records that most of these stars did not themselves direct, though they took a keen interest in many aspects of theatrical production. Those women who ran their own theatres were generally successful for a few years at most, often running up large debts before being forced to close. Part of their failure was attributable to inexperience and incompetence, but much was also attributable to circumstances. Nevertheless, failure of a female theatrical entrepreneur confirmed prejudices that such women were less practical than their male counterparts.

The theatre, however, was not generally regarded as a respectable occupation for women. Many more women sought to use their education to find work in the literary field. Nadezhda Dmitrievna Khovanshchinskaia has been seen as the first Russian woman journalist, already publishing before she arrived in St Petersburg in 1852. She also wrote plays and poems, novels, short stories and essays. Yet she died penniless, recognized by only one provincial newspaper.[39] Thus even a modest education and a respectable occupation did not ensure a woman a living wage. Still, the numbers of women in publishing increased in the later nineteenth and early twentieth centuries, reflecting the demand for work among the upper classes. *The Women's Calendar* published in St Petersburg in the early twentieth century, recorded in 1900 that 131 women in the capital were employed to write for magazines and newspapers. Nor were they restricted to publications directed specifically at women, but wrote regular columns for major newspapers such as *The Russian Word* (*Russkoe Slovo*) and literary journals such as *Russian Riches* (*Russkoe Bogatstvo*). Indeed, it was believed that women gained independence and acceptance in the literary profession before others, including medicine and education.

Certainly, in contrast to the latter, publishing did not require special qualifications, and by the end of the century was relatively well paid (especially compared to schoolteaching). Besides journalism, women also published their own works, including literature (novels, especially romances, short stories and poetry), pedagogy, medical texts, history (especially cultural) and bibliographies.[40] Though some promoted the cause of women, few saw themselves as having political viewpoints; and while the growth of a mass readership provided them with employment opportunities, the rate of female literacy was persistently lower than that of men, while illiteracy remained the common condition of peasant women. The 1897 census revealed that whereas just over 20 per cent of the population was literate, only 13 per cent of women were. Even that comparison is misleading: bearing in mind that literacy can mean simply the ability to sign one's name, while nearly 36 per cent of urban women were literate, only 10 per cent of peasant women were.[41] By 1912, there were only ten literate females for every 24 males.[42]

Peasant women's work

Into the twentieth century, peasant women lived and worked within an extended family consisting of their husbands' parents and generally all the male siblings and their wives. Peasant agriculture put a premium on women's productive as well as reproductive contribution. While all members of the household were subject to the authority of the patriarch, his wife also held a position of power as well as responsibility over the work of her daughters-in-law in the home and on the garden plot. Women were also expected to work in the fields alongside the men in busy periods, such as the harvest, and to replace those men who left in search of cash income with which to subsidize the farm. Besides working on the family plot, by the end of the nineteenth century a quarter of all women wage earners were hired field hands.[43] Thus, while there was a clear division of labour between the sexes in which women were primarily responsible for work within the household (which included the garden and cottage crafts) and childrearing, the survival of the peasant family depended on co-operation between its male and female members.[44]

As noted above, by the late nineteenth century, a peasant girl might be able to delay marriage by proving herself so useful in the parental household that she seemed indispensable. Marriage, however, was almost universal in the village, for there was little scope for individuals to survive on their own. Since the bride would live with her husband's family, great stress was placed on her household skills, proof of which she was expected to display before marriage. The father was expected to provide his daughter with a dowry, but among poor peasants especially, the wife still had to be a capable worker. It was customary at least until the late nineteenth century for the bride to prove her competence and worth to her husband's family by making presents for each member of his household.[45] By the end of the nineteenth century, these gifts often consisted of ready-made objects of urban culture, itself proof that she had earning capabilities. Moreover, concerns about the capacity for work and physical health had given way somewhat to other considerations, reflected in changing views of feminine beauty. Peasant women now wanted to dress fashionably on occasions, as urban women did.[46]

The impression of peasant women's lives is not simply of constant toil, interrupted briefly, if frequently, when giving birth, but of a considerable variety of jobs, the performance of which required a certain organizational ability. The peasant wife had to have at least basic skills in cooking, gardening, tending farm animals, harvesting, producing household commodities and foods, as well as clothing and footwear. She had to be able to process hemp and flax, to bleach linen and to comb wool, to weave and to spin, to sew and to knit. She was not tied to the home, though her status and role were defined by it. She had to be prepared to work not only in the fields, but in the forests, gathering berries and mushrooms. Increasingly by the late nineteenth century, she was expected to contribute to the family's cash income from this agricultural work, for example, by selling the produce of her garden plot and forest gatherings, the marketing of which might have entailed a trip to the nearest town or city.

In addition, and crucially, she had to produce and care for the household's future labour force. Bearing children was vital for the continuity of the peasant household, and its economic basis, since landholding depended on labour. Hence the early marriages and high birthrate. Hence, too, so many marriage customs that were concerned with female fertility: throwing grain or hops at the bride, deliberate profanity, erotic lyrics, and a fur coat turned outward (also a symbol of wealth).[47] Given the high death rate among infants, and the prevalence of gynaecological problems, the extension of modern medicine to the villages in the late nineteenth century was not unwelcome; but peasant women continued to prefer the local untrained midwife to the professionals, partly because the success of the former at uncomplicated deliveries was little different to that of a trained midwife or physician, and partly because the peasant attendant would also perform household tasks while the mother was incapacitated.[48] The female peasantry made their own judgements on what to accept and what to refuse in defence of their traditional way of life.

Given the extensive nature of women's work, it should not be surprising that some aspects suffered at the expense of others. With a rural labour surplus, land hunger and growing peasant impoverishment in the later nineteenth century, the pressure on women to contribute to the family income often adversely affected her ability to care for her infants or young children. Thus, especially during harvest time, breastfeeding would be irregular, and babies were either given juice made from poppies which would suppress hunger, or left to feed themselves on milk strained through a cloth bag, with the attendant dangers of choking, infection and germs.[49] Efforts of urban professionals to teach peasant mothers more scientific methods of childcare were understandable, but without a dramatic improvement in the poor peasantry's standard of living, also unrealistic.

However subordinate, the woman was seen as vital to the continuation of the village as well as the individual household, and a man was not regarded as a complete worker either within the home or the village unless he was married. Still, her value was defined by marriage which meant that women who remained single, especially if childless, were marginal to the village economy. Unless part of an extended family, and any children she might have be able to contribute to, and not simply be a drain upon, its upkeep, a single woman could not survive by farming alone, since it was labour intensive and land was allocated according to the number of males within the household. If she remained within the village, such a woman would have to find ways of augmenting her income, for example, through working at a village craft (such as lacemaking), serving as a healer and midwife, hiring out as a farm labourer or as a domestic servant in a wealthier peasant household, or entering a convent.[50]

Convents were generally open only to those women past the age of childbearing, though some wives of soldiers who were absent for years might enter one temporarily. More often, women who needed to earn wages continued to work on the land as field labour, and though often working alongside men, women earned on average between a third and a half of male rates of pay.[51] In some areas, the difference was much greater: for example, in Saratov, women commanded only a sixth of men's earnings. If these women were entirely dependent on their earnings for survival, they were in a very precarious position. In contrast, Robert Edelman's study of the southwest of the tsarist empire (that is, the right-bank of Ukraine) highlights the regional differences. There, women working in the sugar plantations tended to be the younger members of peasant households who continued to live with the extended family, which meant they had a "safety net". They still earned considerably less than men, but they were recognized as contributing substantially to the survival of their family farm. The wife as well as the children often worked in the beet fields while the husband remained at home cultivating the plot. For Edelman, this extensive female wage labour may have modified the nature of the patriarchal community in this region, and helps explain the highly militant role female field hands played there in the 1905 Revolution.[52] Another study of migrant field labour, however, reveals that in general their lot was deteriorating between 1890 and 1914. Wages of both men and women were depressed partly because of the surplus pool of labour, and partly because of the introduction of machinery.[53]

At any rate, perhaps the main distinction between peasant women and men was that the latter had some leisure time outside of the farm, especially in the winter, whereas the former seem to have been constantly working. This is not to say that women's lives consisted simply of complete drudgery. They enjoyed the company of other women, talking and singing as they worked. Thus paradoxically, while this difference reinforces the image of the female workhorse, it also emphasizes the central role of women in the family economy and that the household was very much women's space. The many and varied tasks performed by peasant women were regarded simply as their "natural" domestic talents, and not skilled in the way that "men's" work was.

Nevertheless, while skill and status was associated with the work done by men, the female crafts were important to the village economy. Peasant women were employed both at traditional handcrafts and in the work put out by urban manufacturers. Better-off rural women were sometimes entrepreneurs. Those who managed a machine (ownership was generally in male hands) employed girls in knitting socks, for example, or making gloves; some kept a tavern and would hire other women as waitresses. If a peasant girl worked in her own home, she might sell her finished articles (such as leather belts, bootlaces, toys, kerchiefs and shawls) through a female agent. Although widespread and providing an increasing proportion of a peasant family's income by the early twentieth century, female entrepreneurship and female crafts were intended to support the farm, and not replace it. Crafts and the putting-out system favoured by manufacturers in the Moscow district allowed women of the wealthy as well as the poor peasantry to remain in the village when the demand for their labour on the farms had significantly decreased, and so helped them preserve the traditional way of life while responding to, and in some cases profiting from, changing economic conditions.[54] However, demand, even from factories, was not constant, and although upper-class fashion might encourage a traditional industry, such as shawl-making, other factors (such as bulk buying for a mass market) diluted women's skills (for example, in the design of lace).[55]

Peasant women, then, produced for both the luxury and the mass markets. Remuneration from such domestic industry was meagre and generally sporadic. Girls learned crafts from an early age (from seven or eight years old). Their cash contribution to the family income allowed mothers to concentrate on the household plot and animals, though all would work at crafts in their "spare" time away from farm tasks. In the light of the varied demands on women, of the variety of jobs that they could perform within the village for the upkeep of the peasant household, it is not surprising that schooling was viewed as less essential than for men who might have to seek work in the city, or in the worst case be conscripted into the army.

Peasant women could also earn money by selling their garden produce in the markets of nearby towns and cities, and in the summer by working on urban garden plots. Whatever form it took, such income-generating work was often seasonal and depended on the whim of the market. It was another means of supporting the family farm, of continuing the traditional way of life. That, however, did not remain unchanged. The growing industrial economy from the 1880s, but especially the 1890s, offered much needed wage labour to peasant men, and fewer but increasing numbers of women. For the former, who generally left wives and children behind in the village, urban employment was looked on as another tactic for preserving the rural household with which they maintained contact, however prolonged their absences. For peasant women who went to work in the cities, migration was more likely an exit from the village which could not support them. As for the majority of women left behind on the land, there was interaction with the towns through occasional visits to, and from, their husbands, through the sale of farm produce on urban markets, and through the impact of the vagaries of urban demand on rural crafts. Even traditional peasant dress was influenced by urban fashion and factory-produced materials.[56]

Whether they remained in the village or migrated to the towns, women began work earlier than men because of the assumption that housework and care of infants were in the female sphere, and because so many of the female crafts (such as sewing, knitting and weaving) were associated with that sphere. One result was that the expertise gained made them attractive as marriage partners, since their labour was proof of their capabilities. Another, as noted above, was that peasant girls were less likely to go to school than boys since the services of the former were so important at home. Neither village culture (which was orally based) nor farm work had much need of literacy or numeracy. What uses they had (such as keeping accounts, communicating with an absent spouse or with an urban manufacturer or middleman or woman, reading aloud for entertainment or religious edification) did not make schooling universally necessary among the peasants. Literacy was more of an asset to boys than girls, since the former were more likely to have dealings with the world outside the village, either through employment or military conscription, where it might help secure a better posting or a promotion. Peasants were not in principle opposed to female literacy, but rather took a utilitarian attitude towards the skill generally. Was it useful in the home, or for employment purposes? If for pleasure, was there time to learn and were there opportunities to read? Would literacy make peasants dissatisfied with their lives?[57] There was a fear that literacy, associated with urban culture, would "seduce" women and weaken their commitment to the traditional way of life, of which they were supposed to be the guardians. One result was that for most of those girls who attended school, it was such a brief experience that it did little to enhance the job opportunities of those who went to the city in search of work while, compared with males, female urban workers rarely improved their level of skill. The minority who were able to continue their education, for example, by training as a nurse or midwife, found that a period spent away from the village acquiring urban skills served to distance them from their "old" life.

Peasant women at work in the city

Necessity forced peasant women, like peasant men, to migrate to the city, but as Barbara Alpern Engel points out in her fascinating study *Between the Fields and the City: Women, Work and Family in Russia, 1861–1914*, whereas patriarchy was weakened by economic developments, the benefits went mainly to younger men who were able to shake off the father's authority. Female peasants, in contrast, left behind a patriarchal family that had "protected and looked after women, even as it constrained and sometimes oppressed them". While Engel's conclusion is perhaps overly pessimistic, she reveals the extent of continuity between the village and the city, showing how patriarchal structures adapted to social and economic change. Her astute observation that married women in the city were sometimes more economically dependent on their men than peasant wives were, leads us to question the view, held by feminists as well as Social Democrats, of the liberating experience of waged labour for women.[58]

There were other factors besides poverty pushing millions of peasant women to the city. Mechanization, increasing division of labour, the dependence on labour intensive production (especially in the Moscow region and the textile industry) rather than on technological advance, and a preference for low-wage earners who were uninterested in taverns, trade unions or politics, combined to result in a massive growth in the numbers of female factory workers in the early twentieth century. Since the turn of the century, their rate of growth had been twice that for male factory hands (at almost 60 per cent for the former and 30 per cent for the latter), and one in three factory workers was a woman by 1913 though men still predominated in the factory labour force.[59] The tendency of employers to replace men with women where possible after the 1905 Revolution confirmed male suspicions that women were a threat to their jobs, wages, skills and status. This fear of the substitution of female for male workers had substance, but was nevertheless exaggerated since most women factory workers tended to remain in sectors traditionally seen as related to their domestic sphere, such as clothing. Thus in 1910, women constituted just under 65 per cent of the workforce in the textile industry, but less than half a per cent in construction, only 1.4 per cent in metals, and 3.3 per cent in machine tools.[60] Men retained their almost total monopoly of the relatively highly paid skilled work, aided by the lower literacy rates among women as well as the latters' own "monopoly" of housework and childcare.

Since women and men generally did different kinds of work in the city, why was there so much unease among men over the perceived competition from female labour by the eve of the First World War? There was, after all, a tendency on the part of employers to categorize jobs in terms of gender suitability: hence the metal industry was seen as masculine, and textiles as feminine. True, that assumption did not mean that these sectors were exclusive to either women or men, but in any industry, women were generally put to work at the lowest paid and unskilled tasks. Outside influences, particularly the revolution of 1905 and the First World War, encouraged employers to take on women not only in increasing numbers, but at tasks previously monopolized by men, though generally not so much within the metal trade, but more within the textile, cotton and clothes industries. Thus by 1910, women made up 62.9 per cent of the textile workforce. In the cotton industry 31 per cent of workers were women and in the garment and shoe industries 48 per cent were women. Women were also moving into printing and chemicals (constituting around 14 per cent of the labour force in each by 1910).[61] By the eve of the First World War, while men clearly dominated in what were traditionally considered masculine trades (such as metal and wood), women constituted a significant and growing percentage of the labour force in a number of areas besides those traditionally associated with the domestic sphere. This is reflected in the following table, showing what percentage of the labour force across a range of industries was female:

	% age
porcelain/ceramic	36.8
glass	19.4
metal/engineering	4.8
woodworking	8.2
chemical	34.8
food	21.4
paper	31.4
linen	53.9
printing	9.1
cotton	56.1
wool	41.6
silk	67.6

Source: E. Milovidova, *Zhenskii vopros i zhenskoe dvizhenie* (Moscow–Leningrad 1929), p. 207.

The minority of politically aware male workers realized that the threat to their position came from technology, new work practices, further division of labour and dilution of skills, rather than women "stealing" men's jobs, but they generally made no demands for sexual equality in pay, promotion or training in the workplace. Any demands for equal pay, made for example by the tailors' union during the 1905 Revolution, were intended to make female labour less attractive to employers, and were often coupled with complaints about women and male apprentices being used to lower wage rates and undermine the position of the skilled male worker.[62] Not only were women's wages never equal to men's, but the gap between the wages earned by the sexes varied widely, with women taking home from as little as a fifth to almost two-thirds of men's average earnings. This was the case even within the textile industry in which women predominated.[63] The gap would have widened as workers aged, since women were much less likely to improve their skills and win promotion than men. Only with war in 1914 did women's wages significantly improve, though they still remained lower than men's, partly due to the skills' gap between the sexes, partly to the assumption that women should command less pay than the male breadwinner. For manufacturing industry as a whole in 1914, women earned 51.1 per cent of the average male wage, but that obscures considerable variations in the daily wages of women workers in percentage terms to those of male workers in the same industry: for example, in the metal industry, women earned only 44.1 per cent of men's average daily wage, whereas in the cotton industry, the percentage was 72.1 per cent.[64] Moreover, if workers married it was generally the wife who was expected to take time off work, with the consequent loss of pay, to attend to domestic concerns, including frequent births and infant deaths.

Thus, while employers looked favourably on women workers as cheap and docile labour, no matter how long a woman remained in employment she was still seen as a housewife and mother first and foremost. In the late nineteenth century, the majority of female migrants had been single women (including widows), but by the turn of the next century increasing numbers of married women with children sought to become wage-earners, since only a minority of highly skilled men were paid enough to support a family by themselves. The 1905 Revolution saw, for the first time, demands for maternity leave and benefit, though it was not until 1912 that the government decreed that a woman could have two weeks off work before giving birth and a month after the baby's arrival. That decree was ignored by employers in the main. In practice, women worked even during labour, often gave birth while still at the workplace, and returned there as soon as possible.[65] Parents might share looking after the baby by working different shifts, or turn to outside help, such as a landlady, neighbour, or a peasant girl (some as young as seven) for whom the job of nanny might be her introduction to urban employment. Alternatively, especially if she had more than one young child, a mother might remain at home, saving on expenses by keeping a garden plot, mending and sewing for the family, taking in a lodger, or working from home (for example, at dressmaking).[66]

Indeed most women did not work in factories. Dressmakers, seamstresses and milliners earned a precarious living, based in a work-shop or at home (and often having to make hats to supplement their dressmaking). Women found jobs as waitresses in taverns and teashops, though, as for dressmakers, the hours were long, while they were vulnerable to the sexual advances of the mainly male customers. There were also positions as shop assistants, though again hours were long and wages low, while the assistants were expected to spend much of their meagre pay making themselves presentable, even fashionable.[67] Millinery, in particular, was subject to the demands of fashion, and female shop assistants were simply sacked wholesale during the low season. Young girls who entered the trade were first taught to trim and alter, and only then allowed into the shops. In high season, they were expected to help the milliners after the shop was closed, in order to meet demand. In St Petersburg and Odessa, for example, which were centres of the hat trade, shop assistants could work up to 19 hours a day throughout the high season. The skilled hat-makers themselves were relatively privileged: they generally worked a ten-hour day, with time off for holidays. Assistants who worked in dress departments were only marginally better off than those who sold hats.[68] In 1908, a shop assistant revealed her difficult, sometimes desperate, situation which she implied was typical:

> Long working hours and low wages push us towards the "shameful business". Our wages are not sufficient to live on, while our employers demand that we dress fashionably. We are powerless to resist, since there are so many in Petersburg ready to take our place, and work 15 hours a day for a slice of dry bread. Shop-owners are only interested in pretty girls. They have their own plans. The majority of girl-assistants are between 17 and 20 years of age. Women over 30 can be encountered only occasionally, and then away from the central shops.[69]

This was also the case for female white-collar workers, such as cashiers, office clerks and stenographers. Though their numbers were lower than for female shop assistants, their position seems to have had similar difficulties, especially for those on the lowest rung of the ladder. While their working day was in general considerably shorter, much depended on the business. In banks and insurance companies, for example, it was usually between seven and nine hours a day, whereas in transport or export companies, it could range between nine and 18 hours. Wages for female white-collar workers were better, and sometimes considerably so, than for shop assistants: whereas the latter might earn 20 roubles a month, a bank clerk could get 40.[70] Such wages were also now attracting women from relatively wealthy families, and there were complaints by the early twentieth century that the latter were providing unfair competition, since they were both better educated and better dressed than lower-class girls.

Yet even on the eve of the First World War, domestic service was the biggest urban employer of Russian women, and for many provided the entrance point to the city. There was considerable variety of situations in domestic service, from caring for the children of a lower-class family in which the mother was employed, to serving in the homes of the upper classes. Some women were hired on a daily basis while others had to surrender their internal passport (without which they could not legally travel) to their employer in whose house they were expected to reside. Since domestic service was often a peasant woman's first experience of city life, competition was fierce, especially when poverty was pushing more and more off the land (notably during the famine of 1901–2). In addition, while many young girls soon moved from being in service to employment in workshops or factories, as women workers grew older and less productive, they often had to return to some form of domestic service. Pay was low and conditions very basic, with servants often expected to sleep in hallways. Heavy physical labour, long hours, social isolation and a ban on visitors, no leisure and poor pay even when compared to women's wages generally, led some to characterize domestic service as "white slavery".[71]

Although factory work was deemed by contemporaries (revolutionaries as well as conservatives) to pose a threat to female morality, and there was widespread sexual harassment of women workers in factories, shops and offices, nevertheless domestic servants were more likely to give birth to illegitimate children.[72] In addition, given the harsh conditions, meagre pay and insecurity, prostitution was an attractive, and sometimes an essential, alternative to domestic service. It was often a supplement to other low wage-earning women, such as seasonal workers (for example, in tailoring), casual day labourers, those who served in the retail sector (as shop assistants, for example, or street hawkers) and some white-collar workers (the lower paid cashiers and clerks, for instance). This should not be surprising since a full-time prostitute could earn between eight and 100 times the average wage of a servant.[73]

Before the 1917 Revolution, prostitution was regulated by the state. The minimum age at which a woman could register with the police as a prostitute was 16 until 1895; by 1909 it had been raised to 21. Many women failed to register, perhaps because they intended to work as prostitutes temporarily or on a part-time basis, while the numbers of young girls (some as young as nine) resorting to prostitution increased greatly in the early twentieth century, and notably as a consequence of the First World War which by 1917 had left many people homeless and children deserted. While prostitution, whether registered or not, was more lucrative than most of the jobs then available to women, few remained in it full-time for more than five years. As in most occupations, the older a woman became, the lower the earnings she could command.[74]

Prostitution was seen by revolutionaries as proof of the degeneracy of capitalism which undermined the family by forcing women to sell their bodies, as Alexandra Kollontai wrote, for a morsel of bread.[75] Yet many working-class women seem to have turned to prostitution not only from dire necessity, or to supplement subsistence wages, but after weighing up alternative job opportunities and wage rates, and even for excitement. In addition, prostitution allowed women to enter the quintessentially masculine space of the tavern. They appear to have decided themselves when to resort to prostitution, and whether to register or not. Those who registered were "career" prostitutes, though as pointed out above, few continued for more than five years. Registered prostitutes were subject to compulsory medical examinations, but many evaded these. The fact that prostitution thrived in the late nineteenth and early twentieth centuries reflected the peculiar pattern of urbanization in Russia in which millions of men migrated for work, leaving their families in the village, resulting in a considerable sexual imbalance in the cities. Thus in Moscow in 1911, 75 per cent of men were supporting rural households. The sexual imbalance was less glaring in St Petersburg, whose inhabitants migrated over longer distances, and indeed in both cities the numbers of women were rising and catching up on the men, notably in the capital: by 1910 women in Petersburg constituted 48 per cent of the population.[76]

Though the gap was closing, autobiographies of male workers reveal that they often lived in a very masculine environment, working alongside, frequenting taverns and sharing accommodation with their countrymen.[77] Besides occasional visits from and to their peasant wives, most working-class men's contacts with women in the city were often limited to transactions for domestic services, such as cooking, cleaning, and washing, and from women as waitresses, hawkers, shop assistants, clerks and prostitutes. Men who became interested in politics met like-minded women, but tended to regard the latter as an unrepresentative minority among their sex. Indeed, radical male workers saw intimate relations with women as a threat to their political idealism, believing that a married woman, especially a mother, would act as a conservative influence on her man. Hence, although revolutionaries saw capitalism as undermining the family, they also considered that institution as a drain on a worker's commitment to the class struggle.

Thus, on the eve of the First World War, there was significant gender inequality in Russia, to which only a few objected, and which seemed even to those critics of the established order a symptom of the general injustice, rather than a priority. For feminists, of course, it was a priority, but one which could be remedied within a reformed legal and political order, and in the struggle to achieve that reform women could prove themselves worthy of full rights of citizenship with men. For those women who had to work for a living, at all social levels, there were increasing opportunities as the economy developed, but in many cases considerable hardship and frustration of their ambitions and talents. The outbreak of war in 1914 was to open doors into male bastions of the economy, and provide what feminists saw as the chance to show their loyalty to the nation in expectation of full equality with men once victory was secured. As the feminist Poliksena Shishkina-Yavein declared in August 1915:

> We women have to unite: and each of us, forgetting personal mis-fortune and suffering, must come out of the narrow confines of the family and devote all our energy, intellect and knowledge to our country. This is our obligation to the fatherland, and this will give us the right to participate as the equals of men in the new life of a victorious Russia.[78]

For the majority of poor women, urban and local, the war was to intensify their inescapable preoccupation with the problems of every-day life, and test their endurance to its limits.

CHAPTER FIVE

From World War to the eve of Revolution

The tsar's decision to go to war in 1914 may be seen as an attempt to forestall a revolution, for although political disturbances had already subsided since the high point of 1912, they had shown how deeply divided Russia was. While the war may be interpreted as a catalyst for revolution in 1917, the latter was not an inevitable consequence of the former. The widespread patriotic fervour that greeted the tsar's declaration of war united the country behind the monarchy. A detailed investigation of the female response to the national emergency reveals how temporary and superficial that unity was as the conflict ultimately fractured the society and so weakened the established political order that it collapsed even before the war had ended.

Women's response to the call to arms in 1914

When asked on her return from the front early in the conflict "did we really need this war?", a volunteer nurse responded in the affirmative. She believed that Russia had become so demoralized and decadent, that the heroic sacrifices demanded by war had been necessary for national regeneration. Some women went further:

> We women don't wish to remain simply bystanders during these great events. Many of us want to join the army as nurses to ease the sufferings of the wounded heroes ... I, too, am full of desire to help my motherland, but I don't have a calling to become a nurse. I want to volunteer to serve in the army as a soldier, and

appeal to wealthy people to respond by providing me with the necessary funds to fulfil my dream of setting up a detachment of women soldiers, of Amazons.[1]

This letter was published in one of the capital's newspapers just after the war had begun. Within a few days, women had replied with understanding and support. What was different, though as we shall see not unique, about this woman's patriotic response to the national emergency was her desire to take on the masculine role. Moreover, although considerably fewer women followed her lead than filled the traditional feminine support roles, she is a salient reminder that, at least in the beginning, the majority of women supported Russia's involvement in the war – to the despair of the Bolsheviks who lamented the poisonous effect of the "drug of patriotism" which blinded women workers from seeing the obvious, that they would escape the horrors of the imperialist war only by overthrowing the political establishment.[2]

The forms of female participation in the war effort were many and varied. The responses of Russian women to the First World War and its impact upon them differed according to class, status, political beliefs and geographical location.[3] Among the lower classes, many rural and urban women became the main breadwinners as they filled the places of their men who were conscripted. A questionnaire among textile workers in St Petersburg in 1907 had revealed that for every 100 families, only eight had mothers who were full-time housewives; by 1914 the impression was that no working-class mother could afford not to be in paid employment.[4] Moreover, although women's wages improved during the war, they remained not only unequal to men's but inadequate for a family's survival in a deteriorating situation of shortages – even of basic necessities such as bread and fuel – and of inflation.

A feminist report delivered to delegates from women's organizations in April 1916 outlined some of the difficulties facing women in agriculture since the mass conscription of their men. While it did not underestimate the problems, the stress was on the opportunities that war afforded the female peasantry, with the argument that their contribution to the war effort merited participation in local government.[5] The reporter, Elena Gal'pern, pointed to the lack of quantitative and qualitative information on the work done by women in agriculture. In the past, the assumption had been that a woman would automatically shoulder more duties to take the place of an absent man; but now it was increasingly necessary to know the impact on farming of conscription on such a massive scale. A local newspaper published in Ukraine in 1915 commented on how startling the changes had been in the villages: no men could be seen, but instead only women and youths were busy in the fields and the threshing mills, in carts and on horses, always working and occupied at every stage of production. The woman was now not only the head of her own household, but effectively in charge of the peasant economy which would collapse without her. According to this 1915 article, the countryside was now the women's kingdom.

Gal'pern's report, which quoted from this article, showed that this situation of women doing men's jobs was universal throughout tsarist Russia. Another newspaper report that she cited, this time from Perm in the Urals, recalled that at first the families of mobilized men worried over how they would cope with the spring sowing without the men, but soon they just got on with the job. Women now cut logs for fuel. Soldiers' wives and young women worked together in pairs. The old people were curious and not a little amused at first to see young women going off to work with axes tucked in behind their belts, as the missing men would have done. Above all their expectations, the women proved very productive, with the result that many of the older or incapacitated men who had been left behind regretted their snide remarks, and felt ashamed at their own lower output.

Then came the time for spring sowing, after the first winter of the war during which many more men had been conscripted. In one village, Gal'pern noted that 200 men had been taken into the army, yet the women still managed to do all the men's work in the fields on top of their traditional work in the kitchen gardens. There was no labour for hire, and no money to pay anyone even if there had been, given the situation of wartime inflation. As the war dragged on, there were refugees and prisoners of war, but there was a lack of data on the former, while bureaucratic regulations concerning the latter meant that only the large estates benefited from such labour. Gal'pern recorded that, again, the peasant women talked among themselves about how they could manage the work. When the women had to cart manure to the fields, they found it most effective to work in pairs, gathering it from each other's house. Some soldiers' wives even scraped the money together to buy light ploughs and started to turn over the soil. This initiative taken by peasant women upsets the general picture of the village woman as a slave to custom, especially since in the past some in southern

Russia had been afraid of machinery, seeing it as the devil's invention. Before, men had used a heavy wooden plough; now their illiterate wives revealed the superiority of the light metal ploughs and harvesters. However, Gal'pern complained that there was not enough agricultural machinery to satisfy demand, and not enough money in the villages to invest in it. Some families of soldiers set up co-operatives to do the field work. Again the other peasants saw that these women were performing no worse than their men.

In addition, peasant women also had to cope with the loss of their livestock to the military. Gal'pern estimated that by early 1916 there had been a 30 per cent cut in the numbers of working cattle.[6] Thus, while able to cope with the fieldwork formerly done by their men, women experienced problems owing to the lack of draught animals and machinery. By February 1917, 2.6 million horses had been either bought or requisitioned, representing 10 per cent of the total number of horses aged four years and above, leaving 30 per cent of households without horses in 13 provinces (a rise of 5 per cent). Most of these farms had no alternative to horse traction, except to rely on the peasants' physical labour. In addition, by early 1917, nearly 23 per cent of peasant households had no cow of their own owing to government requisitioning and excess slaughtering of cattle since the beginning of the war. Such a heavy loss of livestock, alongside the mass conscription of men, left agriculture dependent on women, old men, children and prisoners-of-war. By 1916, 72 per cent of field labour on peasant farms, and 58 per cent on landowners' estates, was female.[7] One consequence of this heavy reliance on women was a halt to female migrant labour, which hit some of the large estates especially the sugar and tobacco plantations in the south.

Increasingly, too, the running of the village could only be done if the women participated. Many were illiterate, but there were local initiatives among the female peasantry to acquire the "three Rs", which they would do in the breaks from farming, often in the evenings, with ten or so sitting around a table with infants on their laps. It seems that women in the villages had become more energetic during the war and in the absence of their husbands. Yet it was doubtful whether the government or society for that matter were aware of, let alone appreciated, the efforts of peasant women, and the enormity of the national task facing the villages. Gal'pern called for more investment in farming, and for agricultural specialists based in the villages. Women should be among them, and not only city-bred professionals, but these peasant women who had proved their worth. "We women city-dwellers were amazed at the strength of a peasant woman, which went hand in hand with her submissiveness: strength of character, and awareness of her duty to the nation."[8] Still, however much they may have reacted out of patriotism to the declaration of war in 1914, the demands of a prolonged conflict, and the heavy loss of life at the front, where the soldiers lacked or had to share essential clothing and equipment, quickly wore down the majority of women.

The actions of such "ordinary" women, which were portrayed in loyal publications as proof of popular support for the war, may be seen instead as reflections of profound concern for their men. Many wives of military men, both officers and rank and file, followed their husbands to the front, working there as nursing auxiliaries, experiencing at first hand the deprivation and danger to which the armies were exposed. A woman worker whose newspaper-seller husband's letters from the front told of his extreme discomfort – of the lack of dry, warm clothing to combat the constant rain – borrowed money so that he could buy some of the basics that the army could not provide. When she heard that he never received it, she went deeper into debt to buy the necessary clothing herself, but the parcel arrived after his detachment had been moved on to another front. This woman was so worried about his condition that she travelled from the Russian capital, Petersburg (now renamed Petrograd because the original sounded too "German") to Austria, a long, arduous and dangerous journey during which she often went hungry. When she finally caught up with him, she delivered the precious clothing and returned to Russia within a few days. At least she had found him alive. A peasant woman whose husband had worked as a doorman at a grand house in Petersburg before the war found him in a battlefield, only to witness his death by a sniper. She returned home to their five-year old son, but later went to work in a field hospital, leaving her son behind in the village.[9]

This woman had responded to the loss of her husband in war by going to the front herself in a support role. More commonly, peasant women, especially those near the front, sometimes with the local female intelligentsia such as the village teachers, set up committees to help the wounded and generally to do as urban women did, which was to collect clothes and bedding, make bandages, and knit socks: the bare essentials that the military machine seemed unable to provide for the millions of men called to arms. Women also collected money, both for soldiers and for their dependents, which revealed further inadequacies of the tsarist authorities. As the war dragged on and conditions worsened, with the breakdown of the transport and distribution systems, such ordinary women increasingly blamed the sufferings of their men on the tsar who had taken personal control of the war effort in 1915.

At least a minority of women felt compelled to follow their husbands to the front, not so much from patriotism or support for the war effort, but from deep emotional attachment, and a belief that a wife's role was to share her husband's trials. One such woman, Lidiia Zakharova, found life without her husband intolerable. After his departure, she said that their flat and her heart felt empty. She found herself consumed by worry over him, exhausted yet unable to sleep, and unprepared to face their two sons, dreading questions from the elder about his father and the constant reminder of her husband from the younger son who bore a striking resemblance to him. She left the boys with her mother, and set out for the front. During the train journey, she befriended a young nurse, Anna Nikolaevna Mosina. By the time they reached the front, Lidiia felt a different person, reflected in the fact that she now asked to be known as "sister", instead of by her own name. One of the tasks she performed was to write letters for the illiterate peasant soldiers addressed to their wives who, in contrast to Lidiia, had little option but to remain behind to look after the children and the farm. Lidiia fell ill and returned home a few months later.[10]

The war afforded the minority of educated women who needed to support themselves increased opportunities for employment in white-collar posts and in the professions. For the wealthy, whose situation did not seem to suffer appreciably during the war, it provided even more scope for their traditional charitable works. Among these upper-class women, patriotism was general and sustained. The few feminists in their number viewed the war as potentially beneficial for women, giving them scope to prove both their talents and their loyalty to the motherland. They were determined to show first, that women had as central and crucial a role to play as men in the defence of their country, and secondly, that once the war had reached a successful conclusion, women had the potential for contributing to the running of their country on an equal basis with men. In her study of Russian feminism in the early twentieth century, Linda Edmondson has shown that the feminist response to the war, while generally supportive, was itself multi-faceted.

For some, their country's struggle called for sacrifices from women as much as from men. For others, such as the feminist physician Mariia Pokrovskaia, war was above all a masculine exercise in barbarism whereas women represented the ideals of a civilized society. She expected women not to oppose the war, but rather to dedicate their sufferings during the war to the salvation and eventual perfection of humanity. In addition, Edmondson has argued that the feminist use of women's contribution to the war effort as propaganda for the granting of equal rights in a reformed society was not simply opportunist.[11] Since the 1870s women from the upper classes had been seeking socially useful work, but the First World War both greatly increased their numbers and gave their efforts an added significance in a public way. Every aspect of women's work, whether paid or unpaid, would strengthen the feminist argument for equal rights:

> Now in the epoch of great war, it becomes clear that, in spite of her present lack of civil rights, woman is strong. The war emphasises this strength. Fathers, brothers, husbands, sons left for the front. According to the obsolete male philosophy, sorrow and helpless tears should have been the destiny of the women left behind. But at this historical moment for Russia, women are proving that they have no time to cry. Merchants' wives are running vast trading businesses, peasant women are responsible for the cultivation of the land, and we now have female tram conductors, points-women, cab-women, female porters and street-cleaners, dray-women, and even female soldiers . . . Now a woman's responsibility to her motherland is great. The war has moved her to the front line of life, and she is taking her final examination. History will later determine her mark . . . Unexpectedly for ourselves and our recent opponents, men, the war has introduced women to those areas of male labour which were beyond our reach in the old days. All we have to do is to prove ourselves in our new jobs so that in the future, after the war, we shall remain in our present, newly gained positions.[12]

The author insisted that no such project could succeed without the full involvement of women, pointing out that a key tactic against the enemy was the boycott of German products and companies in which women as the main consumers would, of necessity, play the central role. Behind the lines, wealthy women turned their usual philanthropic activities into patriotic endeavours, and responded to the massive refugee crises caused by the war, again providing essential services that the government seemed incapable of doing. Conscious that their efforts were vital to both the battle and home fronts, these upper-class women were able to sustain a sense of excitement over what for many was their first experience of being socially useful, and so to retain their initial patriotic enthusiasm for the war far longer than peasant or working-class women.[13]

With millions of men conscripted, industry as well as agriculture became dependent on female labour. War also opened up more and new professional jobs to women as the government desperately needed to make up for shortages of personnel in engineering, transport and essential utilities. In whatever capacity women served the war effort, they were seen as acting from the traditional feminine virtue of selfless devotion. Their motives were more complex than either official or feminist propaganda would allow. It was not simply patriotism or hopes for improvements in the position of women after the war that drew women to the war effort. For some, war afforded unexpected opportunities for adventure outside the confines of domesticity and femininity. Women who did not need to work for wages volunteered to serve as nurses at the front. Female doctors opted to serve in field hospitals, working alongside men. Some found romance at the front. For example, one woman from a very privileged background, Mary Britnieva, served as a Red Cross nurse at the front, and married the chief doctor.[14] However, with millions of men being slaughtered, such women came to be seen by their patients as patching up the men so that they could continue to serve as cannon fodder.

Others of Britnieva's social class trained as drivers for the military. They not only shared the dangers with the troops, but considerable numbers paid the ultimate price with their lives. Nevertheless, such women first had to prove that they were capable before being accepted by the forces on "equal" terms with men. One example is that of the aviator E.P. Samsonova. She had learned to fly in 1911, the same year in which she learned to drive a car. She had wanted to work in a school of aviation, but found obstacles were put in her way because she was a woman. When war broke out, she attended a school for army nurses, while petitioning the minister of war to allow her to join the air force and go to the front. She was refused permission. Samsonova did not give up, but worked in a field hospital, and, finding herself dissatisfied because she was not making as full a contribution to the war effort as her skills would allow, she joined a motor detachment. For over four months, she served as an army chauffeur, working side by side with men, but she still felt unfulfilled.[15]

Taking militant and violent action was not specifically a masculine characteristic, since traditionally peasant women participated in rural unrest and lower class women generally were the major protagonists in bread and conscription riots. Nor was it only poor women who resorted to violence as a form of protest. As we saw in Chapter 3, by the late nineteenth century a minority of radical upper-class women (such as Sof'ia Perovskaia, Vera Figner and Mariia Spiridonova), in despair of achieving reform within the existing system, and impatient with the slow progress of political activities, adopted the tactic of terrorism against the state. What, then, was different about the relationship between women and violence during the First World War? What set this female experience apart was the scale of involvement of women at the front, the fact that although they dressed in male clothes many did not disguise their sex, and the mixture of peasant and aristocratic women (though many more of the former).

Although there had been a tiny number of women before 1914 who had joined the army, usually disguised as men, the main role of women at the front was that of nurse. Nicholas II permitted a number of women to join active service during the First World War, perhaps in the hope that the women's selfless patriotism would encourage their male comrades. Though as many as 5,000 women fought at the front, their involvement was not planned, but rather the result of the women's individual petitions and the tsar's personal decision.[16] Not all were successful. Anna Khrisanfova, from the region of Kazan, was a 21 year old peasant at the time of the outbreak of hostilities. She had spent several years in a convent which she left secretly, dressed as a soldier with close cropped hair. She was finally stopped at Vilno, in Lithuania, and despite her pleading was sent back to the convent. Two younger women, of 17 and 19 years of age, asked to be accepted into the volunteer forces, citing the precedent of the cavalry woman, Durova, from the Napoleonic campaign, and explaining that they wanted to support their brothers. They were refused. Another woman was detained at a Moscow station on her way to the front. Her documents showed that she was a grammar school student. Only when threatened with a medical by a male feldsher (paramedic) did she admit to being female. She was sent home. A 21 year old woman who had made clothes for the wounded, was so worried about her 13 year old brother who was in the army that she tried unsuccessfully to be accepted as a nurse. She met another woman of her age who had also been rejected by the nursing service. Together they borrowed money to travel to a larger city (Tiflis) where they hoped to enlist as privates in the army. More successful was Alexandra Danilova from Baku. The wife of a reservist soldier, she petitioned: "having a strong, burning desire to join the army as a volunteer for the defence of our dear tsar and fatherland, I ask to be accepted into the ranks". Her request was granted.

It seemed to be easier for women to be accepted as volunteers by the army if they were upper-class and resident in the capital. From there, a famous sportswoman, Kudasheva, went to the front on her own horse. The daughter of a senator and two daughters of a colonel also went as volunteers. Another daughter of an army officer (artillery) went to east Prussia with her father. She dressed as an ordinary private, cut short her hair, and participated in several battles. She was awarded a Georgii (St George) Cross for her bravery, soon after which she was sent back to Petrograd, suffering from shell-shock.

Such women may have been accepted because they were from military families, and certainly it seemed to have helped if their fathers were officers or political leaders. These women dressed in military uniforms, as their male comrades did, but did not deny their sex whereas some female soldiers found that the only way they would be accepted by the men was to remain disguised as a man, at least until they were wounded. Others, especially those from the lower orders without a military background, found it necessary to sustain the male impersonation. One such volunteer in 1914 was Anna Alekseevna Krasil'nikova. Both her parents had worked in the Ural mines, and Anna as a child had been set to learn needlework, then as a young woman had entered the factory labour force. She spent a brief period as a novice in a Kazan convent, which she left to find work in a paint shop. When war broke out, she petitioned the governor of Kazan to be allowed to join the army as a private. She decided to circumvent his decision to refuse her permission by enlisting as a man, succeeding on her second attempt. As Anatolii Krasil'nikov, she served initially as a batman before moving up to the front line. By this time she was 21 years of age. She took part in 19 battles, during one of which she was wounded leading men into the attack. She was awarded the order of St George (fourth class) for her outstanding bravery and services. At that time she was a medical orderly. Her injury left her with a permanent limp, but she always regretted being unable to return to the front.[17]

For those women who did not disguise their sex, many still experienced difficulties in winning toleration and respect from the men on equal terms. Often they were assigned duties that seemed little different from domestic service. Men doubted women's capacity for, as well as their skill in, battle. Some men would try to protect any female comrade in arms by shielding them from the fighting. Indeed, Marina Yurlova, who fought with the cossacks, found that the chivalry of the men, especially the older ones, sometimes made her a burden to them during engagements with the enemy. She had joined the cossacks when she was only 15 years old and was taken under the wing of a much older male figure who took on the role of her protector and guide. Yurlova felt that she was valued by her fellow cossacks in her regiment, winning quick acceptance as her company's good luck charm, but many other female soldiers found it hard to be taken seriously by the men who tended to treat them with contempt or condescension.

Certainly, Yurlova was very young when she joined the cossacks compared to the other female combatants. The entry of women into such a quintessentially masculine environment as the army was seen as a potential threat to military discipline. Women who tried to join the army were often suspected of being prostitutes. Hence, whether or not they disguised themselves as men, all female combatants sought to suppress their sexuality. Nor was the danger of sexual harassment limited to the ranks. Yurlova's memoirs show that the main threat to her virtue came from an officer in the rear, who first ordered her to clean his quarters, and then, assuming that she was a lady of easy virtue, made sexual advances to her. From her account of the incident, it was her ladylike fear and trembling which dissuaded him from forcing himself on Yurlova, rather than any overt resistance on her part, while what she seemed to resent most about the incident was that he was not treating her as one of the men: "I did not want to be thought a girl – I was a soldier".[18] Moreover, what she most commented on was not her sexual vulnerability, but the distance between herself as a front-line soldier and this rearguard officer who lived in relative comfort.

Yurlova, like the majority of female combatants, served alongside men, though it was only their presence as individuals that gave the notion that their units were "mixed". These women sought and valued the solidarity of comradeship with the ordinary soldiers, both infantry and cavalry, and the episode of sexual harassment by the officer which Yurlova relates in detail in her memoir stands out on account of its uniqueness. Still, women soldiers were acutely aware of their sexual vulnerability. To protect themselves, they avoided any situation that might compromise their reputation for purity and chastity, remaining aloof even from the casual sexual banter between the men, which served only to isolate the women further. Thus female combatants had to, or felt that they had to, live up to separate and higher standards of behaviour than was expected of males. Moreover, the reception and treatment of women soldiers varied according to the regiment, and seemed to become increasingly hostile as casualties mounted and soldiers' disaffection deepened. Initially trying to gain acceptance from the men through hiding their sex or suppressing their sexuality, the women came to be resented for being held up as role models of devotion and loyalty to the war effort who were meant to shame the men into unquestioning obedience and self-sacrifice. These courageous women were meant to teach their male comrades by example how to act like men.

One patriotic, feminist publication of 1917 recalled the heroism of the left-wing terrorist women such as Vera Figner and Ekaterina Breshko-Breshkovskaia. Rather than enemies of the state, they were now hailed as national heroines from whom Russian women drew civic energy, perhaps because these radicals now supported the war effort. The generally anonymous women who fought in the Russian armies in the First World War were even portrayed as direct descendants of these former terrorists. Yet, while Figner and Breshkovskaia had fought side by side with their male comrades, by 1917 Russian women combatants found that they had to battle on two fronts: against the Germans and against men wearing the uniform of Russian soldiers: "You can't imagine our surprise when we saw empty trenches near us! Our fellow soldiers had left us to our own devices, letting us fight the German assaults by ourselves!" complained a wounded female volunteer.[19]

The most famous female soldier in the tsarist army was Mariia Bochkareva, a peasant woman. She greeted the declaration of war in August 1914 with an enthusiastic, indeed ecstatic patriotism. The war, she felt, drew the people together as no previous war had done. More than that, she believed that the war would save the country, would purify and exalt its spirit. She believed that she had been called to contribute to the nation's survival by serving at the front: "My heart yearned to be there in the seething cauldron of war, to be baptised in its fire and scorched in its lava".[20]

Like the other women who tried to serve at the front, Bochkareva initially met resistance. She was told in November 1914 that women were barred. However, she came up against a sympathetic recruiting officer who advised her to petition the tsar. Unlike so many of the other women, Bochkareva was successful. In common with the other women who sought to enlist, she wore her hair short and dressed as male soldiers did. There were recorded instances of women who had tried to pass as men in the nineteenth and early twentieth centuries, for a variety of reasons: to get better paid jobs than were open to women as a rule, or to escape a violent relationship with a man, as Bochkareva herself had done.[21] In her study of women who dressed as men and served in the armed forces, Julie Wheelwright claims that in assuming the male role, Bochkareva was attempting to shed a feminine identity which she had experienced as a form of enslavement, after a brutal father and two abusive husbands.[22] Yurlova, who did not have a history of violent relationships with men and unlike Bochkareva had never had to work for a living, also suppressed her femininity in this way. As we have seen, even when accepted by the men as one of them, even in the thick of battle, expectations differed for the sexes: women's courage was seen as self-sacrifice, even self-abnegation, whereas men's was seen as dashing heroism. In the memoirs of both Yurlova and Bochkareva, it is clear that each woman wanted to be in combat above all. The ladylike and girlish Yurlova was constantly frustrated by the paternalism of her male peers, while the mature peasant Bochkareva, who was clearly a robust figure used to heavy physical labour, was expected not only to fight alongside the men but also to deal with any women's problems, notably gynaecological, in the villages in which her unit pitched camp.[23] Still, both women fought alongside their male comrades, and both were wounded. Bochkareva was decorated with all four of the prestigious St George crosses for her bravery in combat and in rescuing fallen male comrades.[24] What made her stand out as a female combatant and ensured that her fame was lasting was her military opposition to the Bolshevik seizure of power, which will be discussed in the next chapter.

While heroines such as Bochkareva could be used by both the official and feminist propagandists, they were more at home with the former. They did not call for sexual equality, however much they sought acceptance by the men. They did not set themselves up as role models for their sex, but, especially once the rate of desertion among the rank and file soldiers dramatically increased in 1917, they saw themselves and were portrayed as role models for the men.[25] They did not consider themselves as sisters, but sought to join the fraternity of the men. Female soldiers generally avoided each other's company before the revolution, preferring to be integrated with the men. Their reasons for joining were various and personal, and their enlistment was an individual act. The memoirs of Yurlova and Bochkareva reveal that even as they expressed a desire to be subsumed into their units, they also revelled in their uniqueness.

Upper-class women soldiers, such as Yurlova, were far fewer than recruits from the female peasantry, such as Bochkareva. Although peasant women were perceived to live in total subordination to a patriarchal system, poverty, land hunger and migration to the city for work had given them more opportunities to escape the confinement of the family household than wealthy women such as Yurlova. Being ordinary soldiers did not bridge the gap between them. What they had in common was an emotional, impulsive patriotism, as well as a sense of adventure. They were also alike in finding solidarity with the common soldiers rather than the officers; but unlike the mass of the former, Bochkareva and Yurlova had found something in the army at war that they preferred to life at home. By the summer of 1917, desertion on a mass scale revealed both how war-weary the men were and how much they wanted to return to their families. The war was an escape for the women from the restrictions of their civilian lives, one which offered excitement and a sense of uniqueness that they could never otherwise experience. For the millions of peasant men who made up the bulk of the armed forces, it was a burden of separation from family and farm which the expectations both of the state and of their masculine role demanded that they carry. As for factory workers, any men who protested were liable to be sent to the front as punishment, and as an example to others. As the war dragged on and casualties mounted, cynicism spread among the troops for whom there was no dignified heroism in fighting. Instead, they felt mounting anger as, poorly fed and ill-equipped, they were regarded as expendable for a cause from which they felt increasingly remote.

Although numbered in the thousands, female combatants constituted a tiny minority of women working for the war effort whose main efforts were, as we have seen, on the home front. In whatever role, feminists hoped that such a national emergency would not only prove their case for sexual equality but would also unite women of all classes.[26] Still, in the army women remained isolated individuals, even more so when many male soldiers began to question their own involvement in the mass slaughter. Away from the battle scenes, feminists won the support of some prominent radical women, including as we have seen Figner and Breshkovskaia, and also the prominent former Social Democrat, E.D. Kuskova.[27] In his assessment of the impact of the First World War on Russian women, Alfred Meyer has suggested that the feminists were deluding themselves regarding female solidarity. His study of women's journals published between 1914 and 1917 reveals that whatever hopes feminists placed on women's contribution to the war effort, the gulf between the classes not only remained, it widened. Whatever the philanthropic efforts of wealthy women, however much they talked of making sacrifices for the good of the nation, the collapse of the economic and transport systems seemed to have had a negligible effect on their own living standards. They continued to employ women as domestic servants, and even to criticize declining standards when so many experienced women were drawn into higher paid jobs in industry. Moreover, feminists saw any industrial action and any complaints by lower-class women about food shortages and inflation as threats to morale and, therefore, unpatriotic.[28]

Women, work and war

From the 1890s, but especially since the revolution of 1905, increasing numbers of peasant women had been drawn into the urban labour force. The majority went from necessity. With their reputation for subservience, they proved particularly attractive to employers who had been frightened by the strike wave of the mid 1890s but above all by the revolution of 1905. Although women participated in both, it was men who showed the most sustained interest in developing the labour movement and in radical politics. Hence, from the late nineteenth century, and increasingly from 1905, employers sought to replace male workers with women wherever possible, particularly in the cotton-weaving industry.[29] For male workers, then, women were a threat. Skilled male workers sought after 1905 to build up trade unions to defend their interests against the incursions of the huge pool of unskilled men and women, but especially the latter, which they saw as harmful to the living standards of the working class as a whole. Skilled men saw themselves as the vanguard of their class, and looked down on unskilled men who spent all their spare time in the taverns, and the women who spent theirs before religious icons.

In terms of jobs, the immediate impact of the First World War was to hit those sectors of the economy, such as the luxury trades and crafts, that catered to it, which employed women, both blue and white-collar. As the economy was geared to the needs of the military, however, and with so many men under arms, new jobs opened up for women. In addition, more women were now seeking work, since the allowances allocated to soldiers' wives were paltry and their payment erratic, especially in the villages. With millions of men in uniform, women effectively became heads of households. Although their job opportunities and wages had improved with the loss of so much of the male labour force, women were still regarded by the government and employers as cheap, docile workers. Thus, the First World War quickened this process of female replacing male workers from political expedience and economic necessity.

The proportion of women in industry as a whole soared in Russia from 26.6 per cent in 1914 to 43.4 per cent in 1917; the numbers of factory women rose from 732,000 in 1914 to over a million in 1917.[30] During the war, women and youths found employment in large factories where previously men had predominated. Thus in the Moscow industrial region, the percentage of women workers rose from 39.4 in 1914 to 48.7 in 1917; in the cotton industry from 49.5 in 1914 to 60.6 in 1917; and in the metal industry from 7.4 in 1914 to 18.6 in 1917. The percentage of women employed in the Petrograd district was similar: it rose from 25.3 in 1913 to 33.3 in 1917. Before the war, men had constituted three-quarters of the Petrograd labour force. Towards the end of 1917, they made up less than half the total number of workers employed in the capital. Women and youths penetrated even the metal and chemical industries, which before the war had been male havens. By the eve of the revolution, the former made up at least a third of the workforce in these two areas.[31] However, this trend did not reflect a corresponding increase in the numbers of skilled women workers. For example, women made up 37.5 per cent of the unskilled metal workers in the Moscow province by 1918, whereas men accounted for as much as 99 per cent of skilled toolmakers.[32]

Despite the increasing inroads women made into the factories, they continued to predominate in the more traditionally female areas of light industry and domestic service: in Petrograd by January 1917 there were approximately 80,000 women employed as domestic servants, 50,000 as office workers, and another 50,000 as shop workers, compared to the 130,000 female factory hands. In terms of domestic service, women replaced men as caretakers and gatekeepers. Women, notably soldiers' wives, became street cleaners and porters, and were found to be deficient only in two areas: breaking ice (which demanded considerable physical strength) and keeping accounts (since they lacked education). Women also made incursions into areas that had previously been considered male preserves, both white and blue-collar, including transport (notably the railways) and the service sector (notably the postal service). In 1913, there were only six female cab-drivers in Moscow, one of whom was a young widow who supported her two children by working at night. By 1915, there were 30 cab-women, the majority of whom had husbands at the front, and were supporting large families. They were no longer required to obtain special permission to work on the cabs, but were now seen as more reliable than male cab-drivers, since cases of a female driver being fined for transgressing a company regulation were rare.[33]

Change was more startling in the tram service. Until the war, work on city trams had been clearly identified as "not for women" unless it was cleaning. Yet once war had been declared, women had speedily been taken on to operate the signals and points. Later, they were employed as conductors. To be accepted for the tram service, women had to have a husband who had been an employee of the city and had been enlisted. By 1915, 179 women in Moscow had found new jobs with the city's trams: 79 as conductors, 85 as points and signals operators, 11 as couriers, two as telephonists, and two as delivery women. These were in addition to the cleaners already employed there. All but the cleaners had to sign an undertaking that they would leave when the need for their services came to an end. Interestingly, the manager promised to reconsider that stipulation if this "experiment" proved to be successful.[34]

One woman tram conductor in Petrograd, A.E. Rodionova, described how she became politicized both by her job and by the experience of war and revolution.[35] She came from a working-class family, her mother a laundress and her father employed in a vinegar factory. Both parents were illiterate. Rodionova began work at an early age, by helping her parents: she poured vinegar into bottles, and delivered the laundry that her mother took in at home. Thus, even before she became a tram conductor in 1914, Rodionova had seen quite a bit of the capital city outside of her district, and was aware of the sharp contrasts in living standards between herself and those who employed her mother.

At first, Rodionova worked on the horse-drawn cabs. She soon found that her lack of numeracy skills hampered her, and so she hired a poor student to teach her counting. She quickly became more efficient. Her tram route ran through the working-class Vyborg district, passing the huge Putilov metal works. In winter, it was so dark early in the morning and later in the evening that she could barely see to collect the fares. The workers, however, came to her aid by passing her conductor's cap around and collecting the fares for her. She recalled how calloused and blistered were those hands of her "assistants".

When she had impressed her bosses with her efficiency, Rodionova was upgraded to a mechanical tram, which served the better-off areas of the city, where the wealthy women looked at her in amazement. They did not seem to realize how difficult her job was, working between 12 and 14 hours a day, with no breaks and low pay. By 1916, Rodionova had participated in her first strike when all the tram depots stopped work after their petition for higher wages had been rejected by the engineer who ran the service, whom Rodionova described as a "despot". The tram workers, women and men, were united and not only won increased wages, but forced the sacking of the engineer. Yet Rodionova recalled that their victory did not improve their material conditions.

Rodionova was illiterate. Not only had the war given her a job opportunity that would not normally have been open to a woman, but she had realized that even a little education could improve her chances of promotion. Other jobs demanded some level of schooling above the basics, and these drew educated women in particularly large numbers.[36] In 1915, the Moscow telegraph office employed 1,250 clerks, of whom 700 were women (that is, just under 60 per cent). At the start of the war, the men working for the telegraph were government servants and not subject to the same demands of conscription as elsewhere. Where the most obvious change came was in the schools training telegraph operators: from being between 80 per cent and 90 per cent men, there were only 20 males out of 120 trainees in 1915. The manager of the Moscow telegraph declared himself satisfied that women were precise, accurate and conscientious, and confirmed the trend for his establishment to hire female labour. The post office did not see such dramatic change: by 1915, men constituted 900 of the 1,200 civil servants at the Moscow Post Office. The work demanded of women in the post office was similar to men's: long hours (up to 14 a day) both receiving and despatching parcels, and doing postal deliveries. In addition, professional women gained entry into posts, especially in secondary teaching and in accountancy, which until then had been exclusive to men.

Thus the absorption of so many men into the armed forces and the increasing demand from the war industries for labour drew women and youths even into areas monopolized by skilled male workers until the First World War. The Menshevik Eva Broido recorded that the number of women workers multiplied four or five times in the first two years of the war. In her view, the war had simply speeded up a process that was already in motion before 1914, and which reflected increasing mechanization and a further division of labour. Broido cited the factory inspectorate which noted that in the first decade of the twentieth century, the number of women employed in industry had grown by 33 per cent, in contrast to the growth in the male labour force of only 8 per cent. It was in that decade, Broido wrote, that women began to make small inroads into the metal industry, while during the First World War every metal factory had women workers, though they remained a minority. Broido did not see this development as simply women responding to the needs of the wartime economy, but rather that they acted for the usual reason of economic necessity, having hungry children to feed in an inflationary economy. Indeed, Broido implicitly criticized the feminist claim for the positive results of women entering men's jobs by insisting that it ignored the bitter realities of such work.[37] Not all the women who found work there were "new" workers, since many took the opportunity of better paid and regular factory work and left their traditionally low paid and often seasonal jobs in the service sector. The latter jobs did not disappear, but instead became available to the growing numbers of peasant women seeking work (and higher wages) in the towns. Others who had found themselves unemployed at the start of the war also moved into the higher paid factory jobs.

This tremendous growth in female labour occurred during the disintegration of the economy and the collapse of the transport system brought on by the First World War. It was also only one aspect of the general demographic instability that was a consequence of the war,

131

including millions of troops marching to, and refugees escaping from, the various fronts. By 1917, there were also large numbers of deserting soldiers who sought to return to their villages. Nearly three years of war had fractured the economy, severely disrupting marketing links, both in terms of agricultural produce and labour. Moreover, even as the numbers of female industrial workers grew apace, farming had quickly come to rely almost totally on women. The latter did not worry men as much, or in the same way, as the former did, since farming was based traditionally on the family unit. Skilled male workers, in particular, feared that the combination of wartime emergency and the influx of women would compound the dilution process that had been going on since the beginning of the century with the spread of new, "scientific", work practices. Their fear was not only for their skills and associated superior status in the workplace, but for the trade unions that they had been developing especially since the 1905 Revolution, and which since 1907 had been suffering from concerted efforts by government and employers to weaken any attempts by workers to protect and improve their position. Thus women were perceived as a threat to men on two related fronts: at work and in the labour movement from which women felt excluded since trade unions were for skilled workers, and therefore almost by definition, male.

Nevertheless, a minority of women workers had already displayed an interest in politics, though most felt too badly educated and lacking in confidence to organize themselves. Before war had been declared in 1914, both Bolsheviks and Mensheviks had set up journals that were directly addressed to women workers. The Menshevik *Voice of the Woman Worker* (*Golos Rabotnitsy*) lasted for only two issues; however, the Bolshevik *The Woman Worker* (*Rabotnitsa*) survived for seven issues. *Rabotnitsa*'s editors had to appeal to their male comrades, as well as male workers, to accept that women were a necessary part of the class struggle. Inessa Armand, one of *Rabotnitsa*'s editors in emigration, appealed:

> You, comrade workers, don't forget that the working women's cause is your cause too, that until the masses of women have joined your organisations, until they are drawn into your movement, they will be an immense obstacle on your path. Help them, support this, their first initiative; organise them, conduct agitation among them for the new magazine, collect funds to support it.[38]

While Armand's sympathies were with the women, this quotation reveals that she also viewed the labour movement and the class struggle in masculine terms, and saw only the difficulties of attracting women to the revolutionary cause. *Rabotnitsa*'s editors shared the view of their male comrades that women workers were especially backward and had to be helped both in terms of raising their political awareness and organizational skills. Indeed, the editors argued that unless this help was forthcoming, women workers would continue to think in terms of their individual households rather than the class as a whole, and put pressure on their men to desist from any political activity that might harm the interests of their families.[39] *Rabotnitsa* combined articles written by the editors, notably Nadezhda Krupskaia and Inessa Armand, which discussed the situation of women workers, including their "double burden" (of housework and childcare on top of paid employment), and their place in the struggle of their class. Although the editors tended to gloss over any hostility or abuse to which women were subjected by male workers, they still recognized that men's attitudes towards women had to change, and indeed that the prejudices of male workers helped retard the development of the women. Certainly, given the relatively low levels of literacy among women workers, and their low pay, such journals were a "luxury" that appealed mainly to those who had already reached at least a basic level of political awareness. Nevertheless, these were precisely the women who were expected by *Rabotnitsa* to pass on what they had learned to their less conscious and illiterate sisters.

It is difficult to assess the impact of *Rabotnitsa* in 1914. Of its seven issues, three were confiscated, while the journal itself was suppressed in June because of Bolshevik opposition to the war. Still, towards the end of 1914, a few women sought help from the Bolshevik Party in Petrograd to improve their educational level and organizational skills. The Bolsheviks responded positively, though the group that they established was not restricted to women, while the leadership that they provided was male.[40] The Bolsheviks acknowledged that there was a great deal of doubt among workers (female as well as male) regarding women's ability to organize, and a general assumption that they would be unable to shake off their traditional subservience.[41] There seems to have been a similar notion held by many in the Bolshevik Party itself. Certainly, while sexual equality was championed by the Bolsheviks, they did not question the traditional gendered division of labour, which was reflected in their agitational leaflets addressed to women both as employees and as housewives. As the first, the Bolsheviks expected women workers to fight with men for improved wages and conditions; as the second, the Bolsheviks considered that women as women had domestic skills that could be utilized in the public sphere during emergencies, such as the food shortages.[42]

The Bolsheviks had opposed the war from the beginning. They believed that it would sharpen class differences, and undermine any feminist claim to speak on behalf of all women. Although women seemed to be united by patriotism when war was first declared, the Bolsheviks reasoned that the cost of the war on the home front would weigh heaviest on poor women, and alienate them from their social superiors who remained loyal.[43] If not as enthusiastic as in 1914, the feminists saw that a protracted conflict would make women's contribution even more vital. However, as the economy quickly deteriorated and production for the war effort entailed longer hours and poorer conditions, and as food and fuel were soon in short and irregular supply, problems of everyday life grew for working women who were the sole or main providers for their families.[44]

While the Bolsheviks had realized the material impact of the war on poor women, they had still to come to terms with the growing importance working women would hold politically in a situation in which millions of men were under arms. Despite evidence of militancy by women workers on the eve of the war, such as a strike in a Petersburg rubber factory (over incidents of mass poisoning caused by management's cost cutting) they were still seen as passive, capable only of spontaneous rather than sustained actions, lacking in discipline and unpredictable in behaviour.[45] At the same time as having such a low opinion of the potential of women workers to organize themselves, the Bolshevik Party was also plagued by the fear that feminism might win over some women workers and in the process divide and weaken the working class. Hence, even as it acknowledged that women suffered sexual exploitation, the Bolshevik party saw it as a reflection of class oppression, stressing that female and male workers had to remain united in the face of a common foe.

A leading female Bolshevik, Konkordia Samoilova, came to see the First World War as crucial for the raising of the political consciousness of the female working class.[46] Although many had worked before 1914 to support a family, Samoilova believed that the impact of the war, both in terms of material deprivation and the high death rate of men at the front, forced women to assume the traditionally masculine role of head of household. Moreover, as many more women entered the urban labour force and experienced the harsh conditions of factory work, more also responded like male workers in their increased willingness to protest. Unlike so many of her male and indeed female comrades, Samoilova recognized that these women suffered sexual oppression in addition to (and not just as an aspect of) class oppression, but she too tended, in official party writings, to associate the former with foremen and employers only, and not shop floor workers. The Menshevik Eva Broido acknowledged in 1917 that some of the latter were also guilty of the sexual harassment of women workers.[47] Still, both Broido and Samoilova agreed that women workers suffered a double exploitation, so that their lack of skills and unequal wages made their situation even more desperate than that of male workers. A woman worker, for example, might have recourse to prostitution in order to provide for herself and her family (and prostitution grew enormously during the war). The effect of the war was to intensify the exploitation suffered by women, while also serving to make them more aware of the political inequities of the existing system. Hence women were drawn into the labour movement by force of extreme circumstances, some from a raised consciousness, many out of desperation.

Despite this recognition both of the growth in numbers of the female working class and their new significance for revolutionary developments, women were still generally seen as too downtrodden to act. After all, besides the long hours at work, they spent many more in queues, chasing food (or rumours of supplies) throughout the city. By 1915, Petrograd and cities in the north were already experiencing serious shortages. By the end of 1916, the woman worker was effectively working a double shift as she spent on average 40 hours a week simply searching and standing in line for food, the quality as well as the quantity of which continuously deteriorated, while prices continued to rise and outstrip wages. Broido calculated that wages during the war doubled at most, but that inflation was at least twice that rate. In addition, women's wages were kept down by limiting the majority of them to unskilled work. Broido noted that the wartime economy depended on labour intensive methods and long hours (sometimes up to 16 a day, with overtime unpaid), rather than on skills and machinery.[48]

Soldiers' wives were in an extremely difficult position, since their allowances were not only grossly inadequate, but payment was also at the mercy of an inefficient bureaucracy. Female professionals and white-collar workers, who tended to be unmarried, were trapped by fixed salaries. Even those who won wage increases found that the "extra" was soon eaten up by inflation. Moreover, while certain sectors fulfilling key defence contracts (notably metallurgy and chemicals) saw wage rises of up to 21 per cent by 1916, areas in which women predominated, for example in textiles and woollen goods, actually saw a drop in real earnings (of 3.4 per cent in the former, 16.4 per cent in the latter).[49] It was difficult, therefore, for a single woman of any social class to support herself, but for the lower class family breadwinner without reserves and with a husband at the front, the situation was desperate.

They did not simply blame inflation and shortages on the suppliers and retailers. While some of them were suspected of hoarding in order to push up the prices and profit from the war, it was recognized that others had been forced to cease trading because of the breakdown of the transport and distribution systems, the blame for which was laid at the government's door. As a result of that collapse, the scavenging of women for basic necessities became even more of a burden, forcing them to wander throughout the city, and often to camp out overnight in the hope that bread would be on sale before they had to return to work. Women thus spent hours together, often in atrocious weather conditions since winter aggravated the transport problems, discussing the war, its causes and effects, and the sufferings both of the men at the front and their families behind the lines. These queues, as much as their experience of factory work, may have been responsible for the raising of women's consciousness.[50] Furthermore, they may have deepened class divisions between women, since it was the female poor who waited in line rather than the professional or wealthy women, whose servants did the queuing. As the tsarist secret police recognized before the revolutionaries, such conditions wore down women workers so much that they "cursed god and tsar", but blamed the latter in particular for their wretched lives.[51]

Women and protest before 1917

The fact that women spent so much time trying to ameliorate the conditions of everyday life still convinced conscious male workers as well as the revolutionary groups that, however much their awareness of injustice had been sharpened by the war, women simply did not have the energy for sustained political activities. Preoccupation with bread was traditionally a female responsibility, while revolutionaries had neglected questions of consumption, focusing instead on production. For them, the strike took precedence over the food riot, and indeed was a more sophisticated form of political struggle. Bread riots were seen as spontaneous reactions to a particular situation, whereas the strike was believed to have wider significance. It required some degree of organization and sustained effort. The task for revolutionaries was to shift the ground from material grievances to political demands.

Since the 1880s, but especially since the strike wave of the mid 1890s, the revolutionary movement had concentrated on organizing factory workers in conditions of government repression. Even though trade unions were legalized after the 1905 Revolution, the state and employers had consistently sought to claw back any concessions, so that agitation and organization in the factories remained difficult and dangerous. With the upsurge of the labour movement in 1912, revolutionaries again concentrated their efforts on factory workers. Female membership of trade unions remained insignificant, even in sectors in which they dominated, such as textiles. This did not mean that they were unwilling to take action to protest against their situation. In his study of the St Petersburg labour force between 1907 and 1917, Bob McKean argues that unskilled women workers, not only in textiles but also in food processing and animal products, had been increasingly drawn into the political strike movement in 1913 and 1914, and that they were not responding merely to short-term economic grievances.[52] Certainly, women were less likely than men to sustain such actions, which helps explain why both government and revolutionaries continued to focus concerns on the factories as the potential base for opposition to the state. What revolutionaries as much as the government failed to appreciate was that in the conditions of the First World War, the bread riot was as significant an expression of collective suffering and communal demands as the strike.

Nevertheless, at least a few revolutionaries, such as Alexander Shliapnikov, the leading Bolshevik in Petrograd during the war, recognized that it had brutally raised women's consciousness. In particular, the crisis in food and fuel supplies hit women workers and soldiers' wives very hard. Shliapnikov understood that it was not only the shortages and consequent inflation with which they had to deal, but the demands it placed on their time and resourcefulness. These women became the first to struggle against those who speculated and profited from the war.[53] Shliapnikov grasped the importance of the women's struggle against war profiteers, yet still saw their actions and motivation as essentially apolitical, more a domestic reflection of war weariness than a sign of rising political awareness. This assumption that women were simply too caught up in bread and butter issues to see the wider picture blinded politicians of all shades of opinion to the revolutionary potential of women by 1917. At the beginning of that year, the tsarist secret police had warned that it was precisely these women, mothers of families, exhausted from the endless queues at shops, suffering at the sight of their ill and half-starved children, who were the biggest threat to the regime because they constituted "a mass of inflammable material which needs only a spark for it to burst into flames".[54]

A factory inspector's report of the end of 1915 had recorded large increases not only in the numbers of adult women workers, but of underage youths (males by 37.7 per cent, females by 19.3 per cent). The report noted in particular the growth in numbers of women workers in metal plants, which it related directly to the loss of skilled men to the armed forces. Thus at the beginning of 1915, there had been 3,233 adult female metal workers; by the end, that number had risen to 15,903. The report also recorded the growing diversity of jobs for which women were now deemed eligible, including the masculine preserve of machine operator, so long as not much skill was required. Indeed, management seemed to be taking advantage of the absence of skilled men by employing female labour that was at best semi-skilled, which was not only considerably cheaper but could be used to intensify the division of labour and so dilute skills. In addition, taking on more women in the metal industry yielded the bonus of a workforce less inclined to push demands than their male predecessors.[55] This might have been because the women were recent recruits and did not want to harm their position in what was a higher-wage industry than the more usual "women's" work. Elsewhere, notably in the rubber industry, women were prepared to protest.

As noted earlier, just before war was declared, there had been strikes by female employees of a rubber factory (the Treugolnik) in Petersburg in March 1914 over several cases of mass poisoning, though management and police claimed that the cause was unclear. If anything, the demands of war-time production led to a deterioration in conditions. A district police officer reported on 18 November 1915 that 39 women at the Treugolnik plant had fallen ill, some of whom had lost consciousness. Again no cause was given. Two days later, in the same factory, a 25 year old worker (who had only recently left the village, attracted by the comparatively high wages she could earn in the city) collapsed; within three hours 11 others became ill, eight of whom had to be carried on stretchers to the factory dispensary. Those who had fainted had been unconscious for at least ten minutes, and on regaining consciousness had been unable to speak for another five minutes. Again, the police and employers claimed to be unable to pinpoint the cause, though there were hints that the fainting of so many women might be a form of mass hysteria. Such events were not exclusive to the rubber industry. On 20 December 1915, a colonel in the secret police reported that 20 women working in a pipe-making factory had fallen ill on the afternoon shift, and another 15 in the evening. This time a cause was identified: the women had been working next to the heating system and had been overcome by the carbon monoxide fumes given off by the fuel (coke).[56]

Neither police nor employers saw such events as particularly significant, except in interrupting production. Nevertheless, close attention was paid to the workers' reaction in order to avoid a repeat of the violent unrest of March 1914, so that all the women received medical attention relatively promptly, and were sent home rather than expected to finish their shift. It is not clear whether this apparent concern on the part of management was enough to defuse discontent. What is clear is that women workers generally were becoming more assertive as the war dragged on. To an extent, the Bolsheviks recognized that there was some potential for agitation and organization here. A leaflet for International Women's Day (23 February 1915) was signed by the "Organisation of Women Workers of the RSDLP". It pointed to the impact of the war in destroying workers' organizations, repressing radical newspapers, sending sons, husbands and brothers to bleed to death on foreign fields for the gains of capital. The burden of war had been laid on women's shoulders. How much, the leaflet asked, do you pay for damp flats, for fuel and food? The government even arrested anyone who complained about the doubling of prices. The leaflet called on women workers to stop suffering in silence, and to act to protect their menfolk, ending with the cry "Down with the War!".[57]

Women workers were taking action. On 9 April 1915, 80 female workers in a confectionary factory in the centre of Petrograd petitioned for a wage increase, though they did not strike. Just over a month later, on 19 May, 450 female textile workers (out of a total work force of 1,400 women and men) downed tools and demanded an increase in wages, refusing to leave the workshop. The factory director agreed, but would not give written confirmation until the women restarted production. Within a few hours, he had called in the police to force them to go back to work and to find the ringleaders, but he conceded their demand, and awarded a 10 per cent increase. Although only some of the women, and no men, had taken action on this occasion, the sexes sometimes joined in protest, as male and female tramworkers did in January 1916.[58]

Both the tsar and his opponents ignored the evidence of female disaffection, neither side believing that it could result in more than a riot over "bread and herrings".[59] Even at the end of 1916, a joint report by the governor of Petrograd and the city's chief of secret police claimed that the situation was relatively calm. Although there were strikes of workers in metals, on the trams and in government printing plants, the demands were economic and not political. On 19 December, 996 (out of a total of 1,293) women workers at Petrograd's munitions stores gathered near the canteen after lunch to demand wage increases. On being told by someone from the administration that wages were being reviewed, 952 left for home without finishing their shift. What is interesting here is that only women were taking action, and they were in a minority of the labour force of 5,000. Their demands reflected the considerable gap between male and female wages in the munitions industry. What is also interesting is that, once again, management was prepared to concede a little rather than risk confrontation, or the protest spreading.[60] However, the women lacked the support of the majority of their colleagues, especially the men. When the strikers refused to return to work until their wages were raised, they were threatened with dismissal and the loss of half that month's wages. They returned to work on 21 December 1916.

As noted above, there were also cases of solidarity between male and female workers. They had interests in common: higher (though not equal) pay, the abolition of the right of employers to fine workers as they deemed fit, and the end of compulsory overtime. On 26 January 1917, 700 weavers at one factory demanded the reinstatement of one woman who had been sacked. One of the most protracted strikes was of female textile workers in the Vyborg district of Petrograd, which lasted over a month; another, again in January 1917, lasted five days.[61] By then, the strikes, ostensibly over pay and conditions, had become increasingly political. During the worst winter of the war, in a severe food shortage, when the wealthy somehow got fresh bread daily, women workers' demands for bread were indeed political.

The rise in female militancy did not go completely unnoticed, though revolutionaries saw it as part of the general class struggle. Inessa Armand wrote that during the war, any strikes or demonstrations could only be carried out successfully as long as women workers were involved.[62] In a leaflet of 1915, the Bolsheviks emphasized both the necessity of, and the difficulties in, drawing women into their campaigns:

It is essential to pay close attention to the families of those sent to war, and in particular to workers' wives. [The latter] must play a significant role in the food supply campaign. The struggle to increase wages and shorten the working day is possible only with the full participation of women workers. The task of the day is to assist in raising their class consciousness.[63]

Since at least 1915 Bolsheviks had been responding to workers' protests by addressing leaflets to both female and male workers. The appeals were gender neutral, as in a leaflet of around 14 February 1917 which called for the eight-hour day, the overthrow of tsarism and the establishment of a provisional revolutionary government, and all land to the peasants. This leaflet advised workers to focus their protests on key days, such as 1 May. There was no mention of International Women's Day.[64]

Nikolai Sukhanov, a prominent left-wing critic of the Bolsheviks who was working in Petrograd in 1917, described the general feeling of unease on the eve of the February Revolution, which broke out on International Women's Day, in which the talk of ordinary people concerning the coming political storm was dismissed by seasoned revolutionaries such as himself, particularly if it was "gossip" of office "girls": after all, what could they know of revolution? Sukhanov overheard two typists chatting about the severe food shortages and the search for hoarded food, which included attacks on warehouses. The clerical workers talked about the unrest among the women in the endless queues, the debates and arguments, and concluded that it was the beginning of the revolution. Sukhanov was both sceptical and wistful: "These girls didn't understand what a revolution was. Nor did I believe them for a second." Why not? He thought to himself that not one political group was prepared to overthrow the existing order, that "everyone was dreaming, ruminating, full of foreboding, feeling his way", and that these "philistine" girls did not understand even the basics of politics, so that their judgement was worthless. "Revolution – highly improbable! Revolution! – everyone knew this was only a dream – a dream of generations and of long laborious decades." Still he hesitated, wondering if they might have grasped something which he had missed after all. "Without believing the girls, I repeated after them mechanically: Yes, the beginning of the revolution."[65]

Stuck in his office, he was not aware of the extent of disaffection among the workers in the way that those women who both worked and waited in line outside bakeries were. Rodionova, the tram conductor, saw a great deal as she toured the city. Trams were delayed by the movement of detachments of soldiers going off to war. Working-class areas were crowded with people discussing and protesting at meetings and in queues. Often factories were inactive, having run out of fuel or raw materials. As Rodionova remarked, even someone with very little formal education could understand that such intense social and material discontent had political implications, for the talk in the streets was not just about bread, it was concerned with justice and freedom.[66]

CHAPTER SIX

Women and the 1917 Revolution in Petrograd

It was, then, generally accepted by revolutionaries that women workers were incapable of sustaining either organization or industrial action, and that the cause of any female protest would be material rather than ideological, concerned with problems of everyday life rather than the wider political picture. Still, as we have seen, there was evidence from the early 1880s that a minority of women at least were interested in the labour movement, while large numbers of women were willing to take militant action, as in the textile strikes of the mid 1890s, protests against the conscription of their men in 1904 and political demands in 1905. Indeed the 1905 Revolution was seen as very important for raising the political consciousness of many women, both urban and rural. However, the downturn in the strike movement after 1906, coupled with a still depressed economy (until around 1909–10) and renewed repression from the tsarist government, including attempts to withdraw all concessions made to trade unions and political parties, had again narrowed the focus of revolutionaries to the organized industrial workers, and particularly skilled men.

Jumping forward to 1917, a basic chronology of the revolutionary process would be punctuated by certain key events: the February Revolution and the overthrow of tsarism (23–27 February); the April crisis and the fall of the first Provisional Government over war aims (23–30 April), followed in May by the establishment of a coalition government that included members of the Petrograd Soviet; the disastrous military offensive in June (18 June–2 July); the July Days of demonstrations and riots by workers, soldiers and sailors in Petrograd, which some saw as an attempt by the Bolsheviks to topple the government (3–5 July);

143

the attempted coup in August by General Kornilov, Commander in Chief of the armed forces (26–30 August), which fatally weakened the government and revived the Bolsheviks' political fortunes; culminating in the Bolshevik seizure of power on 25 October.

Above all, these successive crises are related to political and military developments. They may be interwoven with social movements: of the working class (issues of workers' control, development of trade unions and factory committees, the growing militancy of strikes); of the peasantry (who set up their own committees and then determined to solve the land question in their own way, since the Provisional Government postponed radical reform); and in the army (the establishment of soldiers' committees, the diminution of officers' authority, and efforts to replace it with the election of officers). The development of the revolution in the army was closely related to what was happening in both the workers' and peasants' movements (with links between these two, based on continuing contact between workers and their villages and regions of origin). While men predominated, women were active in each of these three strands of the revolutionary process, even, though to a much lesser extent, in the army. Underlying it all after the downfall of the old order in February was the situation of "dual power", by which the Provisional Government held power only so long as it had the support of the Soviet. Much of the narrative of the revolution is taken up with explaining how that unstable situation was resolved, why the Bolsheviks won, and to a lesser extent why Bolshevik opponents and critics lost.

Women scarcely figure in accounts of 1917. Their appearance is generally limited to the February Revolution. Thereafter, political developments appear to be overwhelmingly male affairs: the establishment and collapse of governments; the failure of the summer military offensive; the armed demonstrations against the government in July; the military coup in August; and the Bolshevik assault on the Winter Palace in October. If women appear on the scene after February, it is neither as instigators nor full participants. Rather, they tend to be glimpsed on the sidelines, reacting against revolutionary developments (as in July, when some women accused the Bolsheviks of being German agents, and in October when some resisted the Bolshevik assault on the Provisional Government).

Superficially, then, it appears that women set the revolution in motion precipitately, without preparation, organization, or direction,

144

and then just as quickly withdrew to the wings. However, if we trace the development of the revolution through to October by putting women in the foreground, questions arise as to how "spontaneous" the February Revolution was, what role the unorganized and unskilled workers (who included a majority of female workers) played in the radicalization of the labour movement, and how the Bolsheviks were able to win the support of the masses outside of the trade unions and factory committees (which again included a majority of women workers). Such a perspective will show that the October Revolution cannot be limited to the seizure of power by a minority party. As far as the masses of people were concerned – and notably women who now made up almost half the urban workforce, constituted the bulk of agricultural labour, and were the main consumers for the family – the Provisional Government and its allies had failed them. While it can be argued that the Bolsheviks, once secure in power, "usurped" the revolution, that should not be used retrospectively either to dismiss the masses in general and women in particular from the political process that they undoubtedly helped, and for much of 1917 pushed into shape, or to paint them simply as dupes of the Bolsheviks.

Those masses were not made up of men alone; indeed the First World War had resulted in such a great increase in the numbers of women workers and their significance for the war effort, that their active participation was essential for any protest made by the labour movement to be successful. As we saw in the previous chapter, there was recognition of this development among Social Democrats who, on the eve of the war in 1914, had sought to address women workers directly through specialist journals. Whereas these efforts were quickly suppressed and the revolutionary groups subjected to severe harassment, women workers themselves became more militant. From the second year of the war, there were strikes scattered throughout the country involving female industrial workers protesting not only over pay and deteriorating conditions of work, but also over the lack of respect shown them by foremen and employers. The strikes and demonstrations initiated by women workers that occurred in the capital at the end of February 1917 and which led to the overthrow of tsarism need to be seen in this context of growing popular unrest. Indeed, the protests staged on International Women's Day were preceded by a strike among female textile workers in Petrograd, when one millowner sought to increase the standard shift from 12 to 13 hours. Some of the women had reacted in the traditionally docile manner and been prepared to go along with the management, but the majority refused and forced the latter to withdraw the directive. On this occasion, the militant workers seem to have won over their more passive comrades, since all efforts to neutralize the influence of the former (for example, by transferring those thought to be ringleaders from the shopfloor to the factory's food store in the hope of driving a wedge between the women) failed.[1]

Women and the overthrow of tsarism

Yet, in spite of such actions taken by women workers since 1915, it is generally believed that when revolution broke out at the end of February 1917 on the initiative of women workers and soldiers' wives, no one was prepared. Attention has been focused instead on the strikes by metal workers at the Putilov plant in Petrograd on 18 February, the week preceding the revolution, in which the men demanded higher wages and the re-instatement of fellow workers who had been dismissed. The reaction of management was a lock-out, leaving several thousand men angry and embittered.[2] The men's demands were economic, mirroring the female concern over the worsening material conditions. It was the women, however, both heads of households and housewives, most of whom by 1917 were themselves in full-time paid employment, who spent hours in the dark winter weather queuing for food for the families. It was precisely this double burden that pushed the women to dissolve the already tenuous division between "economic" and "political" demands.

The fact that revolution began on International Women's Day led many later to assume that the women could have provided only the spark, simply making a protest against food and fuel shortages in the traditional way, and that the men would have to assume leadership of this popular protest to give it wider significance and a chance of achieving something. Indeed, in a study of the revolution published in 1990, Richard Pipes argues that the catalytic agents were not women workers at all, but rather those Social Democrats in the Inter-District Committee, who favoured the reunification of Bolsheviks and Mensheviks. Moreover, Pipes insists that rather than the usual depiction of February as a workers' revolt, it was "first and foremost, a mutiny of peasant soldiers whom, to save money, the authorities had billeted in overcrowded facilities in the Empire's capital city".[3]

Most narratives of the February Revolution seem to bear out that general picture, though we disagree with Pipes in our perception of when it began. Since he sees the mutiny of the Petrograd garrison as the key moment, he dates the revolution from 27 February (according to the old style calendar, which would be 12 March). Most historians, however, accept that it began "spontaneously", on the morning of 23 February (or 8 March), when women workers downed tools and took to the streets, and that it culminated on the 27th.[4] A glance at the slogans that were shouted by the female strikers shows that more than material demands were being made: "Down with the war! Down with high prices! Down with hunger! Bread for the workers!" It is also instructive to consider what the women did. They acted in the "irrational" way traditionally expected of female protests, by rioting. They damaged tram cars and looted shops, for example. From the start, however, it was clear that the first priority of the female strikers was to persuade the men, soldiers as well as workers, to join them. Nor were the women prepared to accept "no" for an answer. They pelted factory windows with stones and snow. The fact that so many men joined them immediately was not, or not simply, owing to intimidation from the militant women, but because the women were expressing what their male comrades also felt: enough was enough.[5]

It is also interesting that whereas the Bolshevik leadership in Petrograd had encouraged the women to protest against the war and the slogan denouncing it could be traced to them, they had also tried to dissuade the women from going any further. A leaflet distributed in Petrograd around 14 February called on all workers, female as well as male, to wage a "war on this war", and argued that for a real peace to be achieved, tsarism had to be overthrown.[6] While this leaflet had been addressed to both women and men, the Bolsheviks still saw May Day, the expression of the predominantly male labour movement, as a more appropriate time for political action than International Women's Day, the first of which had been held in Russia only in 1913 and had been a tiny affair. This implicit focus on male factory workers was in spite of the fact that by 1917 women constituted 47 per cent of Petrograd's labour force.[7] The Bolsheviks feared the assumed spontaneity and indiscipline of the women. Indeed, memoirs of male Bolsheviks reveal that they would have preferred there to be no demonstration on 23 February, but reluctantly accepted that the mood of the women could not be ignored.

In fact, it was a few female party members who persuaded the hesitant male leadership to make an effort in the working-class district of Vyborg by holding a meeting on the linked themes of war and inflation. These women, who co-operated with women from the Inter-District Committee, were part of a circle that had been established by the Bolsheviks in Petrograd, in recognition of the growing importance of women workers to the wartime labour movement. This circle, which had been carrying out agitational work in factories where large numbers of women were employed, grasped that the depth of feeling would allow them to make the connection between the women's traditional concern over the food supply and the destructive effects of the war, which the Bolsheviks portrayed as a struggle among greedy capitalists from which the workers had nothing to gain. The leading Bolshevik in Petrograd at that time, Alexander Shliapnikov, recalled that he had not even produced a leaflet for the day, though he put this failure down to problems with the party's printing press.[8] Instead, only a brief appeal was issued, which stated simply that the women were no longer prepared to suffer in silence, but that their pent-up anger at war profiteering had become increasingly political as they realized that the small shop-keepers had not caused the war, and indeed that many of them were suffering too because of the collapse of the transport and distribution systems. Hence, the female Bolsheviks pointed to big business and the government that together they portrayed as a gang of robbers and murderers. The appeal concluded with the characteristic Bolshevik call for an end to the war.[9]

Kaiurov, a skilled metal worker and seasoned member of the Bolshevik Party, addressed a meeting of female workers on the eve of International Women's Day, acknowledging its significance, and touching on the issues of concern to them, both on the woman question in general and on particular ways in which they were affected by the war. He also called on them to do as the Petrograd committee of the party directed, which was to limit their actions and to demonstrate in a disciplined fashion. When he found out, only hours later, about the strike action taken by the textile workers and their efforts to escalate it into a city-wide protest involving the metal industry, in which Bolsheviks such as himself were influential, he was furious. He dismissed at first what he saw as the women's lack of self-control, rather than his own failure to persuade them of his argument. Kaiurov acknowledged that the women had cause for protest, but he nevertheless thought their demonstration to be ill-judged. He believed that the Bolshevik Party had been right to harness its energy for the planned mass day of protest in May. February was not the time for revolution; neither the party nor the working class was prepared for it. Indeed, the fact that the women had ignored his advice convinced him that the Bolsheviks lacked strength in, and any control of, this militant working-class area.[10]

Like most other commentators, Kaiurov portrayed the women's actions as typically emotional, irrational and undisciplined. The only reason he could come up with to explain their behaviour was the food shortages and the endless queues. He overlooked the efforts that had been made by women from the Bolshevik Party and the Inter-District Committee to organize workers and soldiers' wives since the onset of the military conflict in 1914. As popular dissatisfaction with deteriorating living conditions and anger at the heavy military losses spread, such grassroots agitation found an increasingly responsive female working class. At the beginning of the February Revolution, two female Bolsheviks, Nina Agadzhanova and Mariia Vydrina, organized mass meetings of workers and soldiers' wives, workplace strikes and mass demonstrations, searches for weapons to arm the crowds, as well as securing the release of political prisoners, and setting up first-aid units.[11]

Yet Kaiurov still viewed the women's actions on 23 February as a bread riot which the Bolshevik leadership was forced to support because not only had thousands of male workers joined the women in taking their protest to the streets of the capital, but among them were rank and file Bolsheviks who had seized the opportunity to push their more cautious leaders into the open. The women's action may have been spontaneous and leaderless when judged by professional revolutionaries who had struggled for years, in difficult circumstances and at considerable cost to themselves, to raise the political awareness of, and impart organizational skills to, an ill-educated working class. Yet in refusing simply to accept the Bolshevik line, the women had struck an immediate chord in the labour movement. In serving as a catalyst to wider working-class action, the female textile workers and soldiers' wives had effectively taken the lead, and left the revolutionaries standing.

While the male Bolshevik leadership had urged patience on the women, the Mensheviks and SRs had ignored International Women's Day. Nevertheless, however mistaken they regarded the timing of the protest, revolutionaries could hardly stand aside from a protest that was rapidly developing into a political confrontation with the regime. All three parties met together to discuss the turn of events and decided with great reluctance to support the women who had taken strike action. Kaiurov proposed that they try to gain leadership of the strike to ensure that the women would act less precipitately and in a more disciplined fashion. From being left behind, the revolutionaries were now trying to overtake the women and bring order to the protest. Kaiurov felt uneasy because the action had not been planned and did not have an obvious target at which to aim, but he admitted that the working class as a whole was indeed ready (though in his view not prepared) to protest openly against the regime.

Kaiurov and the rest of the revolutionary leadership in Petrograd still did not recognize that what the women had set in motion was a revolution. They seemed blind to the way the "leaderless" women were organizing themselves, assuming that it was a traditional protest that had erupted because of desperation at the extreme shortages and appalling conditions of life. Foreign eyewitness accounts give a similar reading of what happened on 22–23 February. Indeed, and in contrast to Kaiurov's account, the British Consul-General in Russia, R.H. Bruce Lockhart, did not even mention that the initial action had been taken by women, and painted a picture in which male metal workers dominated in the protest movements from the start. Lockhart recalls that the revolution began when:

a long queue of workers waiting for bread lost patience and sacked several shops. On the next day [8 March/23 February] the workers of the famous Putilov arms factory came out on strike. Other strikes followed, and for the first time in the capital since 1905 there were cries of "Down with the autocracy!"[12]

A close reading of Kaiurov's account shows the women acting not so much spontaneously, since after all they had been organizing a demonstration for International Women's Day, but rather against Bolshevik advice and therefore in an undisciplined fashion. Lockhart, on the other hand, sees the February Revolution as spontaneous and leaderless. Lockhart had reason to be critical of the Bolsheviks (he was released from the Kremlin, where he had been imprisoned by them as a spy, only in October 1918), and he was writing many years after the events. His account may have been intended to contrast the popular nature of the February Revolution to the seizure of power by the Bolsheviks in

October. However, historians generally have interpreted the women's actions in this way. Nor does George Katkov, a critic of this thesis of "spontaneity", give the women any more recognition: he believed that a mass movement on this scale and with this momentum "would not have been possible without some kind of directing power behind it".[13] For Katkov this direction was provided by the Bolsheviks backed by German money. What all three overlook are the female members of the Bolshevik Party and the Inter-District Committee who were organizing protests for International Women's Day, including the factory worker, Anastasiá Deviatkina, who had been a member of the former for 13 years, and who organized and led a demonstration on 23 February.[14]

Both contemporaries and historians have based this judgement on the stereotype of the passive, apolitical woman who was incapable of taking the initiative and of sustaining a struggle, despite the fact that the women in February were acting as male workers would do in an industrial dispute which had political as well as economic causes. It was not women in the queues for bread and fuel who began the street protests, but female textile workers from a number of plants in the Vyborg district of Petrograd. They downed tools collectively, left the mills and moved speedily and deliberately in large groups from one factory to another. They did not restrict their search for allies to the textile sector. They demanded from workers in other industries, and notably the metal industry which was regarded as in the vanguard of the labour movement, not just moral support, but active participation. At each stop, the women would cajole and insist that now was the time to cease working and show the employers and government that workers had finally had as much as they were prepared to take. The women rammed home their points by throwing whatever they could lay their hands on (stones, snowballs, sticks) at factory windows and doors, and invading the buildings. Their methods were persuasive enough to convince masses of workers that this was not a simple bread riot, as so many politicians were assuming, but something much wider in scope. Those workers who hesitated to join the demonstrations and simply went home, were skilled men who were afraid of the impact of the strike on their families. Others feared that the movement would be quickly suppressed, and the authorities would punish men by sending them to the front.[15] Perhaps it was the unexpected reversal of gender roles that revolutionaries found difficulty in coming to terms with, so that they ended up by following behind a movement of which they had always assumed they would be in the lead.

The movement gathered pace, however, drawing increasing numbers of men into it. That lockout at the Putilov factory had already put thousands of angry and desperate men on the streets. On 23 February, 20 per cent of all Petrograd's workers were on strike, but of textile workers it was 30 per cent. By 25 February, 52 per cent of the city's labour force had downed tools, but 71 per cent of the textile labour force were on strike. Thus the participation of textile workers was growing at a faster rate than that of the city as a whole.[16] The demand for bread, so closely associated with the February Revolution, was heard from striking textile workers the day before International Women's Day, by which time the women had widened their demands to calling for the return of their men from the front. From the start, they faced the police and troops who tried to prevent them from moving outside their district. Indeed, male workers warned them against trying to reach the centre, arguing that "it is not the business of babas [womenfolk]". The women persisted. In clashes with police and troops, some were killed, buried in common graves, their names unrecorded.[17] The demonstrators realized they had to win over the soldiers.

The women next turned to the city's transportation system, going to the tram depots. The war had forced tram companies to employ increasing numbers of women. Reminiscences of a female tram conductor, who admitted that she feared the outcome of the demonstration, might be taken as proof of Kaiurov's criticism that the women had no clear objective. Yet she also recalled that she shouted along with the rest "Down with the tsar!", which showed that the women understood where political responsibility lay, even if this woman could not envisage what would replace it.[18] Another conductor, Rodionova, revealed how quickly the revolutionary movement grew. On the eve of International Women's Day, armed soldiers stood outside the depots; by the end of 23 February, they had joined the workers inside.[19] The destruction of trams seemed further evidence that elemental forces were simply rioting. In fact, the demonstrators were overturning trams to serve as barricades in order to hinder the movement of police and troops who might be sent to curb the strikes. Moving out of the Vyborg district, the demonstration gathered up more workers (from leather, paper and pipe works), spreading word that the strike was to be a general one. The slogan calling for an end to the war was repeated, and women demanded the return of their men from the front.[20] They did not restrict themselves to shouting slogans, however, but from the start of their action tried to win over the soldiers who were garrisoned in the city, recognizing that they had to convince the troops not to obey any orders to crush the demonstrations. The women realized that the soldiers held the key to the success, or failure, of their protest. Indeed, ever since the start of the war, politically conscious textile workers had established contacts with the garrisons. The conscription of millions of peasant men had led to significant numbers being stationed in the capital, and the women were able to communicate, especially through men who had come from their home village or region. In some cases, close personal relationships developed between soldiers and women workers, so that the barracks were not isolated from the factories when the latter took their action on 23 February 1917.[21]

There were still considerable numbers of troops, in particular the cossacks on whom the regime relied heavily to suppress any unrest. Indeed, while the general view of the February Days was of spontaneity, the government still suspected the Bolsheviks of fomenting unrest. Lenin's elder sister, Anna Elizarova, who played a key role in maintaining the Bolshevik organization in Petrograd during the war (as we saw in Chapter 3), had been arrested in June 1916; released in October, she was arrested again four months later, a week before the revolution.[22] One of the leading Bolsheviks in Petrograd in February, Elena Stasova, was arrested on 24 February, despite the fact that she had been ill and politically inactive since the previous year. At first the only woman in her cell, by the end of the night she was sharing it with 17 others, and the gaol was crowded. They could hear the sound of gunfire. On 27 February, a man appeared, opened the cells and shouted at them to leave. The women hesitated, suspecting that it was a trick by reactionaries and that they would be shot. They turned to Stasova, who was the oldest among them, for advice. She decided to take the chance of escape. The women gathered their pillows and blankets and moved out into the courtyard. To their amazement, they saw crowds of firemen shouting "Liberty!"[23]

While they had been imprisoned, the female protesters on the streets had shown courage and resilience in refusing the calls from the authorities to go home, and in suffering violent attacks from the cossacks, all the time trying to win a hearing from the latter. Rather than flee the mounted soldiers, the women encircled them, and put their case in very simple terms: they were not acting for selfish reasons nor out of lack of patriotism, but in justified anger at being exploited by war profiteers while their men were needlessly slaughtered at the front. Zhenia Egorova, secretary for the Bolshevik Party in the Vyborg district, agitated among the soldiers, appealing to them to disobey orders to shoot down the demonstrators.[24] The women tried to separate the men from their officers. The latter shouted that men should not follow women's lead, and dismissed the women with the insulting term "baba" (which might be translated as "old hag" in this context), but the women refused to give way, and insisted that they be seen as human beings with legitimate concerns for their brothers, fathers and sons serving at the front.

Much to the women's initial amazement, the cossacks listened to them and refused to obey orders to fire, lowering their rifles instead and leading their horses away from the crowds. While these troops had not yet joined the protests, the women had breached the regime's last line of defence.[25] In his study of the February Revolution, Tsuyoshi Hasegawa related that on the afternoon of the 25th, from the crowds confronted by cossacks, stepped a young girl who walked slowly towards the troops. From under her cloak, she brought out a bunch of red roses and held it towards the officer.[26] His unexpected acceptance has been seen as a symbol of both peace and revolution.[27] Thus women workers and house-wives, who were not considered politically conscious enough to be able to lead or organize themselves without male help and guidance, had brought the city's factories and essential services to a standstill and sown confusion in the military garrison.[28]

Within three days, there was a general strike, the army had mutinied and gone over to the revolution and tsarism had collapsed. Caught unawares, politicians of the old regime established the Provisional Government (all male), headed by Prince L'vov, while a council (the Petrograd Soviet) of workers' and soldiers' deputies was established, initially dominated by the Mensheviks and SRs, the vast majority of whom were men. It was soon clear that the Provisional Government could do nothing without the support of the Soviet, but that both the former and the Soviet's leadership saw the revolution as effectively over. While both were immediately preoccupied with strengthening their position as regards each other, the issues over which the women had taken action on International Women's Day – food and fuel shortages – had not been resolved. Indeed, the government's determination to continue the war to a successful conclusion and the soviet leadership's support of a "war of defence" meant that, apart from the end of tsarism, little had changed.

What did the women want now?

Women's role in initiating the February demonstrations, and indeed in maintaining their momentum, had been crucial for the overthrow of the old order, but politicians of all stripes continued to view them as an elemental force, while male workers generally still saw women as a drag on the labour movement. Skilled men dominated the elections for the first Petrograd Soviet and the newly set up factory committees, even being returned in industries in which women were a clear majority of the work force. There were two main reasons for this: women's continuing responsibility for feeding their families in a situation of serious shortages, which the overthrow of tsarism had not eased, and a lack of confidence (shared by women as well as men) in women's abilities either to sustain an activity or to articulate their views. Female political consciousness had certainly been raised, but their level of education and skills remained low. However, a few of those women who had been politically active before February were given some recognition, at least within the Bolshevik Party. For example, in March, in elections to the Narva district committee of the party, one woman was elected. The other 15 were men, which was not surprising since it was an area of metal works, including the great Putilov plant, in which male workers made up the majority of those employed. In another district, Vasil'evskii island, a woman, Vera Slutskaia, played a key role in organizing the elections to the Bolshevik Party committee. By the end of May, she had been elected by the Bolshevik Party to the executive committee of the soviet.[29]

The Social Democrat Sukhanov, who had failed to recognize that the situation in February had revolutionary potential precisely because he had dismissed the discussion he overheard among office "girls" as mere gossip and rumour, paid closer attention to what women had to say after the overthrow of the tsar. While implicitly acknowledging that women were now actors on the political scene, he still saw the role that they played as based on instinct and age-old concerns, without consideration for the outcome. The February Revolution had shown him that any protest over food shortages could have powerful political repercussions in the current material conditions, and he listened with interest to what women were saying in the queues, which had certainly not diminished with the fall of tsarism. The women had not known what kind of regime would replace the old one, but had expected some immediate improvement in their situation. When none was forthcoming, they quickly became disillusioned not only with the Provisional Government but also with revolutionaries like Sukhanov, whose talk of abstract ideals when their families were suffering rang hollow. Tsarism had been overthrown, but otherwise the politicians were following the same policies, and the women lining up for hours suspected that profits from the war were still being made by a few, at their and their men's expense.

This kind of talk worried Social Democrats such as Sukhanov who considered that Russia was nowhere near ready for further popular action, and feared that the outcome could only be either the reassertion of the old order, or victory for the Bolsheviks whose leader Lenin called for a second, socialist, revolution as soon as he returned to Russia from emigration in April. Thus Sukhanov acknowledged that the fate of the revolution lay with the "lower depths" who had forced it in the first place, and that if they were again successful then the Bolsheviks, who ironically had tried so hard to limit the women's actions in February, would be the main beneficiaries.[30] Yet, although both the Provisional Government and the Petrograd Soviet leadership recognized that inflation and food shortages were issues of crucial significance, they did nothing about them. Both were agreed that the ultimate cause was the war, but saw fundamental reforms of the economy as future, or long-term tasks.

Nevertheless, some of the most downtrodden women, the soldiers' wives (*soldatki*), were soon raising their voices in protest at the lack of improvement in their situation. They also revealed that they had more faith in the Petrograd Soviet than in the Provisional Government, since the demonstration of around 15,000 *soldatki* on 11 April was to the Tauride Palace, the headquarters of the former. The chairman of the Soviet was the Menshevik, F.I. Dan. He supported the war as one of self-defence, chided the women for demanding money from an empty treasury, and refused to allow a female Bolshevik member of the Soviet, Alexandra Kollontai, to address the demonstration, though she did so unofficially, urging them to elect their own delegates to the Soviet whose leadership had just rebuffed them.[31] Bolshevik women were already organizing these disappointed as well as hungry women, worn out by the desperate struggle to feed their families on an inadequate and irregular allowance.[32]

Besides the women's continuing domestic worries as a factor explaining the paucity of female representatives elected after February, there was also their peasant inheritance of submission to patriarchal authority and the fact that it was for the most part skilled rather than unskilled workers (and women were mostly among the latter) who had the confidence and experience to put themselves forward. Skill was generally recognized as a masculine attribute, while the skilled male worker was not only better educated but had a wider political perspective than the narrowly family orientated one of the unskilled (both male and female). Still, what February had shown was that the women's domestic focus was not necessarily apolitical, and indeed that the male activists had completely failed to see the revolutionary potential of the women's concern over the price of bread. Although the women's actions had achieved what the revolutionary parties had been aiming at for the previous half century at least, memoirs of skilled male workers such as Kaiurov give the impression that they felt it necessary to retrieve the situation. Bread and butter issues were pushed to the side again as the traditional hierarchy of the labour movement reasserted itself, and reimposed the distinction between economic and political questions.

For a time, the unskilled accepted the leadership of the skilled. The women in particular were acutely aware of their political inexperience and accepted that they needed guidance. P.G. Glizer, a 19 year old seamstress, recalled hearing from a male worker on 27 February that her workshop should stop work because the tsar had been overthrown and they should join the revolution. With the other seamstresses, she made a red banner with the slogan "Long live Freedom!" and listened all night to speeches promising a better life. When nothing had improved by May, Glizer's workshop asked the owners for hot water for their lunches and for ventilators to be installed. When their requests were not met, Glizer went to the militia, only to be told that it was not their job to improve workers' conditions. She heard of a trade union that could help her, but did not know how to find it. Seeing a man in the street who looked as if he might be a tailor, she asked him if he knew the location of the union. Following his directions, Glizer met the union secretary, a female Bolshevik called Sakharova, who sent a union representative. This young girl noted down their grievances and then negotiated with the owners, returning at the end of the day to say that their demands had been met. The following day, the trade union organized a meeting in the workshop, and almost all the women joined. Glizer also became a Bolshevik, was elected chairperson of her factory committee, and in August became a member of the local soviet.[33]

Glizer's workshop was predominantly female, her grievances directly related to her place of work, and the union representatives with whom she first came into contact were women. In general, however, because the labour movement remained male dominated, and the differences in skills, pay, training and job opportunities not only persisted but were championed by the trade unions, female workers still saw the latter as having little to offer them. Since women did not join trade unions or political parties in great numbers, and so few put themselves forward for election by their comrades in the workplace, the caricature of the generally docile but occasionally riotous female reasserted itself. In some factories, male workers even tried to undermine female efforts at self-organization.[34] The Menshevik Eva Broido noted that it was not only in male dominated industries such as metals, in which women were dismissed out of hand as possible representatives of shopfloor workers, but that even in female dominated plants (such as confectionary, food processing and textiles), men rather than women were seen as the most suitable to sit on factory committees.[35]

Nevertheless, some women were elected. In one textile factory in March, five female Bolsheviks and two non-party women were elected to the factory committee. In late spring, women were also elected to the control commission that was to oversee working conditions.[36] In practice, it seems that within the textile industry the majority of those elected did not belong to any particular party. At the Kozhernikov factory in Petrograd, all seven of the members of the committee were uncommitted, five of whom were women. Indeed, a woman, Garezina, chaired that factory committee. Of the Bolsheviks returned from exile, two were women who had worked in this factory, Mariia Nikiforova and Sof'ia Bazulenkova, who were quickly elected to the committee.[37]

At another factory, however, two female Bolsheviks were shouted down by male apprentices and workers, who were particularly hostile to comrade Yadviga whom they suspected of being Jewish. Another female Bolshevik, Olga Chernysheva, was initially defeated in the elections because she was regarded as not representative enough, since she worked in the factory shop. As noted above, employers had shifted women whom they considered as too politicized from the shop floor in an effort to decrease their influence. Eventually, however, Chernysheva was accepted by the workforce.[38] In addition, women made up 11 members of the 20 strong executive committee of the textile union in

March 1917. None of the women was attached to any political party; of the men, only three were (and they were Bolsheviks).[39]

Women were soon showing clear signs of dissatisfaction with the Provisional Government. On 21 April, a crowd of mainly female textile workers demonstrated against the government. They were jeered by pro-government demonstrators, well-dressed women and men, from the other side of the street: "Stockingless! Uneducated riffraff! Ignoble sluts!" One of the workers, Pelageia Romanovna, retorted: "You lot are wearing hats made by our hands!" A fight broke out between the two groups in which banners were torn from the anti-government workers' hands and used to hit them over the head, with the workers retaliating by pulling the hats (and hat-pins) from the heads of the fashionable supporters of the government, and scratching their faces. Before serious harm was done, the workers were escorted to the Petrograd Soviet by a detachment of sailors.[40]

In the summer, women were making their disappointment with the revolution, which they had initiated, clear in a concerted way, by striking. Nor were protests limited to factory women, but spread to the service sector which was notoriously difficult to organize. Thus in May, as many as 40,000 laundresses went on strike over pay and conditions. By then, the first Provisional Government had collapsed, largely over its war aims (which were expansionist), and some leading Mensheviks and SRs from the Soviet had entered a coalition government with former Duma members determined to continue with the war effort. To this government, the laundresses' action was an irritant that endangered their plans for the country. The Bolsheviks, however, recognized the political significance of such actions by previously submissive workers. While their ideal of a working-class militant remained the skilled male worker based in the heavy industry sector, they saw clear evidence of the class struggle among service workers. Hence one of the leading female Bolshevik orators and organizers, Alexandra Kollontai, concentrated much of her effort on working with the laundresses in their May strike, which revealed that women had the capacity for mounting a prolonged protest.

Despite the difficulties of uniting so many women who were scattered throughout the city in thousands of enterprises of vastly different sizes, they had had some experience of organizing protests and setting up a union in 1905, while there were a number of Bolshevik Party members among the laundresses. A key figure in establishing the union was Sof'ia Goncharskaia. Born in 1889 into a coalminer's family, she seems to have joined the Bolsheviks during the 1905 Revolution. One of the first exiles to return to Petrograd after the February Revolution, Goncharskaia had been given the task of organizing the laundresses, whose strike in May was the first under the coalition government. With other female activists from the union, Goncharskaia had gone from one laundry to another persuading the women to join the strike. They would fill buckets with cold water to douse the ovens. In one laundry, the owner attacked Goncharskaia with a crowbar; she was saved by the laundresses grabbing him from behind.[41] Their demands reflected the main aims of the labour movement: improvements in their conditions of work, the eight-hour day, and a minimum wage that they would also receive when absent from work either through illness or on vacation (a linked demand was for annual leave). Their success, though short-lived, raised the prestige of laundresses, who were generally looked on as particularly downtrodden.

Moira Donald concludes from her study of Bolshevik activity among Petrograd's working women in 1917 that it was largely pressure from Kollontai, who spoke at the mass meetings used to organize the laundresses, which persuaded the Bolsheviks to support the strike.[42] However, the content and frequency of reports about the strike in the Bolshevik Party press reveals that the Bolsheviks regarded it almost as a model of militancy, a microcosm of the collapsing economy and bitter class struggle (with violent incidents between strikers and employers, and between the former and the strike-breakers hired by the latter), as well as a reflection of the growing alienation between government and the working class.[43]

Bolshevik reports of strikes and demonstrations by women workers provided a lot of information on how they were organized, on what they were demanding, and what the response was from employers and government. The picture that emerges is one of growing involvement of women workers in strike action and street protests, though few took the step of either joining trade unions, still seen as serving the interest of male workers, or aligning themselves with a particular political party. Sometimes women took action alongside men, as in another strike that took place in May, in dye and cleaning works (involving approximately 350 workers, the majority of whom were female) and sales people (about 150) who worked in affiliated shops, and a June strike of waitresses and waiters in Petrograd's teashops and restaurants. There was considerable interest in these service sector strikes of May and June, but whereas their socialist rivals focused on the material grievances, only the Bolsheviks seem to have realized the political significance of their actions and demands.[44] The former were certainly important. Women workers seemed particularly concerned with wage rises (though they did not seek equal pay with men since generally the sexes were employed at different jobs, and indeed in different industries), improved working conditions (particularly sanitary), maternity benefits, and the abolition of child labour. Their anger at what they felt was sexually demeaning, and indeed often abusive, behaviour in the workplace was reflected in the call for an end to body searches.[45] Such demands were reported to a limited extent in the liberal, and more comprehensively in the non-Bolshevik socialist, press; but both saw them as material, related to the workplace and not the direct concern of government. Besides stressing the political significance of such protests, however, the Bolsheviks also noted the significance of concerns with the behaviour of not only employers and foremen towards workers, but of customers too. For example, the waitresses and waiters who struck in June were preoccupied with questions of dignity, and one of their demands was that they be shown respect as human beings, including an end to tipping and to being addressed with the familiar, rather than the formal, "you". Certainly, all service sector employees, including domestic servants, resented the latter familiarity which they associated with the degradation of serfdom, abolished as an institution only in 1861.

Hence, the Bolsheviks paid close attention to the grievances of service sector workers, while their opposition to the war led them to highlight the miserable situation of soldiers' wives. Kollontai in particular sought to organize these women once she returned to Russia in April.[46] The ground had been prepared, however, by working-class Bolsheviks such as Anastasiá Deviatkina, who had focused her political energy on soldiers' wives since the beginning of the war, and who played a key role in setting up a union of soldiers' wives after the February Revolution.[47] In the Vyborg district, Krupskaia took over the running of the local Committee for the Relief of Soldiers' Wives in May. Her predecessor, Nina Gerd, had been an old student friend and colleague in the Sunday school movement in the early 1890s, but had since abandoned Marxism for liberalism. As she relinquished her post, she said to Krupskaia:

> The soldiers' wives do not trust us; they are displeased with whatever we do; they have faith only in the Bolsheviks. Well, you take the work over; perhaps you will be able to do it better than we did.[48]

Thus the Bolshevik Party maintained a hard core of support within the leadership of the labour movement, while forging close links with the militant masses. They also tried to persuade the former to assist the latter, and to draw them into the organized labour movement. In previously male dominated areas where women had made inroads that could not be undone, trade unions tried to recruit them by convincing the women that their specific needs would be taken into account, for example by setting up special women's committees within the union.[49] Women workers, nevertheless, harboured suspicions that their male comrades' underlying aim was to protect the male-dominated labour aristocracy, even in industries in which women predominated. Whatever the men's intentions, their behaviour towards their less politically experienced and aware comrades was overweening, mirroring the disrespectful treatment that they received from foremen.[50]

Still, although such complaints can be seen as representing conflicts of interest within the working class between women and men, experience predisposed rank and file workers to resent any authority figure, while there were few positive role models to guide any worker, female or male, who was promoted. Indeed a dispute in the summer of 1917 at a rubber factory in Moscow saw female shop-floor workers taking sides against, and forcing the dismissal of, 20 forewomen whom they accused of disrespectful treatment. The foremen sided with their female counterparts.[51] At a textile factory, there was tension between the women on the factory committee and the male apprentices. One of the latter refused a summons to attend the committee, and swore at the women. They forced his dismissal, and refused any demands from the apprentices that he be reinstated. The male apprentices even took strike action. When the women would not yield, the apprentices returned to work and sought the support of the union, which they assumed would be forthcoming. However, the union sided with the women.[52]

Organizing women workers after
the February Revolution

Not only was news of female workers' protests against employers reported throughout the Bolshevik Party press but, in addition, the journal specifically directed at women workers, *Rabotnitsa*, which had been founded in 1914 and suppressed with the outbreak of war, was revived in May 1917. No matter how late the Bolsheviks may have been in recognizing the political potential of working-class women, and how great the divisions within the party over the best way in which to organize them, the leadership was convinced by March 1917 that they had to make special efforts to win over women. Although these special efforts were to be contained within the party's organizational framework, they nevertheless entailed the establishment of a bureau charged with specializing in work among women.

One reason for this development was that the Bolsheviks' rivals, the Mensheviks and the SRs, were rapidly gaining members, whereas the Bolshevik insistence on political education and experience before being considered for membership meant a slower growth in the size of the party. Indeed, this would be the case especially among women: hence the need for special efforts to recruit them, both to draw women into the party and to increase party membership overall. Anna Loginova, a textile worker sympathetic to the Bolsheviks, described the Menshevik and SR efforts to recruit workers by having small groups of agitators stand outside factories waiting for the end of a shift. She compared these revolutionary parties to merchants in a market who stood outside their little shops trying to attract customers inside: they were impossible to ignore. She claimed that if any of the workers talked to the Mensheviks or SRs, their names would be put on the list of members. She believed that the members these two groups signed up in 1917 comprised mainly those liable to be called up into the armed forces, and that they were mainly peasants recently arrived from the countryside or lower-middle-class men trying to evade military conscription by working at munitions plants.[53] The implication is that these new members were predominantly male.

Certainly, while the initiative for a bureau devoted to work among women came from Bolshevik women, many Bolsheviks, female as well as male, continued to resist the notion of special work among women. Leading Bolshevik women such as Krupskaia, Kollontai, Samoilova,

Stal' and Slutskaia, insisted that such theoretical purity was holding back the class struggle on two counts: first, in not recognizing that women were a force to be reckoned with by building on their militancy, and secondly, that however militant, women workers were backward, in terms of political consciousness and organizational experience, compared to men. Of those female Bolsheviks who championed special work among women, Kollontai is the most famous. Still, she was not the voice in the wilderness that her memoirs and admirers imply.[54] Even before she returned to Russia from exile and suggested that such a women's department be set up, others who had arrived earlier, such as Slutskaia and Samoilova, had already made similar proposals, revolving around the revival of *Rabotnitsa*. Moreover, when Kollontai made her suggestion in April, it was to a meeting of female delegates during a conference of the Bolshevik Party on Lenin's return to Russia, also in April.[55] Kollontai received little support in the party, but then neither did Lenin for his *April Theses*. Indeed, one of his few supporters was Kollontai, while Lenin is portrayed as an advocate of a women's department in 1917.[56]

Such was the Bolshevik fear of feminism dividing and weakening the working class that the organization of agitation and propaganda among women workers was left to the editorial board of *Rabotnitsa*. The idea for a journal devoted to women workers had initiated with women from the intelligentsia who dominated the editorial board, which was expected to pass on its grasp of political theory and any advice on, or experience of, organization to the readership. The editors certainly toed the party line, but besides reporting on the situation of women workers, they encouraged the latter to write themselves, and drew some working women onto the board. From the beginning, there were concerns that *Rabotnitsa* would fail to have much of an impact on the majority of working-class women because it was run too intellectually, and because of the party's dogmatic opposition to the separate organization of female workers.[57] What is more, Stal' claimed that the initial efforts to establish a department for work among women were sabotaged by party comrades who insisted that the interests of female and male workers were essentially the same and would be harmed by having special sections for women.[58] The editors persisted, however. The journal itself served as an organizational centre, with the editors calling and addressing meetings of soldiers' wives and women workers (in the service sector as well as in factories), and generally carrying on extensive agitational work among women.

The tram conductor, Rodionova, whom we met in the previous chapter, decided to give three days' wages to help get *Rabotnitsa* started, at a meeting which gathered 800 roubles. She was asked to take the money to Bolshevik headquarters, where she was given copies of the paper as well as leaflets to take back to her depot. She did this regularly, working late into the night, on top of her job on the trams. Soon Rodionova was asked to write for *Rabotnitsa*. Given her only recently acquired literacy, she had little confidence in her ability to commit her thoughts to paper, but was encouraged to write about what she knew, her job as a conductor. Rodionova was a keen reader of what other workers wrote, and recalled preserving a cutting of an appeal from seamstresses to their husbands and brothers at the front, in which they tried to explain their situation, blaming their misfortunes on the war as well as their employers. That summer, she became a Bolshevik.

Samoilova also initiated short study courses for, and eventually conferences of, women workers.[59] The aim was not to separate women from men within the party, but ultimately to integrate women into the male dominated revolutionary movement. However limited the success in achieving the latter, Samoilova insisted that the time devoted to women workers paid off in terms of the heightened political awareness shown by them in the months after February when they increasingly took organized action and demanded better living and working conditions, and ultimately an end to the war.[60] Krupskaia had noted, on her return to Russia in April, that there had been significant development in the political awareness of working-class women since the 1905 Revolution. Indeed, these women were now prepared to take the initiative: "The first to carry on Bolshevik agitation among the soldiers were the sellers of sunflower seeds, cider, etc.; many were soldiers' wives." Krupskaia found herself inspired by these women: "I had quite a lot of work to do among the women. I had already got over my former shyness and spoke wherever it was necessary."[61]

Thus while the focus remained the factory, even before the laundresses' strike in May some at least in the Bolshevik Party sought to mobilize women workers and wives of workers on a wider scale, while from May *Rabotnitsa* set out not only to address women, but also to remind male comrades, and indeed the male working class generally, that women were an essential part of the labour movement. On the one hand, this entailed challenging the stereotype of the passive, conservative woman and insisting on the principle of sexual equality. On the other hand, it focused on "women's" issues (such as crèches, nurseries, maternity benefits and protective labour legislation), as well as those "domestic" problems associated with the war (such as food and fuel shortages), partly to attract women, and partly to show that such concerns should be integrated into the general demands of the working class. One result was to draw women into the class struggle in increasing numbers, but in the process to reinforce the belief that they had different interests and priorities from men. Thus there was no weakening of (and no attempt to undermine) the sexual division of labour, although Krupskaia recorded that at least the revolutionary youth had radical ideas on domestic issues, as will be discussed below. Instead, and in time, it was assumed that the "women's sphere" of housework and childcare would be taken over by the state. Besides having to meet the criticisms that special work among women smacked of the feminist claim for the battle being between the sexes rather than the classes, the Bolsheviks associated with *Rabotnitsa* were trying to raise the levels of women's political awareness in a situation of extreme instability, without alienating them (or their men) by attacking traditional gender relations. Not surprisingly, the Bolsheviks focused on issues of immediate relevance to the women and their families, recognizing that concerns with the effects of economic problems (such as inflation) on families, predisposed women in the longer term to Bolshevik propaganda against the war.[62]

In addition, while clearly limited by the perceived need to unite rather than divide the working class, *Rabotnitsa* and the other Bolshevik publications were also calling on men to accord women respect and recognition as their comrades. It was realized by the Bolsheviks that not only did traditional patriarchal attitudes towards women serve to divide the working class, but that male workers also used the needs of their families to defend their position against the encroachments of cheaper female labour, despite the fact that so many women now headed households. Hence, agitation and propaganda on the women question was not limited to female workers. The Bolshevik Party fought to have women represented on factory committees in industries where they constituted a significant portion of the workforce (notably textiles), which involved persuading men to vote for them.[63]

That was an important task, because fears of unemployment in 1917 owing to the collapsing economy led male workers, who dominated factory committees and trade unions, to protect their position against employers' efforts to replace them with cheaper female labour, notably in the munitions industry. Female metal workers in Petrograd knew of cases where men would not accept a woman as factory representative.[64] Indeed, the men went further and targeted wives and sisters who worked in the same factory as their men. From June, there were calls from male workers' representatives to deal with job losses and layoffs by protecting men's jobs at the expense of women's, on the grounds that the former were the main family breadwinners, while the latter's wages were supplementary.[65] The Bolsheviks acted with the metal workers' union to challenge such patriarchal attitudes and tactics that discriminated against women. However, since the aim was to unite workers against employers and the government, the stress in Bolshevik arguments was on class solidarity rather than sexual equality.[66] Moreover, while superficially championing the right of women to work in the metal industry, the metal workers' union was trying to limit their attraction to employers as cheap (and docile) substitutes for men.

Patriarchy was not simply about the subordination of women. There was in addition also the issue of age, of the demand that the youth defer to their male elders. Skilled men were also worried that youth, especially through the apprenticeship system, were being used to undermine their position in the labour hierarchy which they had worked so hard to attain. This was another constituency on which the Bolsheviks expended special efforts to recruit members. Krupskaia and Slutsksaia were charged with youth work, and collaborated with three young Bolsheviks, one of whom was a woman, Liza Pylaeva, who was the only female on the eight-member inter-district committee of the Socialist Union of Working Youth in Petrograd which held a conference on 18 August. Of the eight, there were four Bolsheviks, two non-party, and two anarchists.[67] Pylaeva had joined the Bolshevik Party in February, on the recommendation of Mariia Ul'ianova, who worked for both *Rabotnitsa* and *Pravda*. Pylaeva quickly realized the importance of winning over young people. In June, *Pravda* published an appeal directed at 18 and 19 year old workers to set up a socialist youth organization. Pylaeva had addressed that meeting, and though not an accomplished speaker, her enthusiasm drew the attention of the audience. From there, she became a key organizer of the Socialist Union of Working Youth, the forerunner of the communist youth organization *Komsomol*. Three thousand attended the first meeting of the union on 1 July, at which Pylaeva made a speech, and was elected to the executive committee. She also joined the Red Guards.[68]

Initially, the youth league had been called "Light and Knowledge", and had included not only Bolsheviks, but Mensheviks and anarchists, as well as some who were not affiliated to any political group. Krupskaia found the discussions among the revolutionary youth very interesting:

> For instance, one of the items was that all members must learn to sew. Then one young fellow, a Bolshevik, asked: "Why should everyone learn to sew? Girls, of course, must be able to sew, otherwise, later on, they will not be able to sew buttons on their husbands' trousers, but why should we all learn?" These words raised a storm of indignation. Not only the girls, but everybody expressed indignation and jumped up and down from their seats. "The wife must sew buttons on trousers? What do you mean? Do you want to uphold the old slavery of women? The wife is her husband's comrade, not his servant!" The lad who proposed that only women learn to sew had to surrender.[69]

Such issues, however, were not taken up within the Bolshevik Party as a whole, which was preoccupied with building a base among the working class, and resolving internal differences over the way forward for the revolutionary process. Like the other revolutionary groups, though initially more slowly, the Bolsheviks grew enormously after the February Revolution, and despite their expectation of some political apprenticeship before membership, in the circumstances of 1917 that was minimal. The majority of new recruits, therefore, lacked the kind of preparation that established members had experienced. Moreover, the new members were predominantly male, harbouring traditionally patriarchal attitudes.

The actions of textile workers in February and of laundresses in May had shown that women of all ages were capable of taking the political initiative. The difference between what was seen as a spontaneous bread riot in February and the prolonged strike in May, moreover, revealed that women were learning through their own practical experience how to organize themselves. Still both the Bolsheviks and the female workers themselves considered women to be more politically backward than men and also, because of their lower educational levels, more susceptible to counter-revolutionary propaganda. This was confirmed early in July, after the disastrous summer offensive launched by Alexander Kerensky, who both headed the Provisional Government and was Minister of War. Intended to strengthen the Provisional Government, the offensive turned into a rout when the Germans counter-attacked. The Russian army effectively disintegrated, while thousands of soldiers and sailors in Petrograd staged armed demonstrations, demanding that the Soviet take power, a demand that the Bolsheviks had been making since April. The Bolsheviks joined the demonstrators, though Lenin considered that not only was a rising premature, but that it would benefit the Mensheviks and SRs, since the Bolsheviks were still in a minority in the Soviet. The demonstrations were crushed, leaving hundreds dead, while Kerensky claimed that Lenin was in the pay of the Germans. Lenin went into hiding in Finland, while other prominent Bolsheviks (including Kamenev and Kollontai as well as Trotsky who now joined the Party) were imprisoned. The crisis of the July Days was a disaster for the Bolsheviks, yet it also weakened the Mensheviks and SRs both in the Provisional Government, since they had been unable to control the masses, and in the Petrograd Soviet, since the brutal crushing of the demonstrations, followed by the appointment in August of the hardline General Kornilov as Commander-in-Chief of the armed forces and the increasing intransigence of employers, led workers to desert those socialists who collaborated with the government. This meant that the Bolshevik Party, with the exception of the leadership, was increasingly a working-class organization. It was also, and even more than before 1917, predominantly male.

The immediate aftermath of the July Days, however, was grim for the Bolsheviks. They had to face not only government harassment, but the anger of workers who thought that they bore some responsibility for the debacle at the front. Of course, since it was women who constituted the majority in the lengthening queues, they were more exposed to rumours, such as the claim in July that the Bolsheviks were spying for the German government, and that their political campaigns were intended to undermine the Russian war effort. A few female Bolsheviks were physically as well as verbally attacked.[70] One, E. Tarasova, described her reception at a factory in the Vyborg district on 5 July: as soon as she entered, she was pelted by nuts and bolts thrown by women workers who screamed at her that she was a German spy. When her face and hands began to bleed profusely, however, the women stopped hitting her, and some even helped clean and dress her cuts. She had been organizing a first-aid unit there before the July demonstrations. The women explained their initial hostility as they bandaged her, saying that while she had been in hiding the previous two days, a Menshevik woman had agitated against the Bolsheviks.[71] This wavering among women workers seems to have been widespread. Samoilova was aghast when considerable numbers of women workers who had recently joined the Bolshevik Party renounced their membership. She saw their actions as further evidence of profound political naïvety among women workers, and became even more convinced of the need for special efforts to be made to raise their consciousness.[72]

On the other hand, Bolshevik women had been active in July. The youth organizer, Pylaeva, along with two friends, Nina Bogoslovskaia (who worked for the city committee of the party) and Lisa Koksharova (who was a member of a Red Guard first-aid unit) had spent the night before the demonstrations began at party headquarters. The Provisional Government's efforts to suppress the Bolshevik organization forced them into hiding on 5 July, and with Bolshevik soldiers and sailors, the three young women hid out at the Peter and Paul Fortress, armed and prepared to resist government forces. The women were carrying many party documents as well as considerable funds and a briefcase belonging to a leading party member, Sverdlov, who along with Stasova formed the nucleus of the Bolshevik Party secretariat. The young comrades were determined that the money and documents should not fall into the hands of the government forces. The fortress was under siege for a few hours before the women managed to escape, disguised as nurses. When they were stopped by government troops and challenged to identify what was in the baskets they were carrying, Pylaeva replied with a smile, "dynamite and revolvers!" When the soldiers glanced into the basket and saw only bandages and medical aids lying on top, they did not dig any deeper, but instead told off the young "girl" for her joke, which they said was in poor taste.[73]

These three young women had only recently joined the Bolsheviks, having first proved themselves by studying political literature, as well as carrying out various practical tasks (such as distributing party leaflets, acting as couriers, and raising funds). They were young and energetic, had already come into contact with the Bolsheviks before the February Revolution, and did not have family responsibilities to distract them from political participation. It should not be surprising that the Bolshevik Party in 1917 would concentrate efforts on winning such members. Bolshevik work among women, however, is generally seen as reactive rather than pro-active, in contrast to the work among youth. Key figures, such as Kollontai, are credited with taking the initiative and forcing the Bolsheviks to pay attention to women outside of the party. The Bolshevik Party had to perform the difficult task of catching up with the militancy of the women workers that had left them standing in February and which so impressed them in May, and shaping these women's political consciousness in order to make them more willing to be led by the party. Ironically, with government repression of the Bolsheviks in July, the party for a time depended on *Rabotnitsa*, since the main newspaper *Pravda* had been raided. When the police turned to *Rabotnitsa*, they found its editorial office empty. The women workers had taken the journal to the factories during the night.[74] Not all Bolshevik women avoided arrest: police searching for Lenin took into custody his wife, Krupskaia, his sister Anna's husband and the domestic servant, as well as Kollontai.[75]

Whereas western studies of women workers during the 1917 revolution tend to focus on Kollontai and insist that the Bolsheviks only belatedly and reluctantly paid attention to women, soviet studies stress the significance of Bolshevik women, working in conjunction with their party, for the organization of female workers. Interestingly, the attitudes and activities of other revolutionaries in this area are overlooked. Certainly, both Mensheviks and SRs had been even more cautious than the Bolsheviks in regard to International Women's Day. Moreover, once the overthrow of tsarism had been achieved, both of the former decided to support the Provisional Government that was formed, accepting the need to continue with the war and assuming that the revolutionary movement had gone as far as it should. Thus Mensheviks and SRs lobbied from their position as leaders of the Petrograd Soviet for reforms, in exchange for which they would support the government.

Yet the key reform that would have satisfied the latter's constituency, female and male alike – the redistribution of the land among the peasants – was postponed by the government, even when a leading SR (Victor Chernov) became Minister of Agriculture in the coalition government of May 1917. The two most prominent SR women, Ekaterina Breshkovskaia and Mariia Spiridonova, both returned to Petrograd from exile in Siberia, the former in March, the latter in June. Both women had spent years isolated from their party. The revolution for which they had worked tirelessly for so long had taken place, but in the city rather than the countryside, and during a war to which, theoretically, they were opposed. The two female terrorists, however, like their party, split over the latter issue. Breshkovskaia was persuaded that the war had to be continued to a successful conclusion, and was even more convinced that Lenin, with his call for an immediate peace, was a German spy. Spiridonova, on the contrary, called for peace, recognizing that the pursuit of war would mean postponing key reforms. Spiridonova was elected not only to the Petrograd Soviet, but also as president of the First Congress of Peasants' Soviets. While Breshkovskaia denounced the Bolsheviks and supported the Provisional Government, Spiridonova tried unsuccessfully to persuade her party to call an armistice and legislate for land reform. As leader of the Left SRs, she was increasingly drawn to support the Bolshevik position.

By entering the government in the summer, the Mensheviks and SRs could be held accountable for any of its failures and for popular disappointments at the slow pace of reform. In his seminal study of the women's movement in Russia between 1860 and 1930, Richard Stites made an acute observation regarding the difference between Bolsheviks and Mensheviks in their relations with working-class women during the revolutionary year of 1917: whereas they were in agreement on viewing women first and foremost in terms of their class, the Bolsheviks nevertheless paid closer attention to the specific needs of women workers and put more energy and resources into helping their struggles.[76] This difference was related to fundamental political disagreements between them, notably on the issues of attitudes towards the Provisional Government and the war, which were not directly related to women workers, but which served to draw the latter increasingly closer to the Bolsheviks. Since the Mensheviks and the SRs supported, and indeed served in, the government and accepted its policy of continuing the war, any reports that they made of strikes, demonstrations, and protests over shortages of basic necessities and rising prices were limited in scope, sympathizing with the material grievances of the workers, but avoiding any links between their complaints and the wider political situation, above all the impact of the war. What is more, since the Mensheviks and the SRs were members of the coalition government, they had to seek compromise between employers and employees, to effect conciliation between protesters and government.

Both these parties had adopted the strategy of working within the system in contrast to the Bolshevik position of outright opposition, which allowed them to champion the workers' demands. Hence the Bolsheviks could identify completely with the workers whereas the Mensheviks and SRs always sought to modify what they saw as extreme, unreasonable or politically inappropriate demands. While the Bolsheviks would support strikers' demands (such as those of the laundresses in May) for nationalization of their workplace, Mensheviks preferred to negotiate less drastic change. For example, Eva Broido called for the establishment of a female factory inspectorate that would also have powers to investigate the living conditions, as well as the workplace, of all women workers and their children.[77]

Thus Mensheviks were seen as conciliators who sought moderate reform, while the SRs, whose support had a wider social base than either the Bolsheviks or the Mensheviks, were increasingly divided over the war and the government. Certainly both the Mensheviks and the SRs were in the leadership of the Soviet that emerged from the February Revolution, but gradually a gulf of understanding grew between them and the Petrograd working class as the latter made increasingly radical demands on the Provisional Government which the Soviet leadership struggled to modify. As the strike movement gathered pace after February, the Mensheviks and SRs called for a return to work, confusing the people who saw them as working-class representatives, rather than in the role they had adopted as mediators between the people and the government. Increasingly, workers turned away from the Mensheviks and SRs and towards the Bolsheviks. The latter agreed with the logic of the female textile workers in 1917 who accused a Menshevik deputy of betraying them.[78] All Menshevik and SR efforts at winning a compromise were interpreted by desperate workers as siding with the masters and with the allies. By September, the Bolsheviks had taken over the leadership of the Soviet in both Petrograd and Moscow.

As we shall see, events after July – associated with an attempted military coup in August, the government's continuing support for the war, the closure of factories and lock-out of workers by employers – brought increased female support for the Bolsheviks, as well as, and perhaps more so than, the efforts of the latter to win over women workers. Though compared to men who joined, the numbers of female recruits were much fewer, such efforts were nevertheless important in helping publicize and organize female protests, especially as by August real wages had declined and food shortages had worsened.[79] Indeed, however limited Bolshevik work among women was in 1917, it was greater than the efforts of the other revolutionary groups. Certainly, there were reports of women workers' strikes in Menshevik and SR newspapers, but given their conditional support for the government both parties were alarmed by the destabilizing potential of such unrest which they saw as aiding the Bolshevik calls for an end to the war and the Soviet to take power. Moreover, both Mensheviks and SRs shared the Bolshevik fear of dividing the lower orders along the battle lines of sex.

Although certainly in a minority within their organization, there were more female Bolshevik members who were in a position to influence their party into making a special effort to organize women workers than was the case in either of its main socialist rivals. For example, the prominent female Menshevik, Eva Broido, took a line that was very similar to that of Kollontai.[80] Both women insisted on the need for men to accept women as equals in the class struggle; both aimed at the inclusion of women in trade unions and in their respective parties to fight for improvement in the lives of their class; and both saw the need to pay particular attention to raising women's political consciousness and convince both sexes that women's backwardness was the result of social and cultural conditioning, and not prescribed by nature. Kollontai, besides being renowned as an orator, had been organizing women workers since at least 1907, and was able, alongside the efforts of other leading Bolshevik women, to goad her party into concentrating at least some of its forces on women's struggles. Broido, however, seems to have been even more isolated in her party than Kollontai felt she was among the Bolsheviks. In a study of Menshevik leaders in 1917, Ziva Galili omits to mention not only any efforts to organize female workers, but even Menshevik women, with the exception of Lydia Dan, who is included as sister of one prominent Menshevik (Martov) and wife of another, each of whom led a different faction. Indeed, Lydia Dan is noted only for serving tea to Menshevik leaders who came to her apartment in the evening to debate.[81]

As far as women were concerned, there had been gains after the February Revolution, notably in terms of universal suffrage in July, for which the feminist movement had renewed campaigning after February.[82] However, such gains as sexual equality in politics and the civil service, law and the professions had little immediate impact on the majority of women who sought more tangible changes in their situation. Moreover, while the feminists gained from the revolution initiated by women workers, the latter grew increasingly frustrated and disillusioned with the government's concentration on the pursuit of the war, while the economy continued to deteriorate. The feminists remained committed to the Provisional Government's war efforts and the Allies, which served to distance them from the working-class and peasant women who increasingly called for peace. The SRs and the Mensheviks were committed to a war in defence of Russia, but their entry into a coalition with pro-war parties compromised them in the eyes of the workers in Petrograd, especially when some leading female members such as Figner and Breshkovskaia appeared on feminist platforms and at rallies in support of the war.

Since the female terrorists had shown little interest in the women question before the February Revolution, this was an interesting development. By 1917, Breshkovskaia and Figner had been reduced to symbols of revolutionary heroism, and had little influence in the SR Party. They were seen as part of the glorious but past struggle and out of place in the halls of power. The former, in particular, came to resent this and to see it as a reflection of women's political powerlessness, writing in 1921 that she did not expect statesmen to pay much attention to what she had to say "as is always the case between men and women".[83] Perhaps even more so than Breshkovskaia, who had been associated with the SR Party since its formation, Vera Figner had been cut off from revolutionary political organizations since her imprisonment and exile in the early 1880s. Since both women welcomed the downfall of tsarism, and expected land reform from the Provisional Government, especially once the SRs had entered into the coalition, any demand for the extension of the political community to include women as citizens on equal rights with men seemed logical. They were also persuaded by the feminist argument that women deserved the vote because of their contribution both to the war effort and to the revolutionary movement, of which Figner and Breshkovskaia were living symbols. As Poliksena Shishkina-Yavein, a physician who since 1910 had been president of the Russian League for Women's Equality (founded in 1907), declared to the male leaders of the Soviet and the Provisional Government on 20 March, after a massive demonstration (estimated at around 40,000) calling for female suffrage:

We have come here to remind you that women were your faithful comrades in the gigantic struggle for the freedom of the Russian people; that they also have been filling up the prisons, and boldly marched to the galleys. The best of us looked into the eyes of death without fear. Here at my side stands V.N. Figner, who has been struggling all her life for what has now been obtained.[84]

Feminist arguments in favour of continuing the war also echoed the female terrorists' disdain for Marxist materialism. As another feminist physician, Mariia Pokrovskaia, insisted, women should fight with men for liberty rather than bread, should be "guided by ideals and aspirations, but not by coarse material incentives"[85]:

> We do not accept that for the masses the main thing in the revolution is bread, land, and economic improvement, rather than electoral rights, freedom of speech and a parliament. The Russian people value spiritual things . . . We must explain to them the significance of rights and liberties . . . To repeat to the people that "the revolution will give you a better piece of bread" is to appeal to the worst part of the people.[86]

Women, war and revolution

The hostile reaction of many women workers against the Bolsheviks during the demonstrations in July, when the latter seemed to be making a premature attempt to seize power, helped convince the non-Bolshevik revolutionaries and the feminists of the efficacy of their cautious campaigns for reforms in co-operation with the government. The war, however, overshadowed everything, and ultimately it was the government's determination to pursue it vigorously, with the tacit support of the feminists and non-Bolshevik left, which radicalized the workers and peasants. Indeed, in less than a month the still deteriorating economy and a threat to the revolution from the right – in the shape of an attempted military coup – pushed many women back towards the Bolsheviks. The prime minister, Alexander Kerensky, had been determined to pursue the war effectively. To that end he had made a new appointment as Chief of Staff: General Kornilov, who had a reputation as a disciplinarian and whom Kerensky hoped would bring order back to the armed forces, which had been suffering a high rate of desertion since March. Kerensky's planned summer offensive had quickly collapsed. Still, the July demonstrations had allowed the prime minister to move against the Bolsheviks, who were the main opponents of the government's war policy. Thus Kerensky had seemed to strengthen his position, despite the military disaster.

In fact, it was an illusion of power, highlighted by his next failure to unite the governing classes at a specially convened conference in

Moscow. The Allies, especially the British who had been Kerensky's sponsor, quickly became disenchanted with him and favoured a "strong man" such as Kornilov, to take power and crush the anti-war Bolsheviks.[87] To complicate matters, the general believed that when he marched on the capital in August, ostensibly to crush the Bolsheviks, he had the support of the prime minister. The latter took fright, suspecting that the general wanted to seize power for himself, declared Kornilov a traitor to the revolution, and freed the leading Bolsheviks who had been imprisoned in July so that they could help organize the defence of Petrograd against the general's forces.

Women workers responded to the attempted military coup in a very different way from their confusion over the July days. Then Kerensky had been able to manipulate their patriotism by accusing Lenin of being in league with the Germans. A month later, when the question was not the increasingly unpopular war but the defence of the revolution which female workers had begun, women worked with men to repel the general's forces, building barricades and organizing medical aid, in the form of Red Sisters.[88] Kornilov's attempted coup was opposed by the workers and soldiers of the capital, among whom the Bolsheviks were seen to play a key role, and defeated even before he arrived. Not only had the Bolsheviks recovered ground lost in July, but there was now deep suspicion of the prime minister who was seen as implicated in the coup, which harmed his government and raised the standing of the Bolsheviks at the expense of their socialist rivals.

The government's post-July days' repression had struck not only at the Bolsheviks, but also at the machine-gun regiment which had taken part in the armed demonstrations. The regiment was publicly disarmed and disgraced, as a warning to the rest of the armed forces. Krupskaia, who observed the scene, remarked:

As they led their horses by the bridle so much hatred burned in their eyes, there was so much hatred in their slow march, that it was clear that a more stupid method could not have been devised. And as a matter of fact, in October, the machine-gun regiment followed the Bolsheviks to a man, the machine-gunners guarding Lenin at Smol'ny.[89]

This makes the agitation, which she had already noted women workers were carrying on among the soldiers, seem even more astute: no longer as in February to neutralize them, so that they would not defend the old order, but rather to win them over as active participants in the coming revolution. Moreover, the Bolsheviks now benefited from a split in the SRs, with the Right SRs remaining on the side of the government, and the Left, headed by Spiridonova, taking a much more radical stance, demanding immediate land reform and joining Bolshevik calls for an end to the war.

In addition, the Bolshevik anti-war propaganda gradually won popular support, at the expense not only of their revolutionary rivals, but of the liberals and feminists. Along with the government, the feminists approved strongly of the female soldier, Mariia Bochkareva. As discussed in the previous chapter, she had volunteered to fight at the front from a deep sense of patriotism and a belief that the war would prove to be a force for the renewal of Russian society. Although she had been a loyal subject of the tsar, she had become convinced that he was mismanaging the war effort, and even grew to doubt the patriotism both of the royal family and the tsar's ministers and advisers. With the collapse of tsarism as a result of the February Revolution, Bochkareva decided to switch her loyalty to the Provisional Government because of its policy of pursuing the war to a victorious conclusion.

Until 1917, female combatants had been scattered throughout the armed forces and, by preference, had served as isolated individuals to prove their worth as soldiers to their male comrades. After the February Revolution, however, but especially after the rout by the Germans of the Russian summer offensive, the rate of desertion soared. Because little seemed to have changed for the better in the countryside since the revolution in February, and with local administration dominated as before by the landed elite, the peasant-soldiers wanted to return to their villages and ensure that their families benefited from the promised land reform, postponed by the Provisional Government until after the war. The peasants were not only unwilling to wait, they were determined not to allow the great landowners to shape the reform in their interests as they had done with the abolition of serfdom in 1861, the outcome of which the peasants still regarded as fraudulent. Indeed, as war weariness deepened, and as disillusionment with the Provisional Government led many peasants to take matters into their own hands, increasing numbers of soldiers simply left the front so that they could play a part in the settlement of the land question.

In this situation, female soldiers took on a new significance: they were to serve as models of military heroism to their male comrades who were to be shamed into remaining in their posts. Already in May, Bochkareva had petitioned the government to allow her to set up, under her command, a battalion of women soldiers. She likened Russia to a mother who was in dire need of help, without which she would perish. She insisted that only women "whose tears are pure crystal, whose souls are pure, whose impulses are lofty" could save Russia. Their example of self-sacrifice would force men to acknowledge their patriotic duty and fight for their country.[90] It was also meant to be an example to any female waverers:

> While admiring the heroism and self-sacrifice of those women whose hand has raised the sword in the people's defence, we, their sisters remaining on the home front, must be worthy of them. We must remember that fortitude will reign at the front and our army's actions will succeed only by ensuring that fortitude and a readiness for energetic and unselfish work will reign on the home front. We must ensure that our army does not feel detached from, and forgotten by, the people. There are countless ways in which millions of Russian women could ensure that. We must set up various women's organisations to look after soldiers, to care for the children of fallen warriors – let these orphans become the charges of the entire people, as in France where all orphaned children during this war have been adopted by the nation . . .
>
> We must also ensure that the leading role in the soviets of workers' and soldiers' deputies and in their executive committees is played by those who, from the very beginning, were loyal to the motherland and tirelessly called on the people to defend it, and not by those who fraternised with the enemies, renounced defence of the motherland and now try to pass themselves off as "true" patriots.
>
> More importantly, there is the constant struggle against despondency and cowardice, against those preaching betrayal and treachery. A woman who now, at this fatal hour for Russia, writes letters to her husband, son, or brother fighting on the front line which only convey to him feelings of weakness, betrayal of his motherland's interests and thoughts of throwing down his arms and returning home, such a woman sins not only against herself, but against Russia, her people and freedom.[91]

There was an immediate outpouring of support from the upper classes to the peasant Bochkareva's patriotic appeal, and as many as 2,000 women volunteered. However, she insisted on not only devotion to the cause, but total obedience to her and such high standards of behaviour and strict training regime, that in Petrograd only around 300 lived up to Bochkareva's stringent requirements. The latter included irreproachable honesty and a serious attitude towards the cause; cheerfulness, politeness, kindness, affability, cleanliness and tidiness; respect for other people's views, complete trust between each other; and noble aspirations.[92] Feminists at home and abroad, and notably Mrs Emmeline Pankhurst in England, applauded Bochkareva's battalion of women soldiers.

Indeed, Mrs Pankhurst had welcomed the February Revolution, suspecting that the tsar had been unduly influenced by pro-German court intrigue. Lloyd George, then prime minister, arranged for Mrs Pankhurst to travel to Russia on a special mission in June. She was to encourage the women's battalion in their example to the male waverers among the Russian troops, and provide support for the Russian government's war policy. However, fearing that her extreme pro-war stance would be too provocative to Bolshevik supporters, the Provisional Government refused permission for Mrs Pankhurst to address public meetings in Petrograd. She met instead with feminist leaders (among whom Anna Shabanova was her host), addressed several meetings in private houses, and helped raise funds for the women's battalion. She declared it a terrible situation when women who brought children into the world should feel compelled to fight because their men were deserting. Mrs Pankhurst insisted that women would never be slaves to Germany, and that it was better to die fighting, though she implied that combat was a man's job which men were shirking. Women at least knew their duty, while their courage would shame the men. She remained in Russia for three months, leaving in September when the Provisional Government seemed vulnerable to the Bolshevik advance. On her return to London, she advised Lloyd George to intervene to prevent a Bolshevik seizure of power. She seemed convinced that the Bolsheviks were German agents, and felt vindicated when they prepared to sign a separate peace with Germany, after they had taken power. In addition, she used fear of socialism in Britain to try to stem the rising criticism of the war, both in the armed forces and on the home front, among factory workers and women protesting against price increases.[93]

Although Bochkareva did not see herself as championing the cause of women, some feminists at least saw another opportunity for women to prove their equality with men.[94] Richard Stites records the first and last Women's Military Congress, which brought together in Petrograd women devoted to the war effort, both combatant and non-combatant, feminist and revolutionary (including Breshkovskaia), at the beginning of August.[95] Feminists such as Olga Nechaeva and Ariadna Tyrkova had tried to build on Bochkareva's May initiative by proposing to the prime minister that women aged between 18 and 45 be drafted into state service, in order to replace men who could then be available for military conscription. Nothing seems to have come of it, however, while the feminists' overt support for the war effort widened the gulf between themselves and the very women they intended to exempt from the draft: workers, peasants, and mothers of children aged under five.[96]

Bochkareva was not alone in seeking permission to establish women-only combat units. Besides Petrograd, there were similar initiatives in the cities of Moscow, Saratov, Tambov, Mariupol', Baku, Ekaterinburg, Kiev, Tashkent, Ekaterinodar, Odessa, Minsk, Pskov, Riga and Ufa.[97] Perhaps because the capital was the centre of revolution and Bochkareva left a memoir of her exploits, it is her "battalion of death" that had the biggest impact on contemporaries and which figures most prominently, indeed almost exclusively, in historical accounts.

The general attitude towards these women's battalions among the ordinary, war-weary Russians in 1917, perhaps not surprisingly, was of contempt, that turned to outright hostility as opposition mounted against any further sacrifices in a conflict that seemed both incomprehensible and, as explained by the Bolsheviks, unjust and exploitative. Sightings of the women's battalion marching through Petrograd were punctuated by jeers and insults about the sexual purity and proclivities of the female troops. Indeed, fears for the women's safety resulted in male guards being posted around the female soldiers' barracks.[98] While this might give the impression that the women's battalion was not a serious enterprise, Bochkareva was determined to prove its worth. Her troops took part in Kerensky's abortive offensive against the Germans on the western front in June, and suffered heavy casualties, a few of which it has been claimed were at the hands of embittered men on their own side.[99] Far from serving as an example of patriotism and military duty to the men, the loss of many lives in what was seen as a hopeless, even vainglorious cause only served to speed up the rate of desertion and the growth in support for Bolshevik calls for an immediate peace. Bochkareva herself was wounded, and retreated to Moscow to recuperate.[100]

Women and the October Revolution

Thus Bochkareva's troops withdrew from the front to serve as the last line of defence of the Provisional Government against the Bolsheviks in October. Of the 3,000 troops who were based in the Winter Palace in Petrograd to protect ministers of the Provisional Government, approximately 200 were from the women's battalion, with the rest made up of two companies of cossacks and some officer cadets. By then, the government had become so isolated that there was little confidence in its survival. Moreover, the male defenders felt uncomfortable at being stationed with a female battalion. Cossacks generally regarded soldiering as a man's job, and were both dismissive of and scandalized by Bochkareva's women. The latter along with the officer cadets tried to build barricades from the winter supply of wood around the main entrance of the Winter Palace, but their materials were flimsy. The military defenders lacked provisions, and soon there were desertions through hunger and demoralization – though not from the women's battalion. They had been told repeatedly by their officers that "a fate worse than death" awaited them if they surrendered to the Red Guard. However, they did so once the Winter Palace was attacked, being unprepared to face the superior arms and numbers of their opponents.[101]

The fact that the military defence of Kerensky's government depended partly on women was, and indeed still is, generally taken as a sign of its weakness, as if it had been emasculated. Certainly, when the battleship *Aurora* fired a blank round on the palace as a signal for the Bolshevik rising, resistance speedily collapsed. The government ministers threw themselves, or fainted, onto the floor, while their defenders surrendered with little resistance. Yet rather than focus attention on the men who deserted their posts, the spotlight has fallen on the women's battalion. Only their behaviour has been described as hysterical.[102] Robert Daniels, in his study of the Red Guard and the October Revolution, is more sympathetic, but still condescending: "The girls can hardly be blamed for being no more ready to face artillery and machine-gun fire than the cossacks were."[103]

The hopes which patriotic feminists had placed in Bochkareva's battalion were dashed partly because its very presence was seen as a sign of the government's terminal condition. In addition, the women, portrayed as damsels in distress at the mercy of uncouth men who greatly outnumbered them, were useful to the propaganda assault on the Bolsheviks. Thus the British ambassador in Petrograd, Sir George Buchanan, wrote that the women were brutally treated by the Red Guards who had taken them prisoner, and were only saved by the British General Knox from the terrible fate that would surely have befallen them had they remained in the hands of the Bolsheviks overnight.[104] General Knox had been told by Lady Buchanan that two officer instructors of the women's battalion believed that 137 female soldiers had been taken prisoner and "beaten and tortured, and were now being outraged". Another British observer, M. Philips Price, had seen the women being marched away but "speedily released and sent home to their mothers". Knox, however, believed Lady Buchanan, and effected the release of the women through discussions with the Bolsheviks. He claimed that the women had been roughly handled and that "blackguards among the soldiery had shouted threats that had made them tremble for the fate that night might bring", though he later contradicted his story.[105] While charges of mass rapes of the female soldiers in Petrograd were greatly exaggerated, it appears that there were at least three cases of sexual assault, and one woman was believed to have committed suicide.[106] Stites, moreover, records considerable violence against the women's battalions outside Petrograd, among the frontline troops. When Bochkareva had returned to the front in the autumn, "she was threatened and insulted and twenty of her women were lynched by Russian soldiers".[107] With the rate of male desertions soaring, Bochkareva acknowledged defeat at the front by disbanding her unit.

The Bolsheviks both denied the accusations of severe ill-treatment of the women defenders of the Provisional Government, and portrayed Bochkareva, who went on to fight against the Bolsheviks with General Kornilov after the October Revolution, as perversely kissing the chains that bound her and her class. They considered the troops under her command to be either class enemies or, like Bochkareva, victims of false consciousness. Certainly, the women who had responded to Bochkareva's call had come either from the upper classes or the peasantry. Their motives in volunteering for combat were not seen as noble by the revolutionaries, but rather as misguided; their patriotism was manipulated. Some sought revenge for the loss of male relatives at the front. Others saw combat as either an escape from their existing problems or an adventure. A few saw the shedding of blood as a purgative necessary for society's regeneration.[108]

The Bolsheviks did not completely dismiss the notion of the woman under arms, but rather judged her by the cause for which she fought, and saw her actions as a response to a particular crisis. During 1917, women had taken violent action against people and property, but especially the latter, in both town and countryside, while some female Bolsheviks took up arms as members of the Red Guard for the attack on the Winter Palace in October. Such women, though more numerous than Bochkareva's battalion, were nevertheless in the minority on their own side. This is not to diminish the part that they played in the October Revolution. Prominent Bolshevik women such as Krupskaia, Kollontai, Samoilova, Stal', Nikolaeva and Kudelli had city-wide responsibilities, while others concentrated on local preparations. Thus, Slutskaia played a key role in organizing the rising in the Moscow district of Petrograd, as L.R. Menzhinskaia and D.A. Lazurkina did in the First City district, and A.I. Kruglova in the Okhta district. The Party's youth workers Liza Pylaeva and Evgeniia Gerr were members of the Red Guard.

It was more common, however, for Bolshevik women to fill a support role, in communications, as messengers and in the medical brigades, of which they constituted the majority.[109] Their contribution to the success of the revolution was still vital. T.A. Fortunatova, for example, was a feldsher-midwife who played a leading role during the October Revolution by organizing women workers as medics and stretcher-bearers.[110] Krupskaia recalled that 50 women workers prepared for the insurrection by spending the night at the Vyborg soviet, taking instruction in first aid from a female physician.[111] The tram conductor, Rodionova, had hidden 42 rifles and other weapons in her depot when the Provisional Government had tried to disarm the workers after the July days. In October, she was responsible for making sure that two trams with machine guns left the depot for the storming of the Winter Palace. She had to ensure that the tram service operated during the night of 25 to 26 October, to assist the seizure of power, and to check the Red Guard posts throughout the city. She was also a member of the sanitary detachment defending the city.[112]

Such women are generally missing from the historical account, and often from memoirs of male participants, such as Trotsky, who concentrates on setting the record straight as to his own role, which he puts at centre stage. The fact that so many women went on to defend the new soviet republic during the civil war against both counter-revolutionary forces and the intervening foreign powers, between 1918 and 1920, gives some indication of the strength of commitment of female Bolsheviks, and indeed of non-party women workers, to the cause of the revolution. According to Kollontai, by the end of the civil war there were around 66,000 female Red Army personnel, of whom approximately 1,850 had either been killed or captured.[113] Again the majority were in support roles, but still there were many more female combatants than during the First World War.[114] Few women, however, remained in the Red Army once the war was over. Except in extreme circumstances, woman was reproducer, man defender of the state.

While some attention is paid to women's actions in historical accounts of the overthrow of tsarism, usually limited to a mention of the strikes and demonstrations on 23 February, the focus in studies of October, if it plays on women at all, falls on the women's battalions. Both diminish the participation of women to the stereotypes of spon-taneity and innate conservatism. In terms of women's involvement in the revolutionary movement of 1917, many more participated in February, but in October women acted in a more overtly political way, with a clear direction. In the former, women served as the catalyst, and briefly took the lead as male workers and revolutionaries hesitated. From March, the unrest of women workers reflected not only the impact on them of the continuing economic collapse, but also their growing radicalization and opposition to the war. Female activists, both liberals and non-Bolshevik socialists, urged restraint and sought reform within the sys-tem. They had little success, however, and what they did achieve (such as female suffrage on the same terms as men) seemed irrelevant given the urgency felt by working-class women faced with basic questions of everyday life, which the war exacerbated. The attempted military coup in August and Bolshevik victories in elections to the Soviets in Septem-ber in both Petrograd and Moscow, left the Provisional Government exposed. Refusing either to end the war or to legislate fundamental reforms until the war was over, the governing coalition lost public confidence. In October, in contrast to February, men led the way in the overthrow of the government. Nevertheless, Bolshevik women performed essential logistical and support roles that required initiative as well as courage, and a few at least held positions of responsibility within the Bolshevik Party, notably at local level. By then, leadership of the revolutionary movement was again firmly in male hands.

CHAPTER SEVEN

Conclusion

A conservative opponent of the February Revolution insisted that it had begun in Petrograd as an apolitical riot, with the mob composed of hungry women and children demanding bread and herrings, wrecking tram cars and looting small shops, and that it was only the male working class and the politicians who turned the February events in the capital into a revolution that toppled the tsar.[1] Writing in 1920, however, the Bolshevik Konkordiá Samoilova insisted that the experience of the First World War had had a deeper impact on women than hunger and cold. The military conflict had been so costly in terms of lives that it had opened women's eyes to the oppression of the political system headed by the landed aristocracy and big capitalists. She wrote that the army too had been politicized, so that instead of blindly obeying the officers to crush the rebellious crowds, the troops in Petrograd had listened to the arguments of the female strikers and demonstrators, and been persuaded to join them. Samoilova also believed that by "cooking them in the factory pot", the war had quickened the political development of many women.[2] Essentially, she was reminding both women and men that the former had played a significant part in the overthrow of the old order and in the eventual victory of the Bolsheviks, implying that women's role had been forgotten only three years after the revolution.

Most studies of the 1917 Revolution, including this one, concentrate on Petrograd, then the country's capital and seat of political power. Yet it was hardly representative of the tsarist state. Not only was the vast majority of the population peasant, but Petrograd had been established (as St Petersburg) only at the beginning of the eighteenth century by the westernizing tsar, Peter the Great, who had tried to enforce reforms in relations between the sexes along western lines. In fact, it was really the late nineteenth-century development in the economy that brought change to, but no transformation in, the lives of women. In his study of the peasantry in 1917, Graeme Gill saw two revolutions, one in the countryside and the other in Petrograd. In his view, the former was a traditional protest against "privileged Russia" in which the peasantry turned their backs on urban influences, and in which their only concern with the capital was that whoever was in power should accede to their demands.[3] A study of the Volga countryside by Orlando Figes bears out Gill's conclusion. Figes agrees that the role of the peasantry was decisive in 1917 (as Lenin himself realized). Essentially, by destroying the political and military basis of the old order, the peasants allowed the Bolsheviks to take and then consolidate their power with the support of only a minority of the population.[4] The peasantry did so without changing their old, patriarchal way of life. While urban women pushed successfully for the female franchise on the same basis as men, peasant women proved unwilling to take advantage of that right, at least in the local elections of May 1917, an attitude that held more significance for the construction of the post-revolutionary order than for the revolution itself.[5]

Women outside of Petrograd

Donald Raleigh's study of the provincial city of Saratov reveals that, as in Petrograd, the First World War had a profound impact on the population. Whereas before war broke out in 1914, there had been 102.5 women for every 100 men in Saratov, two years later, there were 121.8 women; and by 1917, 47.3 per cent of the province's able-bodied men had been conscripted, and 30.7 per cent of all households in the countryside were without male labourers.[6] Although a small and relatively unindustrialized city, there had been considerable revolutionary activity in Saratov in the early twentieth century, and by 1915 strike activity had increased. Both the city and the surrounding countryside quickly accepted the downfall of tsarism at the end of February, while three Bolshevik women, E.K. Romanenko, E.N. Bogdanova and E.R. Peterson, formed a women's department of the party in Saratov, and concentrated on organizing and recruiting working-class women.[7] As in Petrograd, the most militant working women in 1917 were in the service sector, while workers in general were increasingly drawn to the Bolsheviks, as the Mensheviks and SRs appealed for discipline and moderation.

Raleigh recounts an incident that occurred after the overthrow of the tsar and reflected popular frustration at the deterioration in their living conditions. In August, an estimated 2,000 women and youths, blaming the Provisional Government and the privileged classes for the scarcity of food and essential consumer goods, looted the shoe store where they had been queuing, and were only dispersed forcibly by a combination of soldiers and men from the fire department.[8] There was also a detachment of female soldiers formed after the February Revolution to defend the Provisional Government, but as in the capital, they were considerably outnumbered by women taking action against it. The peasant seizure of land in the Volga countryside and failure to send supplies to the cities provided the basis for the urban revolution. Unlike Petrograd, women in Saratov had not acted as catalysts for the end of the old order, while the relatively underdeveloped nature of the city's economy and the close interaction between Saratov and the Volga countryside ensured that the new regime would be influenced by traditional patriarchal culture, no matter how active Bolshevik women were.

The ancient Russian capital, Moscow, was a much larger city than Saratov, but like the latter it had close contact with the surrounding countryside. Indeed, in contrast to Petersburg, such cities have been described as "islands in an ocean of peasants".[9] Whereas geographically, Petersburg was at the western periphery of Russia, its "window on the west", Moscow was in the heart of the country, in the Central Industrial Region. Moscow was certainly much more industrialized than Saratov. Moscow's industry, on the other hand, was less mechanized than Petersburg's, with a lower level of productivity, and a tendency to rely on plentiful and cheap unskilled labour. Before the revolution Moscow's main industry was textiles, which continued to expand during the war, though by then other sectors of industry had grown considerably. By 1917, women predominated not only in textiles, but also in the chemical, tobacco and food processing industries.[10] There were, in addition, efforts made by the upper classes to combine production for the war effort (at which they considered the tsarist government very inadequate) with help for the families of those men who were conscripted. It has been estimated that in Moscow around 200,000 women may have been employed in these small workshops making essential clothes and footwear for the poorly supplied troops.[11]

The majority of women in Moscow before and during the revolution were employed in the service sector, as they were in Petersburg. Both Petersburg and Moscow grew through in-migration of workers from the countryside, but Moscow's population tended to maintain closer links with their home villages. In both cases, males outnumbered females, but the war led to a greater increase in the latter: thus in 1912 there were 843 women to every 1,000 men in Moscow, but by 1917 this figure had risen to 982.[12] Diane Koenker concluded from her study of Moscow in 1917 that "there was more diversity and less polarity within society and the working class" than in Petrograd.[13]

As in Saratov, Moscow's local government collapsed as soon as news of the February Revolution in Petrograd was received. Also as in Saratov, the local Bolsheviks expended special efforts on organizing and recruiting women workers. Koenker argues that although "women workers generally were much more passive than men politically", nevertheless the record for Moscow shows that the revolution was not an exclusively male affair, that women too were drawn into the revolutionary process.[14] Krupskaia recorded that Armand was a key figure behind the establishment of *Rabotnitsa* and that from its revival in Petrograd in 1917 Bolshevik women addressed female workers not only through this specialist journal, but also in pamphlets and meetings dedicated to women's issues, and in the pages of the party's newspapers, urging women to become involved in the struggle against counter-revolution, and in support of Bolsheviks. They believed that systematic work among women by female delegates from the party was vital if peasant and working-class women were to be absorbed into active participation in the building of a new society.[15] However, in his biography of Armand, R.C. Elwood has shown that in 1917 *Rabotnitsa* was very much a Petrograd initiative, while Armand spent most of the year, after her return to Russia in April, in Moscow. There, Armand, Varvara Iakovleva and then Sof'ia Smidovich tried to conduct work among factory women first through their new, but short-lived, journal, *Zhizn' rabotnitsy* (*The Woman Worker's Life*), and then through the Moscow region's "Commissions for Agitation and Propaganda among Working Women". Thus, while in Elwood's view the Moscow journal was a pale imitation of *Rabotnitsa*, the commissions resembled those sections that Kollontai had unsuccessfully proposed in Petrograd in May. Armand was returned as a Bolshevik representative in the May elections to the city's duma, and the following month was elected to the executive commission of the party's Moscow committee. Armand soon withdrew to her family estate to care for her 13 year old son, who was seriously ill.[16]

The fact that, with the exception of Armand, there was no Bolshevik woman in Moscow of comparative stature to Kollontai in Petrogad, with similar oratorical skills, who left a significant body of writing, may explain the lack of interest in the party's work among women in Moscow. An examination of some of the female Bolsheviks who took part in the revolution in Moscow shows similarities with Petrograd: more working-class women joined after becoming radicalized by the war and the February Revolution, but overall women were outnumbered by the flood of male recruits in 1917. Nevertheless, women played leading roles in the Moscow party, including the Red Guard, and many went on to play key roles in the new soviet republic.[17] One woman who had joined the Bolsheviks in Siberia less than a year before the revolution was the daughter of literate peasants. She had moved to Moscow and found a job in a dye factory, where there were frequent cases of poisoning as a result of poor health and safety conditions and increased demands on productivity during the war. In the February Revolution, she had transported weapons to a working-class suburb. In May, she married a comrade, and returned to Siberia to visit her family. When her husband was conscripted there, she went to work in Omsk for the party newspaper, where her husband later joined her.[18]

Another peasant woman, P.G. Zamogil'naia, worked from the age of ten in a confectionary factory in Moscow, joining the Bolsheviks in 1917. Like the previous woman, Zamogil'naia's father was interested in politics and wanted his daughters as well as his sons to be literate. During the February Revolution, Zamogil'naia participated alongside her father in mass demonstrations. Through him, she was introduced to the Bolsheviks. The first lecture she attended was on the topic of "woman and socialism", where the majority of the audience was male. She admitted finding the theoretical arguments difficult to follow, but she grasped that women had an important role to play in the revolutionary struggle, which persuaded her to devote her life to the cause. She joined the Bolshevik Party on 5 May. As a young member (she was then 17 years old), Zamogil'naia's task was to try to attract the youth to the Bolsheviks. She organized Bolshevik speakers for youth meetings, supported them from the crowd, and provided protection against anyone trying to pull a Bolshevik from the platform. She had a male mentor, who encouraged her to read the party newspapers and to learn how to speak in public. Like the women in Petrograd, Zamogil'naia participated with men in the general work of the party, while unlike the men she also helped her mother make tea and sandwiches for party members who worked late into the night. She joined the Red Guard in July and learned basic first aid. During the October rising, she was the one who liaised with the centre from her post in the suburbs, organized weapons and loaded machine guns for comrades, and led them safely through the streets of Moscow. She still found time to prepare a hot meal for the Red Guards.[19]

Like so many working-class female Bolsheviks, the revolutionary activity of these Moscow women was a family affair. Yet they were not simply moulded by their parents or siblings. Their experiences and observations of home and work, and the impact of the February Revolution prompted a growing political awareness, as well as excitement, in them. So too did the existence of female role models, which indicates that Bolshevik work among women, however reluctantly accepted by many members, was a significant factor in winning the active support of a militant sector of the working class. This growth in consciousness is reflected in the biography of Anna Litveiko, a worker who joined the Bolsheviks in Moscow in 1917.[20] She had started work at the age of 12, and by the outbreak of the revolution was employed at a factory in Moscow making electric light bulbs. Aged 18, she found the work monotonous, with little hope of learning a skill. Her father was a worker who drank heavily and physically abused his wife. When he cut his wife's shoulder and chest with his razor, Litveiko and her sister chased him out of the house. Litveiko's mother took in washing, cleaned wealthy people's apartments, took in student lodgers, and prepared wood as fuel for the block of flats in which the family lived. Litveiko listened to the students' political discussions, and read their books. She was particularly influenced by one of the young men who was conscripted during the war but kept in touch by letter, describing the horrors of the front and the growing disillusionment with the war effort. With her two close girl friends, Litveiko had dreamed of leaving the factory, gaining a serious education, training to be a feldsher and "going to the people", though she had no idea of the realities of village life. When the tsar was overthrown in February, she realized that there was no need to leave the city with which she was familiar, and which had now become so interesting.

Litveiko had little knowledge of political parties, but soon realized that she leaned towards the Social Democrats, seeing the SRs as a party for the peasantry. She was initially impressed by a Menshevik speaker, but with her co-workers saw his calls for moderation as out of touch with their situation. Litveiko was elected to her factory committee, where she came into contact with a Bolshevik, Natasha Bogacheva, a soldier's wife and a mother in her thirties. Litveiko was impressed by her vitality and forthrightness, and noticed that all the Bolsheviks in her factory were workers, while the Mensheviks who came to address their meetings were invariably intellectuals. In contrast to the Mensheviks and SRs, the Bolsheviks offered uncompromising opposition to the employers. When a foreman at her factory struck and burned a woman with a hot rod, the Bolshevik Bogacheva called a meeting to discuss his behaviour. The outcome was that the women put him in a wheelbarrow and drove him out of the factory. Humiliated, he never returned, which gave the women a sense of their power.

This was a traditional form of punishment resorted to by workers, but it took on a political meaning in the conditions of 1917. Litveiko's growing political consciousness and militance led her to the Bolsheviks, but she found that joining the party was no simple affair: she had to show why she wanted to become a Bolshevik and not join another revolutionary group, and she was expected to study party literature and participate in discussion groups. She grew in confidence, and was elected as a Bolshevik representative to the district soviet. Litveiko still did not feel brave enough to make speeches, but she would join with others in barracking anyone who opposed the Bolshevik line. Finally, Bogacheva persuaded Litveiko to report to the soviet. Having overcome her fear, Litveiko went on to teach other female workers how to speak out in public.

Like Pylaeva in Petrograd, Litveiko concentrated on youth work, recruiting young women workers, including her close friend, Tania, to the Bolsheviks. Party work became dangerous when the Bolsheviks were accused of being German spies, and during the July Days in Moscow, Litveiko was unable to prevent Bogacheva from being pulled off the platform when she was addressing female textile workers. In August, when Bolshevik fortunes were still at a low ebb, Litveiko and Tania demonstrated outside the hall where Kerensky was holding a state conference. The two young women not only participated in the political events of the city, they began to attend evening classes, to get the education they had dreamed of before the revolution. The recovery in Bolshevik fortunes after the Kornilov coup led Litveiko's mother to canvas for the Bolsheviks among her neighbours.

Litveiko and her friend took an active part in the October Revolution, transporting weapons throughout the city. Again like Pylaeva in Petrograd, they were considered by Bolshevik opponents to be too young and girlish to be interested in politics; indeed liberals warned them of the Bolshevik menace to youth. The "girls", however, embraced the revolution, serving as scouts, seeking out counter-revolutionaries. They also searched for food and fuel as well as weapons; they collected the wounded and carried them to medical points, where they were shown by professional nurses how to tend to them. Bogacheva ran a feeding-point for the fighters, where her five year old daughter assisted her.

After the October Revolution, Litveiko's male student friend returned from the front, and asked her to become his wife. She could understand why he wanted to establish a family after experiencing such a bloody conflict. He had not thought to ask her what she wanted, nor noticed how much she had changed. She realized that she would suffocate in his little domestic world. Instead, she went on to fight counter-revolution. In 1919, she married a comrade who shared her beliefs and worked with her for the Communist Party.

Women and the 1917 Revolution

Why have women been left out of accounts of the events between the two revolutions of 1917? One explanation is that they did not play a prominent role in bringing the Bolsheviks to power, and most historians investigate those eight months to find "answers" for the outcome. Even social histories tend to overlook any active part played by women in favour of a consideration of gender as a fundamental influence on the working class, more important as a legacy for the way in which the communist state developed from the 1920s, than for the revolutionary process in 1917. Yet after the February Revolution, the Bolsheviks paid particular attention to the organization of women, resulting in the women's department (*zhenotdel*) which survived throughout the 1920s. There was much to be done. At a congress of poor peasants held shortly after the Bolsheviks came to power, all of the delegates were male. Asked by a leading member of the party, Grigorii Zinoviev, why this was the case, the peasants indicated that they did not consider it a fit place for a woman: "We will discuss serious matters here, and perhaps curse." For Zinoviev, the peasantry had to be forced to think about the woman question, and had to be rebuked until women were accepted as men's equals: "It is time for [the male peasant] to forget that men represent some sort of special estate, or the idea that he alone is called to be concerned about politics and socialism. Make way for women!"[21] However, the Communist Party's alienation of the peasantry by the end of the civil war meant that the former had to placate, rather than challenge, the latter.

In her study of *zhenotdel* Elizabeth Wood argues that "this was emphatically not a feminist revolution" and that the Bolsheviks always had a negative view of women: the most downtrodden and conservative part of the working class, backward, passive, a brake on the revolution.[22] Female workers may have set the revolution in motion, but the Bolshevik fear was that women were inherently counter-revolutionary. Hence, the post-1917 regime saw even more need to mobilize women, to transform them into defenders of the revolution. In the post-revolutionary period, the Communist Party found that women responded most positively to issues that directly concerned them, which in turn perpetuated and strengthened the gendered division of labour. The argument Wood puts forward, that at every stage of the revolution the Bolshevik Party (and indeed the women's sections) understood the political order in gendered terms, is convincing. This failure to challenge gender definitions helps explain both the revolutionary process and the construction of the communist state, but it should not lead us to dismiss, or diminish, what women did in 1917, simply because they acted in accordance with those definitions. Women expressed themselves forcefully, they took direct action, they did not wait to be told what to do or how to do it, and they challenged men. The Bolsheviks were indeed reluctant to organize women separately, and when they did it was to mobilize them for the party; but the relationship was not just one-way. At each stage of the revolutionary process, women goaded the Bolsheviks into action, while the activists who worked with the women learned from them and did not simply mould them. Kollontai wanted to create "new" women, but Krupskaia drew strength from the traditional babas who not only made their voices heard in 1917, but gave Krupskaia, a revolutionary since the 1890s, a new confidence to speak in public.

Zhenotdel was abolished by Stalin in 1930, a year after he had embarked on the forced collectivization of agriculture, under the pretext that the women's department had achieved its goals and there was no more need of it. Ironically, the decision was announced on International Women's Day. Perhaps part of the reason for the neglect of women from considerations of the revolution is that the figure of Stalin looms over the history of the Soviet Union, so that the implicit focus for so many studies of 1917 is the question posed by Alec Nove, "was Stalin really necessary?"[23] It is interesting that Stalin does not figure largely in any of the histories of the 1917 Revolution, with the exception of the special study by Robert Slusser, *Stalin in October: The Man Who Missed the Revolution*.[24] Sukhanov, in his memoir of 1917, saw Stalin's role after he returned to Petrograd in March as "modest", and wrote that Stalin gave "the impression of a grey blur, looming up now and then dimly and not leaving any trace. There is really nothing more to be said about him".[25] Zhenia Egorova, who played a key role in the Bolshevik Party in 1917, had quite a different experience, one which presaged ill for the post-revolutionary order:

> In July 1917 Zhenia Egorova was working at the office of the party's Vyborg district committee in Petrograd. There weren't enough people to do everything, and she spent almost all her time there. One day she closed the office and went to lunch as usual. When she came back she found someone she didn't know standing in the doorway. Those were troubled times, and Egorova was on her guard: "Excuse me. Did you want to see someone?" The visitor didn't reply. She opened the office. The stranger followed her in and headed straight for the desk.
>
> "Who are you? I didn't let you in."
>
> Comrade Koba [i.e. Stalin] shoved her rudely out of the way. But she was a big, solidly built woman and she knew how to stand up for herself. A fight started.
>
> It turned out that Central Committee member Stalin needed a quiet place to look over some materials for *Pravda*. And here some woman was getting in the way and demanding his name.[26]

Egorova (like Sukhanov) was a victim of Stalin's purges. In 1937 she was executed.

The 1917 Revolution has been the subject of intense scrutiny and impassioned debate since the Bolsheviks took power. Yet despite the development of feminist history in the 1970s, there has been little examination of the role women played in the development of the political process. What studies there have been have focused on the Bolsheviks and their relations to women workers, with the underlying assumption that the party's attitude was one of condescension and neglect; that only a few women, and most notably Kollontai, saw the need for special efforts to organize women workers, and then because they were a drag on the labour movement; and that the Bolsheviks underestimated the capacity of these women to act in a rational, "political" way.[27] What is underestimated are the sustained efforts of rank and file members to organize women workers, which continued despite the suppression of *Rabotnitsa* in 1914 and the harassment of the party because of its anti-war stance. Indeed, in her study of the attitude and practices of the Bolshevik Party towards women workers between the 1905 Revolution and the end of the civil war in 1920, Anne Bobroff argues that the formation of a women's section of the party was as a result of the actions, and not the "backwardness" of women, quoting Vera Slutskaia: "In view of the fact that at the present time an appreciable movement has come into existence among them [working women], it is desirable to direct the said movement into the channels of political action . . .".[28]

What is also overlooked is that the socialist rivals to the Bolsheviks, the Mensheviks and the SRs, but especially the latter, paid little attention to the organization of women workers. While these parties reported female protests and strikes in detail, they failed to grasp that they represented not simply material grievances, nor even the development of the women's organizational abilities, but a rise in their political consciousness. In their study of perceptions and realities of working-class unrest between the two revolutions, Diane Koenker and William Rosenberg remark on the attentiveness of the Bolshevik press to those service sector workers, particularly the women, whom all revolutionaries had previously dismissed as impervious to politics. It was not that the Mensheviks ignored such strikes – far from it. It was more that they missed their political import.[29]

In her study of Moscow in 1917, however, Diane Koenker suggests that working women there tended to support the Mensheviks, though she admits that the evidence is flimsy.[30] She speculates that the most likely female working-class voters in elections to the provincial duma in June were older, experienced workers. What is interesting is that the Bolsheviks were concentrating on winning over the youth and on organizing the inexperienced workers. Koenker suggests that these Moscow women voters may have felt more comfortable with the older and more moderate Menshevik Party.[31] It was precisely that moderation – which in the context of 1917 might also be seen as vacillation – that led to a haemorrhage of their support once they were in government.

How "moderate" were the Mensheviks? In *Rethinking the Russian Revolution*, Edward Acton points to the radical policies of those in the Provisional Government in which they participated, and defends the Menshevik and SRs against charges of poor organization, deep internal divisions, and lack of effective leadership.[32] Yet even as they accepted the need for thoroughgoing political and social change, they drew back in order to cement an alliance with the liberals, who resisted any such transformation, at least while the war continued. Both the moderate socialists and the liberals refused to consider a separate peace, assuming that the people remained patriotic, and fearing that Russian withdrawal would pave the way for a German victory in the west. However plausible these arguments, the moderate socialists showed a remarkable incapacity to grasp the mood of the soldiers and workers. Indeed, they seemed afraid of the very people whom they claimed to represent. Sukhanov, who sided with the Mensheviks in 1917, expressed his fear of the peasant-soldiers.[33] He was also, as we have seen, afraid of the women workers, predicting that if their dissatisfaction with the February Revolution continued, it could result in a Bolshevik victory:

> People who used to assert that Moscow was burned down by a copeck [penny] candle were fond of repeating in 1917 that the women in the queues made the revolution. I wondered what these women wanted to do now. What would it bring forth, this talk [of shortages and profiteering] – reaction or future Bolshevism? . . .
>
> It seemed that in the new conditions, the "lower depths" were in deadly earnest about the questions of prices and the struggle against the high cost of living.[34]

Given that the average real wage of unskilled workers (among whom were the majority of women workers, who earned less than men) had dropped by almost a third in June 1917, it is perhaps not surprising that their protests against the lowering of already low standards of living led them to see the Mensheviks, who from government were calling for restraint, as traitors to the working class and to the revolution that they had set in motion.[35] The defeat of the July demonstrations, and the reaction of women workers against the Bolsheviks, seems to have given hope to the moderate socialists, but that apparent respite masked the basic weakness of their position. The July Days showed the liberals and the right that they could no longer rely on the ability of their socialist partners to rein in the masses through the Soviet. Yet the Mensheviks and SRs persisted in their efforts to co-operate with those now bent on confrontation, including the prime minister, Alexander Kerensky.

In his reconsideration of the Bolshevik victory in October, Edward Acton gives little space to women, though he sees them as constituting a large part of the unskilled and recent migrant workers from the country-side.[36] Acton sees skilled workers in the vanguard of the strike movement from May, overlooking (or perhaps judging to be less significant) the massive protests of female service sector workers.[37] In their studies of the Petrograd working class in 1917, Stephen Smith and David Mandel pay particular attention to women, but see their participation as essentially a kind of pressure group forcing the skilled male workers and the Bolsheviks to take more radical actions.[38] It is indeed tempting to narrow the focus to the articulate skilled workers who demanded not simply higher wages, but also recognition for trade unions and factory committees, respect between employers and bosses and a voice for the former in the decisions of the latter. Yet examination of the struggles of women workers in 1917 shows similar concerns, which is all the more remarkable given the male-dominated nature of the labour movement, and the assumptions about the irrational and apolitical nature of women.

The Bolshevik women Nikiforova, Pan'kina and Chernysheva re-called the way that women workers had developed their strike strategy from 23 February, undeterred by attacks from cossacks who at first used whips to try to disperse the thousands of women. In one textile factory (Novaia Bumagopriadil'naia) in March, the first person elected to chair the committee was a woman, Galina Lotkova. Under her, the factory committee played an important role not only in organizing the workers, but in running the factory itself, since the manager (a William Howard) and his key workers left for England in March. In this "Moscow" district of Petrograd, the Bolsheviks organized women as well as youth from textile, metal and shoe factories. During the October Revolution, women in that district concentrated on organizing supplies and setting up feeding points for the Red Guards.[39] Nor did such tasks end with the Bolshevik seizure of power, since the onset of civil war by 1918 forced many women to use their domestic skills for the war effort: foraging for food and fuel not just for their families, but to keep their factories going; ensuring that the Red Army was supplied; caring for the wounded, the refugees and the abandoned children; and generally filling the places of those men, and considerable numbers of women, who went to the various fronts. As one female textile worker in Moscow recalled with pride at the end of the war: "we carried the revolution on our shoulders. And we didn't give in!"[40]

We are back at the domestic and support roles that women filled in the background, and which they continued to occupy throughout the existence of the Communist state. After the October Revolution, few women, and fewer working-class women, attained positions of responsibility in the new state structure, though many of those who had been active in 1917 were drawn into the administration. They were thus separated from their female constituency by virtue of becoming representatives of the state. Moreover, the role of secretary seemed to have changed significantly, becoming more of an administrative than a political post as the Bolsheviks ceased to be an organization of professional revolutionaries and became a mass party of state. The civil war (1918–20) confirmed the importance of women for the military as well as the economic defence of the revolution. Though few women remained in the Red Army after 1920, the victorious Communist regime expected them not only to fulfil the traditional domestic role of housekeeper and mother, but to take an active part in public life as well, according to the belief that through economic independence they could become "new" women.

The persistence of patriarchal attitudes and practices during the Communist regime has resulted in the underestimation both of the role women played in the 1917 Revolution, and of how far those women who had joined the Bolshevik Party had come in terms of their political awareness. However narrow Bolshevik theory and limited its practice on the woman question, the meetings that they had held for female workers in 1917, though focusing on immediate concerns, also included discussions of the position of women. These "midwives of the revolution" were poorly educated and drawn to simple explanations for their plight, but they were not simply blank pages on which the Bolsheviks could write. Rather, they eventually turned to the Bolshevik Party because it alone seemed to articulate their concerns as women and as workers, and to appreciate that they wanted these addressed as a matter of urgency. That the women who supported the 1917 Revolution seem to have been influenced more by class than by gender, and that they did not fundamentally challenge gender roles but tended to justify what they did by reference to their traditional domestic responsibilities, should not blind us to the active role that they played in the revolutionary process.

Notes

Chapter 1

1. R. Stites (1991) *The Women's Liberation Movement in Russia: Feminism, Nihilism, and Bolshevism, 1860–1930* (2nd edn). Princeton, NJ: Princeton University Press, p.289.
2. L.H. Edmondson (1984) *Feminism in Russia, 1900–1917*. London: Heinemann, pp.170, 174.
3. P. Sorokin (1950) *Leaves from a Russian Diary*. London: Hurst & Blackett, p.3.
4. Stites, *The Women's Liberation Movement*, p.290.
5. E.N. Burdzhalov (1987) *Russia's Second Revolution: The February 1917 Uprising in Petrograd*, D.J. Raleigh (trans.). Bloomington, Indiana: Indiana University Press; see introduction by D.J. Raleigh. See also E.N. Burdzhalov (1956) "O taktike bol'shevikov v marte-aprele 1917", *Voprosy istorii*, **4**, pp.38–56.
6. N.N. Sukhanov (1983) *The Russian Revolution 1917: A Personal Record*, J. Carmichael (ed., trans., and abridg.). Princeton, NJ: Princeton University Press, p.5 for the quotation; p.34 for the "first day of the revolution: February 27th".
7. Quoted in Burdzhalov, *Russia's Second Revolution*, p.87.
8. See M. Melancon (1998) "Who wrote what and when? Proclamations of the February Revolution in Petrograd, 23 February–1 March 1917", *Soviet Studies*, **40**, 3, pp.479–500; J.D. White (1989) "The February Revolution and the Bolshevik Vyborg District Committee (in response to Michael Melancon)", *Soviet Studies*, **41**, 4, pp.602–24; D.A. Longley (1989) "The Mezhraionka, the Bolsheviks and International Women's Day: in response to Michael Melancon", *Soviet Studies*, **41**, pp.625–45.

9. C. Read (1996) *From Tsar to Soviets: The Russian People and their Revolution, 1917–1921*. London: UCL, p.43.

10. M. McAuley (1991) *Bread and Justice: State and Society in Petrograd 1917–1922*. Oxford: Oxford University Press, p.23.

11. R.G. Suny (1987) "Revising the old story: the 1917 revolution in light of new sources", in D.H. Kaiser (ed.) *The Workers' Revolution in Russia, 1917: The View from Below*. Cambridge: Cambridge University Press, ch.1, p.3.

12. See, for example, D. Koenker (1981) *Moscow Workers and the 1917 Revolution*. Princeton, NJ: Princeton University Press; S. Smith (1983) *Red Petrograd: Revolution in the Factories 1917–1918*. Cambridge: Cambridge University Press.

13. See R. McKean (1990) *St. Petersburg Between the Revolutions: Workers and Revolutionaries June 1907–February 1917*. New Haven, CT: Yale University Press.

14. B.E. Clements (1994) *Daughters of Revolution: A History of Women in the U.S.S.R.* Arlington Heights, Illinois: Harlan Davidson, p.29.

15. T.J. Uldrieks (1974) "The 'crowd' in the Russian Revolution: towards reassessing the nature of revolutionary leadership", *Politics and Society*, **4**, 3, pp.397–413, 406.

16. R. Pipes (1990) *The Russian Revolution 1899–1919*. London: Fontana, p.xxiv.

17. R. Suny (1983) "Toward a Social History of the October Revolution", *The American Historical Review*, **88**, 1, pp.31–52.

18. See M. Donald (1982) "Bolshevik Activity Amongst the Working Women of Petrograd in 1917", *International Review of Social History*, **xxvii**, pp.129–60. However, B. Farnsworth (1980), in *Aleksandra Kollontai. Socialism, Feminism, and the Bolshevik Revolution*, Palo Alto: Stanford University Press, p.42, acknowledges that other female Bolsheviks shared Kollontai's commitment to the woman question "if not her single-minded intensity".

19. See for example S.A. Smith (1981) "Craft consciousness, class consciousness: Petrograd 1917", *History Workshop Journal*, **11** (Spring), pp.33–56; William G. Rosenberg (1978) "Workers and Workers' Control in the Russian Revolution", *History Workshop Journal*, **5** (Spring), pp.89–97.

20. See W.G. Rosenberg (1974) *Liberals in the Russian Revolution: The Constitutional Democratic Party, 1917–1921*. Princeton, NJ: Princeton University Press.

21. See for example E. Acton (1990) *Rethinking the Russian Revolution*. London: Edward Arnold; E. Frankel, J. Frankel and B. Knei-Paz (eds) (1992) *Revolution in Russia: Reassessments of 1917*. Cambridge: Cambridge University Press; Pipes, *The Russian Revolution*; J.D. White (1994)

The Russian Revolution 1917–21: A Short History. London: Edward Arnold; O. Figes (1996) *A People's Tragedy: The Russian Revolution, 1891–1924*. London: Jonathan Cape.

22. See, for example, Kaiser, *The Workers' Revolution in Russia*; Smith, *Red Petrograd*; D. Mandel (1983) *The Petrograd Workers and the Fall of the Old Regime: From the February Revolution to the July Days 1917*. London: Macmillan and D. Mandel (1984) *Petrograd Workers and the Soviet Seizure of Power (July 1917–June 1918)*. London: Macmillan.

23. See L.H. Haimson (1964–5) "The problem of social stability in urban Russia, 1905–1917", *Slavic Review*, **23**, pp.619–42, and **24**, pp.1–22.

24. O. Figes (1989) *Peasant Russia, Civil War: The Volga Countryside in Revolution (1917–1921)*. Oxford: Oxford University Press, pp.32, 37.

25. See, for example, S. Bridger (1996) *No More Heroines? Russia, Women and the Market*. London: Routledge; L. Attwood (1996) "The post-Soviet woman in the move to the market: a return to domesticity and dependence?", in R. Marsh (ed.), *Women in Russia and Ukraine*. Cambridge: Cambridge University Press, ch.17.

26. D. Godineau (1998) *The Women of Paris and their Revolution*. Berkeley Calif.: California University Press, p.xvi.

27. B.E. Clements (1997) *Bolshevik Women*. Cambridge: Cambridge University Press, p.17.

28. B. Fieseler (1989) "The making of Russian female Social Democrats 1890–1917", *International Review of Social History*, **xxxiv**, 2, pp.193–226, 218–20; Stites, *The Women's Liberation Movement in Russia*, pp.276–7.

29. B. Fieseler (1995) *Frauen auf dem Weg in die russische Sozialdemokratie, 1890–1917 (eine kollektive Biographie)*. Stuttgart: Steiner.

30. E.A. Wood (1997) *The Baba and the Comrade. Gender and Politics in Revolutionary Russia*. Bloomington, Indiana: Indiana University Press, p.75. See Kollontai's writings on the new morality and the working class, *Novaia moral' i rabochii klass* (Moscow 1918), and on the family under communism, *Sem'ia i kommunisticheskoe gosudarstvo* (Moscow 1918). See also Farnsworth, *Aleksandra Kollontai*, pp.143–67.

Chapter 2

1. See V. Dunham (1960) "The strong woman motif in Russian literature", in *The Transformation of Russian Society*, C.E. Black (ed.). Cambridge: Cambridge University Press, pp.459–83.

2. B. Heldt (1987) *Terrible Perfection: Women and Russian Literature*. Bloomington, Indiana: Indiana University Press, p.12.

3. See *Sbornik pamiati Anny Filosofovoi* (Petrograd 1915), vol.2, pp.102–3; T.A. Bogdanovich (1929) *Liubov' liudei shestidesiatykh godov*. Leningrad, p.95.

4. See S. Tsederbaum (1927) *Zhenshchina v russkom revoliutsionnom dvizhenii 1870–1905*. Leningrad, p.8; E. Shtakenshneider (1934) *Dnevniki i zapiski*. Moscow, p.325; E.N. Vodovozova (1964) *Na zare zhizni* (2 volumes). Moscow, vol.2, pp.186–202.

5. N.G. Chernyshevskii (1961) *What is to be done?*, introduced by E.H. Carr. New York: Vintage; E.A. Wood (1997) *The Baba and the Comrade. Gender and Politics in Revolutionary Russia*. Bloomington, Indiana: Indiana University Press, p.24.

6. H. Hoogenboom (1996) "Vera Figner and revolutionary autobiographies: the influence of gender on genre", in R. Marsh (ed.) (1996) *Women in Russia and Ukraine*. Cambridge: Cambridge University Press, p.85.

7. See for example, Bogdanovich, *Liubov' liudei shestidesiatykh godov*, pp.16–17; A.V. Amfiteatrov (1908) *Zhenshchina v obshchestvennykh dvizheniiakh Rossii*. Geneva, p.31; M.V. Kechedzhi-Shapovalov (1902) *Zhenskoe dvizhenie v Rossii i zagranitsei*. St Petersburg, p.145.

8. B.A. Engel (1983) *Mothers and Daughters: Women of the Intelligentsia in Nineteenth-Century Russia*. Cambridge: Cambridge University Press.

9. A. Herzen (1956) *From the Other Shore, and the Russian People and Socialism*, introduced by I. Berlin. Oxford: Oxford University Press, pp.12–13.

10. Herzen, *The Russian People and Socialism*, pp.185–6.

11. ibid., pp.190–91.

12. A. Herzen (1968) *My Past and Thoughts: The Memoirs of Alexander Herzen*. London: Chatto & Windus, vol.2, p.829.

13. A. Herzen (1984) *Who is to blame?*, M. Katz (trans.). Ithaca, NY: Cornell University Press.

14. See A.N. Shabanova (1911) *Ocherk zhenskogo dvizheniia v Rossii*. St Petersburg, p.7.

15. E. Zhukovskaia (1930) *Zapiski*. Leningrad, pp.22–3.

16. M.N. Vernadskaia (1862) *Sobranie sochinenii*. St Petersburg, pp.71–146.

17. N.I. Pirogov (1900) *Sochineniia*. St Petersburg, vol.1, pp.24–76.

18. ibid., pp.39–43.

19. E. Likhacheva (1899–1901) *Materialy dlia istorii zhenskogo obrazovaniia v Rossii*. St Petersburg, vol.2, pp.7, 17, 156, 456–62.

20. E. Yunge (1913) *Vospominaniia 1843–1860gg.* St Petersburg, pp.479–81.

21. M.L. Mikhailov (1903) *Zhenshchiny: ikh vospitanie i znachenie v obshchestve*. St Petersburg. See R. Stites (1969) "M.L. Mikhailov and the emergence of the woman question", *Canadian Slavic Studies*, **3**, 2, pp.178–99.

22. S.S. Shashkov (1871) *Istoricheskie sud'by zhenshchiny*. St Petersburg, pp.212–13.

23. V. Figner (1964) *Zapechatlennyi trud*. Moscow, vol.1, pp.116–20; B.S. Itenburg (1965) *Dvizhenie revoliutsionnogo narodnichestva*. Moscow, pp.142–4; Amy Knight (1975) "The Fritsche: a study of female radicals in the Russian Populist Movement", *Canadian Slavic Studies*, **9**, 1, pp.1–18. See also J. Meijer (1955) *Knowledge and Revolution: The Russian Colony in Zurich, 1870–1873*. Assen, The Netherlands: Van Gorcum.

24. V. Figner (1929) *Polnoe sobranie sochinenii*. Moscow, vol.5, p.39.

25. Figner, *Zapechatlennyi trud*, vol.1, p.122.

26. See B.A. Engel and C.N. Rosenthal (eds) (1975) *Five Sisters: Women Against the Tsar*. London: Weidenfeld & Nicolson.

27. V. Figner (1927) *Memoirs of a Revolutionist*. New York: International Publishers, pp.13, 44–5, 62.

28. See M. Maxwell (1990) *Narodniki Women: Russian Women Who Sacrificed Themselves for the Dream of Freedom*. New York: Pergamon Press.

29. A. Koni (1933) *Vospominaniia o dele Very Zasulich*. Moscow, p.139. See also J. Bergman (1983) *Vera Zasulich: A Biography*. Palo Alto, Calif.: Stanford University Press.

30. J.D. White (1996) *Karl Marx and the Intellectual Origins of Dialectical Materialism*. London: Macmillan, pp.273–4. See also A. Walicki (1979) *A History of Russian Thought: From the Enlightenment to Marxism*. Oxford: Clarendon Press, pp.407–8.

31. E.B. Nikanorova (ed.) (1990) *Naslednitsa: stranitsy zhizni N.K. Krupskoi*. Leningrad, pp.60–61.

32. V.I. Zasulich (1925) *Stat'i o russkoi literature*. Moscow, p.96.

33. V.I. Zasulich (1929) "Zhenshchiny v russkom rabochem dvizhenii", *Katorga i ssylka*, **6**, 55, pp.41–3.

34. R.A. Kazakevich (1960) *Sotsial-demokraticheskie organizatsii Peterburga kontsa 80kh-nachala 90kh godov*. Leningrad, p.148.

35. See *Rabochee dvizhenie v Rossii v xix veke* (4 volumes). Moscow, 1955–61, vol.3, pp.115–21.

36. Vera Karelina, "Vospominanii: na zare rabochego dvizheniia v S-Peterburge", *Krasnaia letopis'* (1922), **4**, pp.12–21:12.

37. *Rabochee dvizhenie v Rossii v xix veke*, vol.3, pp.578–9, 746–8.

38. Karelina, "Vospominaniia", pp.12–21; *Literatura Moskovskogo Rabochego Soiuza*. Moscow, 1930, p.68; R.L. Glickman (1984) *Russian Factory Women: Workplace and Society 1880–1914*. Berkeley, Calif.: California University Press, p.179.

39. Nikanorova, *Naslednitsa*, pp.69–70.

40. V.E. Bonnell (1983) *Roots of Rebellion: Workers' Politics and Organizations in St. Petersburg and Moscow, 1900–1914.* Berkeley, Calif.: California University Press, pp.80–6.
41. See *A Radical Worker in Tsarist Russia: the Autobiography of Semen Ivanovich Kanatchikov*, R.E. Zelnick (ed. and trans.). Palo Alto, Calif.: Stanford University Press, p.103; A. Buzinov (1930) *Za nevskoi zastavoi: zapiski rabochego.* Moscow, pp.20–21.
42. *Literatura Moskovskogo Rabochego Soiuza*, pp.163–70.
43. *Zhenshchina v revoliutsii.* Moscow, 1959, p.21.
44. A. Bebel (1918) *Zhenshchina i sotsializm.* Petrograd, p.iv.
45. A.M. Kollontai (1918) *Novaia moral' i rabochii klass.* Moscow, pp.29–30.
46. ibid., p.32.
47. ibid., pp.22–3.
48. ibid., p.13.
49. ibid., p.26.
50. ibid., p.60.
51. ibid., pp.6–7, 35.
52. V. Figner (1921) *Zapechatlennyi trud.* Moscow, pp.70–71.
53. See V.V. Stasova (1899) *Nadezhda Vasil'evna Stasova: vospominaniia i ocherki.* St Petersburg, p.189.
54. N. Mirovich (1908) *Iz istorii zhenskogo dvizheniia v Rossii.* Moscow, pp.4–10, 41.
55. A.M. Kollontai (1921) "Avtobiograficheskii ocherk", *Proletarskaia revoliutsiia*, **3**, pp.261–302: 267–71.
56. Karelina, "Vospominaniia", pp.19–20.
57. P.F. Kudelli (ed.) (1926) *Rabotnitsa v 1905g. v S-Peterburge: Sbornik statei i vospominanii.* Leningrad, pp.64, 67.
58. Glickman, *Russian Factory Women*, pp.184–5.
59. L.N. Lenskaia (1908) "O prisluge", *Doklad chitannyi vo vtorom zhenskom klube v Moskve v Fev. 1908 goda.* Moscow, pp.20–21.
60. See Stites, *The Women's Liberation Movement in Russia*, pp.198–210.
61. N. Mirovich (1908) *Iz istorii zhenskogo dvizheniia v Rossii.* Moscow, pp.6–10.
62. ibid., pp.12–13.
63. ibid., pp.13–18.
64. See A. Shabanova (1912) *Ocherk zhenskogo dvizheniia v Rossii.* St Petersburg.
65. Mirovich, *Iz istorii*, pp.27–54.
66. E. Bochkareva and S. Liubimova (1967) *Svetlyi put'.* Moscow, p.26.
67. R. Stites (1991) *The Women's Liberation Movement in Russia: Feminism, Nihilism, and Bolshevism, 1860–1930* (2nd edn). Princeton, NJ: Princeton University Press, pp.270–4.

68. Quoted in A. Geifman (1993) *Thou Shalt Kill: Revolutionary Terrorism in Russia, 1894–1917*. Princeton, NJ: Princeton University Press, p.171. See also A. Knight (1979) "Female Terrorists in the Russian Socialist Revolutionary Party", *Russian Review*, **38**, 2, pp.151–3.

69. V. Bilshai (1956) *Reshenie zhenskogo voprosa v SSSR*. Moscow, p.65 and L. Edmondson (1984) *Feminism in Russia, 1900–1917*. London: Heinemann, p.71. For Kollontai, see her *Sotsial'nie osnovy zhenskago voprosa* (St Petersburg 1909).

70. See *Trudy pervogo vserossiiskogo s'ezda pri Russkom zhenskom obshchestve v Sankt-Peterburge 10–16 dekabria, 1908* (St Petersburg 1909); N.V. Orlova (1911) *O zhenskom dvizhenii v Rossii*. St Petersburg; Stites, *The Women's Liberation Movement in Russia*, pp.215–19.

71. *Trudy*, pp.791–2.

72. Alexandra Kollontai (1977) *Selected Writings*, translated and introduced by Alix Holt. London: Allison & Busby, pp.58–73: 59. See also A.M. Kollontai (1921) "Avtobiograficheskii ocherk", *Proletarskaia revoliutsiia*, **3**, pp.261–302: 268–78.

73. A. Tyrkova-Vil'iams (1952) *Na putiakh k svobode*. New York, pp.343–5.

Chapter 3

1. B.A. Engel (1983) *Mothers and Daughters: Women of the Intelligentsia in Nineteenth-Century Russia*. Cambridge: Cambridge University Press, pp.202–3.

2. V.I. Zasulich (1931) *Vospominaniia*. Moscow, p.15.

3. L. Trotsky (1970) *My Life*. New York: Pathfinder Press, p.150.

4. J. Bergman (1983) *Vera Zasulich: A Biography*. Palo Alto, Calif.: Stanford University Press, p.26.

5. See V. Figner (1927) *Memoirs of a Revolutionist*. New York.

6. M. Perrie (1972) "The social composition and structure of the Socialist-Revolutionary Party before 1917", *Soviet Studies*, **24**, 2, pp.223–50: 236; A. Knight (1979) "Female terrorists in the Russian Socialist Revolutionary Party", *Russian Review* **38**, 2, pp.139–59: pp.144–5.

7. ibid.

8. ibid., p.145; B. Fieseler (1989) "The making of Russian female Social Democrats, 1890–1917", *International Review of Social History*, **xxxiv**, pp.193–226: p.211.

9. V. Perazich (1927) *Tekstili Leningrada v 1917g.* Leningrad, pp.35–6.

10. A.S. Blackwell (ed.) (1919) *The Little Grandmother of the Russian Revolution: Reminiscences and Letters of Catherine Breshkovsky*. Boston: Little Brown; E. Breshko-Breshkovskaia (1931) *Hidden Springs of the*

Russian Revolution: Personal Memoirs. Palo Alto, Calif.: Stanford University Press.

11. Knight, "Female terrorists", pp.148–52.

12. I. Steinberg (1935) *Spiridonova: Revolutionary Terrorist.* London.

13. B.E. Clements (1994) *Daughters of Revolution: A History of Women in the U.S.S.R.* Arlington Heights, Illinois: Harlan Davidson, p.26.

14. R. Stites (1991) *The Women's Liberation Movement in Russia: Feminism, Nihilism and Bolshevism, 1860–1930* (2nd edn). Princeton, NJ: Princeton University Press, p.313.

15. J.D. White, *The Russian Revolution, 1917–1921.* London: Edward Arnold, p.292.

16. E. Goldman (1924) *My Disillusionment with Russia.* New York, ch.16.

17. M. Maxwell (1990) *Narodniki Women: Russian Women Who Sacrificed Themselves for the Dream of Freedom.* New York: Pergamon Press, p.283.

18. Stites, *The Women's Liberation Movement in Russia,* p.313.

19. C. Rice, *Russian Workers and the Socialist Revolutionary Party through the Revolution of 1905–07.* London: Macmillan, p.195.

20. See B.A. Engel and C.N. Rosenthal (eds) (1975) *Five Sisters: Women against the Tsar.* London: Wiedenfeld & Nicolson.

21. B.E. Clements (1997) *Bolshevik Women.* Cambridge: Cambridge University Press, p.17.

22. B.E. Clements (1979) *Bolshevik Feminist: The Life of Aleksandra Kollontai.* Bloomington, Indiana: Indiana University Press.

23. ibid., p.110.

24. G. Haupt and J.-J. Marie (eds) (1974) *Makers of the Russian Revolution: Biographies of Bolshevik Leaders.* London: Allen & Unwin.

25. *Entsiklopedicheskii Slovar' Russskogo Bibliograficheskogo Instituta Granat.* Moscow 1927–9.

26. Haupt and Marie, *Makers of the Russian Revolution,* p.17.

27. V. Poliakova (ed.) (1967) *Geroi Oktiabria.* Leningrad, vol.1, p.375.

28. L. Kunetskaia and K. Mashtakova (1979) *Mariia Ul'ianova.* Moscow, pp.148–79.

29. Haupt and Marie, *Makers of the Russian Revolution,* pp.21–2.

30. Clements, *Bolshevik Women,* p.110.

31. R. McNeal, *Bride of the Revolution: Krupskaia and Lenin.* London: Victor Gollancz.

32. Haupt and Marie, *Makers of the Russian Revolution,* p.156.

33. McNeal, *Bride of the Revolution,* p.188.

34. D. Volkogonov (1994) *Lenin, Life and Legacy.* London: HarperCollins, p.35.

35. N. Krupskaia (1930) *Memories of Lenin.* London: Lawrence & Wishart, p.102.

36. ibid., p.43.
37. Volkogonov, *Lenin*, p.33.
38. Trotsky, *My Life*, p.152.
39. Clements, *Bolshevik Women*, p.110.
40. Haupt and Marie, *Makers of the Russian Revolution*, p.157.
41. Krupskaia, *Memories of Lenin*, p.104.
42. ibid.
43. A. Walicki (1980) *A History of Russian Thought: From the Enlightenment to Marxism*. Oxford: Clarendon Press, pp.411–12; J.D. White (1998) " 'No, we won't go that way; that is not the way to take': the place of Alexander Ul'ianov in the development of Social-Democracy in Russia", *Revolutionary Russia*, **11**, 2, pp. 82–110.
44. P. Kudelli (1936) "Svetloi pamiati Anny Il'inichny Elizarovoi-Ul'ianovoi", *Krasnaia letopis'*, **1**, pp.200–204.
45. Kunetskaia and Mashtakova, *Mariia Ul'ianova*, pp.148–79.
46. Krupskaia, *Memories of Lenin*, p.257.
47. McNeal, *Bride of the Revolution*, p.73. Clements, in *Bolshevik Women*, p.140, disagrees with McNeal that Krupskaia was replaced by Stasova in 1917, and suggests instead that Krupskaia may have wanted to get back in touch with Russia.
48. Krupskaia, *Memories of Lenin*, p.261.
49. *Geroi Oktiabria*, vol.1, pp.597–600.
50. Krupskaia, *Memories of Lenin*, p.269.
51. Haupt and Marie, *Makers of the Russian Revolution*, p.358.
52. For the *zhenotdel*, see C.E. Hayden (1976) "The *Zhenotdel* and the Bolshevik Party", *Russian History*, **3**, 2, pp.150–73; R. Stites, "*Zhenotdel*: Bolshevism and Russian Women, 1917–1930", *Russian History*, **3**, pp.174–93; E.A. Wood (1997) *The Baba and the Comrade. Gender and Politics in Revolutionary Russia*. Bloomington, Indiana: Indiana University Press.
53. For Kollontai, see A.M. Kollontai (1921) "Avtobiograficheskie ocherki", *Proletarskaia revoliutsiia*, **3**, pp.261–302; A.M. Kollontai (1972) *Autobiography of a Sexually Emancipated Woman*. London; Clements, *Bolshevik Feminist: The Life of Aleksandra Kollontai*; B. Farnsworth (1980) *Aleksandra Kollontai: Socialism, Feminism and the Russian Revolution*. Palo Alto, Calif.: Stanford University Press; R. Stites, "Alexandra Kollontai and the Russian Revolution", in *European Women on the Left*, J. Slaughter and R. Kern (eds). Westport, CT: Greenwood Press, pp.101–23; B. Williams (1986) "Kollontai and after: women in the Russian Revolution", in S. Reynalds (ed.), *Women, State and Revolution*. Brighton: Wheatsheaf, pp.60–80.

54. R.C. Elwood (1992) *Inessa Armand: revolutionary and feminist*. Cambridge: Cambridge University Press.
55. ibid., p.145.
56. L. Katasheva (1934) *Natasha: A Bolshevik Woman Organiser*. New York: Workers' Library Publishers, pp.5–6, 24.
57. ibid., p.24; Wood, *The Baba and the Comrade*, p.75; *Zhenshchiny v revoliutsii*, Moscow 1959, pp.96–8.
58. ibid., Clements, *Bolshevik Women*, pp.55–6.
59. K. Samoilova (1920) *Rabotnitsy v rossiisskoi revoliutsii*. Moscow, p.7; *Zhenshchiny goroda Lenina*, Leningrad 1963, pp.90–94.
60. L. Stal' (1922) "Rabotnitsa v Oktiabre", *Proletarskaia revoliutsiia*, **10**, p.299.
61. E. Broido (1917) *Zhenshchina-rabotnitsa*. Petrograd, p.4.
62. Quoted in L.H. Haimson (ed.) (1987) *The Making of Three Russian Revolutionaries: Voices from the Menshevik Past*, in collaboration with Ziva Galili y Garcia and Richard Wortman. Cambridge: Cambridge University Press, pp.80, 82.
63. E. Broido (1967) *Memoirs of a Revolutionary*. London: Oxford University Press, p.20.
64. ibid., pp.34–5.
65. M.M. Mullaney (1983) *Revolutionary Women: Gender and the Socialist Revolutionary Role*. New York: Praeger, p.59.
66. See *Geroi Oktiabria*, vol.1.
67. ibid., pp.41–3.
68. ibid., pp.44–5.
69. ibid., pp.271–2.
70. ibid., pp.305–6.
71. ibid., pp.457–8.
72. ibid., pp.64–5.
73. *Kommunistka*, 1924, No.4, pp.8–10.
74. *Geroi Oktiabria*, vol.1, pp.318–19.
75. ibid., pp.595–6.
76. See E. Vechtomova (1981) *Zhenia Egorova*. Leningrad.
77. Haupt and Marie, *Makers of the Russian Revolution*, p.269.
78. E.D. Stasova (1988) *Stranitsy zhizni i bor'by*. Moscow, p.147.
79. See Clements, *Bolshevik Women*, p.17; M. McAuley (1991) *Bread and Justice: State and Society in Petrograd 1917–1922*. Oxford: Oxford University Press, p.31; Wood, *The Baba and the Comrade*, pp.34–5, 69–70.
80. W.H. Chamberlain (1929) "Daughters of the Russian Revolution", *Yale Review*, **18**, pp.732–48.
81. V. Zubkhov and Yu. Medvedev (1974) *Komsomol'skie Vozhaki*. Moscow, pp.5–10.

82. *Geroi Oktiabria*, vol.1, p.535.
83. ibid., pp.453–4.
84. ibid., pp.579–81.
85. Haupt and Marie, *Makers of the Russian Revolution*, pp.404–9; Stites, *The Women's Liberation Movement in Russia*, p.319; Cathy Porter (1988) *Larissa Reisner*. London: Virago.
86. *Geroi Oktiabria*, vol.1, pp.436–7.
87. Krupskaia, *Memories of Lenin*, p.269.
88. W. Chase and J.A. Getty (1978) "The Moscow Bolshevik cadres of 1917: A prosopographical analysis", *Russian History*, **5**, pp.84–105: 93–4.
89. B.E. Clements (1985) "Baba and Bolshevik: Russian Women and Revolutionary Change", *Soviet Union/Union Sovietique*, **12**, 2, pp.161–84: p.167.
90. I. Kor (ed.) (1934) *Kak my zhili pri tsare i kak zhivem teper'*. Moscow, pp.32–3.
91. Fieseler, "The Making of Russian Female Social Democrats".
92. N.N. Sukhanov (1983) *The Russian Revolution 1917: A Personal Record*, J. Carmichael (ed., trans. and abridg). Princeton, NJ.: Princeton University Press, p.556.
93. B.T. Norton (1989) "The making of a female Social Democrat: E.D. Kuskova's conversion to Russian Social Democracy", *International Review of Social History*, **xxxiv**, pp.227–47.
94. B. Fieseler (1995) *Frauen auf dem Weg in die russische Sozialdemokratie, 1890–1917 (eine kollektive Biographie)*. Stuttgart: Steiner, p.24.
95. Clements, *Daughters of the Revolution*, p.27.
96. Krupskaia, *Memories of Lenin*, p.268.
97. R.H. McNeal (1971–2) "Women in the Russian Radical Movement", *Journal of Social History*, **2**, pp.143–63: 160; R. Pethybridge (1994) *Soviet Studies*, **26**, 2, pp.294–5.
98. R.C. Elwood (1974) *Russian Social Democracy in the Underground: A Study of the RSDRP in the Ukraine, 1907–1914*. Assen, The Netherlands: Van Gorcum, pp.67–8.
99. Fieseler, "The making of Russian female Social Democrats", p.226.

Chapter 4

1. V.A. Aleksandrov (1976) *Sel'skaia obshchina v Rossii (xvii – nachalo xix v)*. Moscow, p.176.
2. ibid., pp.303–5.
3. V.V. Bervi-Flerovsky (1958) *Izbrannye ekonomicheskie proizvedeniia*, (2 volumes). Moscow, vol.1, p.88.
4. Aleksandrov, *Sel'skaia obshchina v Rossii*, pp.111–70, 314–15.

5. See Y.A. Kantorovich (1896) *Zhenshchina v prave*. St Petersburg, pp.50–59.

6. See E.D. Morgan and C.H. Coote (eds) (1886) *Early Voyages and Travels to Russia and Persia*. London: Hakluyt Society, p.38; D.M. Wallace (1961) *Russia on the Eve of War and Revolution*, edited and introduced by C.E. Black. New York: Vintage Books, p.279; G. Brandes (1889) *Impressions of Russia*. New York: Cromwell, p.65.

7. J. Hubbs (1988) *Mother Russia: The Feminine Myth in Russian Culture*. Bloomington, Indiana: Indiana University Press, p.81.

8. M. Zebrikoff (1984) "Russia", pp.396–7, in T. Stanton (ed.), *The Woman Question in Europe*. New York; Aleksandra Efimenko (1884) *Issledovaniia narodnoi zhizni, vol.1: obychnoe pravo*. Moscow, pp.84, 89; P.G. Mizhuev (1906) *Zhenskii vopros i zhenskoe dvizhenie*. St Petersburg, pp.61–2; M. Kovalevsky (1891) *Modern Customs and Ancient Laws of Russia*. London, pp.44–6.

9. Hubbs, *Mother Russia*, p.81.

10. ibid.

11. P.N. Tarnovskaia (1902) *Zhenshchiny-ubiitsy*. St Petersburg.

12. M. Bulgakov (1990) *A Country Doctor's Notebook*, M. Glenny (trans.). Glasgow: Collins, pp.45–6.

13. H. Lange (1871) *Higher Education of Women in Europe*. New York, p.130.

14. See S.S. Shashkov (1871) *Istoricheskiie sud'by zhenshchiny*. St Petersburg, pp.312–13; E. Yunge (1913) *Vospominaniia 1843–1860gg*. St Petersburg, p.481; E.N. Vodovozova (1964) *Na zare zhizni* (2 volumes). Moscow, vol.2, pp.99–100; J. Meijer (1995) *Knowledge and Revolution: The Russian Colony in Zurich, 1870–1873*. Assen, The Netherlands: Van Gorcum.

15. E. Likhacheva (1890–93) *Materialy dlia istorii zhenskogo obrazovaniia v Rossii*. St Petersburg, vol.2, pp.530–35; S. Satina (1966) *Education of Women in Pre-Revolutionary Russia*, A.F. Poustchine (trans.). New York, pp.74–5, 124–5; L.D. Filippova (1963) "Iz istorii zhenskogo obrazovaniia v Rossii", *Voprosy istorii*, pp.209–18.

16. I. Brainin (1974) "Bestuzhevskie", *Novyi mir*, **9**, pp.242–3.

17. Likhacheva, *Materialy*, vol.2, pp.486–7; N.V. Shelgunov (1904) *Sochineniia*. St Petersburg, vol.2, pp.217–66.

18. O. Bulanova-Trubnikova (1928) *Tri pokoleniia*. Moscow-Leningrad, pp.80–81; E.A. Shtakenshneider (1934) *Dnevniki i zapiski*. Moscow, p.394.

19. A.V. Tyrkova (1915) *Sbornik pamiati Anny Pavlovny Filosofovoi*. Petrograd, vol.1, pp.125–36; Shtakenshneider, *Dnevniki i zapiski*, pp.349–57.

20. See C. Johanson (1987) *Women's Struggle for Higher Education in Russia, 1865–1900*. Montreal: McGill-Queen's University Press.

21. See *A Radical Worker in Tsarist Russia*, p.93.
22. See B.A. Engel and C.N. Rosenthal (1975) *Five Sisters: Women Against the Tsar*. London: Weidenfeld & Nicolson.
23. See B.A. Engel (1983) *Mothers and Daughters: Women of the Intelligentsia in Nineteenth-century Russia*. Cambridge: Cambridge University Press.
24. *Vospominaniia vrachei Yulia Kviatkovskaia i Mariia Pavlovna Rachkovich*. Paris 1937. The information here refers to Kviatkovskaia.
25. See N.M. Frieden (1981) *Russian Physicians in an Era of Reform and Revolution, 1856–1905*. Princeton, NJ: Princeton University Press; B. Ekloff (1986) *Russian Peasant Schools: Officialdom, Village Culture, and Popular Pedagogy*. Berkeley, Calif.: California University Press.
26. See E.V. Aptekman (1884) "Iz zapisok zemskogo vracha", *Russkaia mysl'* **12**, pp.48–82.
27. See B.E. Clements, B.A. Engel and C.D. Worobec (eds) (1990) *Russia's Women: Accommodation, Resistance, Transformation*. Berkeley, Calif.: California University Press; E. Kingston-Mann and T. Mixter (eds) (1991) *Peasant Economy, Culture and Politics of European Russia, 1800–1921*. Princeton, NJ: Princeton University Press.
28. See Aptekman, "Iz zapisok zemskogo vracha".
29. See V.N. Povalishina (1925) *Tridtsat' let kul'turnoi raboty uchastkovogo vracha v derevne*. Moscow.
30. T. Stevens (1891) *Through Russia on a Mustang*. London, p.321.
31. C. Kelly (1996) "Teacups and coffins: the culture of Russian merchant women, 1850–1917", in R. Marsh (ed.), *Women in Russia and Ukraine*. Cambridge: Cambridge University Press, ch.4.
32. ibid., pp.65–7.
33. A. Gudvan (1925) *Ocherki po istorii dvizheniia sluzhashchikh v Rossii, chast' 1: "Do revoliutsii 1905g"*. Moscow, p.105.
34. See A.J. Rieber (1982) *Merchants and Entrepreneurs in Imperial Russia*. Chapel Hill, North Carolina: University of North Carolina Press.
35. See J.A. Ruckman (1984) *The Moscow Business Elite: A Social and Cultural Portrait of Two Generations, 1840–1905*. De Kalb, N. Illinois: Northern Illinois University Press.
36. See, for example, *Zhenskii Kalendar'*, St Petersburg 1903.
37. C.A. Schuler (1996) *Women in Russian Theatre: the actress in the silver age*. London: Routledge.
38. For a study of a starring concert performer, see L. McReynolds, "'The Incomparable' Anastasiia Vial'tseva and the Culture of Personality", in H. Goscilo and B. Holmgren (eds), *Russia Women Culture*. Bloomington, Indiana: Indiana University Press.
39. Vl. Zotov (1889) "Nadezhda Dmitrievna Khovanshchinskaia", *Istoricheskii vestnik*, **38**, pp.93–108: 103.

40. See V.R. Leikina-Svirskaia (1971) *Intelligentsiia v Rossii vo vtoroi polovine xix veka*. Moscow, ch.6.

41. Rashin, *Naselenie Rossii*, pp.293, 305–6.

42. H.P. Kennard (ed.) (1912) *The Russian Year-Book for 1912*. London: Eyre & Spottiswoode, p.88. See also Jeffrey Weeks (1985) *When Russia Learned to Read: Literacy and Popular Literature, 1861–1917*. Princeton, NJ: Princeton University Press.

43. A.G. Rashin (1956) *Naselenie Rossii za sto let*. Moscow, p.158.

44. See, for example, S. Benet (ed. and trans.) (1970) *The Village of Viriatino*, New York: Anchor Books.

45. Y.M. Sokolov (1971) *Russian Folklore*. Detroit: Gale, p.207.

46. Bervi-Flerovsky, *Izbrannye ekonomicheskie proizvedeniia*, vol.1, pp.517–18.

47. Sokolov, *Russian Folklore*, pp.204–7.

48. S. Ramer, "*Zemstvo* and Public Health", in *The Zemstvo in Russia: An Experiment in Local Self-government*, T. Emmons and W.S. Vucinich (eds). Cambridge: Cambridge University Press, pp.279–34: p.303.

49. N.K. Krupskaia (1988) *Izbrannye proizvedeniia*. Moscow, p.13.

50. For crafts, see *Zhenskie Promysly Moskovskoi Gubernii*, Moscow, 1882; J. Pallott (1990) "Women's domestic industries in Moscow Province, 1880–1910", in Clements, Engel and Worobec (1990), *Russia's Women*, pp.163–84. For healing and midwifery, see R. Glickman, "The peasant woman as healer", in Clements et al. (ibid.), pp.148–62, and S. Ramer, "Childbirth and culture: midwifery in the nineteenth century Russian countryside", in D.L. Ransel (ed.) (1978) *The Family in Imperial Russia*, pp.218–35. Urbana: University of Illinois Press. For convents, see B. Meehan-Waters (1992) "To save oneself: Russian peasant women and the development of Women's Religious Communities in pre-revolutionary Russia", in B. Farnsworth and L. Viola (eds) *Russian Peasant Women*. Oxford: Oxford University Press, pp.121–33.

51. Rashin, *Naselinie za sto let*, p.158.

52. R. Edelman (1987) *Proletarian Peasants: The Revolution of 1905 in Russia's Southwest*. Ithaca, NY: Cornell University Press, pp.77–80, 156–7.

53. T. Mixter (1991) "The hiring market as workers' turf: migrant agricultural labourers and the mobilization of collective action in the Steppe grainbelt of European Russia, 1853–1913, in E. Kingston-Mann and T. Mizter (eds), *Peasant Economy, Culture and Politics of European Russia, 1800–1921*. Princeton, NJ: Princeton University Press, pp.294–340.

54. See Pallot, "Women's domestic industries in Moscow Province, 1880–1900".

55. Kennard (ed.) *The Russian Year-Book for 1912*, p.711. See also Pallot, "Women's domestic industries in Moscow Province, 1880–1900".

56. See E.A. Oliunina (1914) *Portnovskii promysel v Moskve i v derevniakh Moskovskoi i Riazanskoi gubernii: Materialy k istorii domashnei promyshlennosti v Rossii*. Moscow, pp.57, 94; A. Hilton (1995) *Russian Folk Art*. Bloomington, Indiana: Indiana University Press, p.96.

57. Ekloff, *Russian Peasant Schools*, especially pp.255–79.

58. B.A. Engel (1994) *Between the Fields and the City: Women, Work and Family in Russia, 1861–1914*. Cambridge: Cambridge University Press, pp.239, 240.

59. A.G. Rashin (1985) *Formirovanie rabochego klassa v Rossii; istoriko-ekonomicheskie ocherki*. Moscow, pp.185–95, 214–17.

60. Rashin, *Naselenie Rossii*, table 276.

61. ibid.

62. For tailors in 1905, see Oliunina, *Portnovskii promysel*, pp.276–317.

63. See M. Davidovich (1912) *Peterburgskii tekstil'nyi rabochii v ego biudzhetakh*. St Petersburg, pp.5–6.

64. E. Milovidova (1929) *Zhenskii vopros i zhenskoe dvizhenie*, Moscow–Leningrad, p.211.

65. See, for example, S. Lapitskaia (1935) *Byt rabochikh Trekhgornoi manufactury*. Moscow, pp.42–51.

66. See, for example, E.O. Kabo, *Ocherki rabochego byta*. Moscow 1928.

67. See V. Bonnell (ed.) *The Russian Worker: Life and Labour under the Tsarist Regime*. Berkeley, Calif.: California University Press, p.195.

68. Gudvan, *Ocherki po istorii dvizheniia sluzhashchikh v Rossii, part 1: "Do revoliutsii 1905g."*, pp.152–4.

69. ibid., p.137.

70. ibid., p.139.

71. See L. Lenskaia (1908) *"O prisluge", Doklad chitannyi vo vtorom zhenskom klube v Moskve v fev. 1908 goda*. Moscow, p.13. See also R. Glickman (1984) *Russian Factory Women: Workplace and Society, 1880–1914*. Berkeley, Calif.: California University Press, p.60.

72. See D. Ransel (1982) "Problems in measuring illegitimacy in pre-revolutionary Russia", *Journal of Social History* **16**, 2, p.122; D. Koenker (1981) *Moscow Workers and the 1917 Revolution*. Princeton, NJ: Princeton University Press, p.41; R.E. Johnson (1979) *Peasant and Proletarian: The Working Class of Moscow in the Late Nineteenth Century*. Leicester: Leicester University Press, p.96.

73. See Bonnell, *The Russian Worker*, p.195; Gudvan, *Ocherki po istorii dvizheniia sluzhashchikh v Rossii, chast' 1*, p.139; Oliunina, *Portnovskii promysel*, p.267; R. Stites (1983) "Prostitution and society in pre-

revolutionary Russia", *Jahrbücher fur Geschichte Osteuropas*, **xxxi**, 3, pp.348–64: 352.

74. See A. Dubrovsky (1890) *Prostitutsiia v Rossiiskoi Imperii*. St Petersburg; B.A. Engel (1989) "St Petersburg prostitutes in the late nineteenth century: a personal and social profile", *Russian Review*, **48**, pp.21–44; L. Bernstein (1995) *Sonia's Daughters: Prostitutes and their Regulation in Imperial Russia*. Berkeley, Calif.: California University Press.

75. A.M. Kollontai (1921) *Prostitutsiia i mery bor'by s ney*. Moscow.

76. See J. Bradley (1988) *Muzhik and Muscovite: Urbanisation in Late Imperial Russia*. Berkeley, Calif.: California University Press, p.134; J.H. Bater (1986) "Between old and new: St Petersburg in the late Imperial era", in M. Hamm (ed.), *The City in Late Imperial Russia*. Bloomington, Indiana: Indiana University Press, p.52.

77. See, for example, *A Radical Worker in Tsarist Russia: The Autobiography of Semen Ivanovich Kanatchikov*, R.E. Zelnick (trans. and ed.). Palo Alto, Calif.: Stanford University Press; A. Buzinov (1930) *Za nevskoi zastavoi: zapiski rabochego*. Moscow; Bonnell, *The Russian Worker*.

78. Quoted in Stites, *The Women's Liberation Movement*, p.282.

Chapter 5

1. V.V. Brusianin (1917) *Voina, zhenshchiny i deti*. Moscow, p.6.

2. E. Blonina (Inessa Armand) (1920) *Bor'ba rabotnits za poslednie gody*. Kharkov, p.29.

3. A.G. Meyer (1991) "The impact of World War I on Russian women's lives", in B.E. Clements, B.A. Engel, C.D. Worobec (eds), *Russia's Women: Accommodation, Resistance, Transformation*. Berkeley, Calif.: California University Press, pp.208–24.

4. E. Broido (1917) *Zhenshchina-Rabotnitsa*. Petrograd, p.4.

5. The following discussion is based on Elena Gal'pern, *Zhenshchina-krest'ianka v nyneshnei voine i reforma volostnogo samo-upravleniia* (Moscow 1916).

6. ibid., p.7.

7. J. Keep (1976) *The Russian Revolution: A Study in Mass Mobilization*. London: Weidenfeld & Nicolson, p.32.

8. Gal'pern, *Zhenshchina-krest'ianka v nyneshnei voine*, p.16.

9. Brusianin, *Voina, zhenshchiny i deti*, p.67.

10. L. Zakharova (1915) *Dnevnik sestry miloserdiia na peredovykh*. Petrograd, pp.11–47.

11. L. Edmondson (1984) *Feminism in Russia 1900–1917*. London: Heinemann Educational, pp.159–63.

12. *Zhenshchina i voina*, No.1, 1915, pp.3–4.
13. See Meyer, "The impact of World War I", p.209.
14. M. Britnieva (1934) *One Woman's Story*. London.
15. *Zhenshchina i voina*, No.1, 1915, p.2.
16. The following discussion is based on Brusianin, *Voina, zhenshchiny i deti*, chs viii and xvi.
17. *Zhenshchina i voina*, No. 1, 1915, p.11.
18. M. Yurlova (1934) *Cossack Girl*. London: Cassell, pp.126–7.
19. T. Aleksinskaia (1917) *Zhenshchina v voine i revoliutsii*. Petrograd, np.
20. *Yashka: My Life as Peasant, Exile and Soldier*, by Mariia Bochkareva, Commander of the Russian Women's Battalion of Death, as set down by I.D. Levine (1919). London: Constable, pp.64–5.
21. See A. Amfiteatrov (1905) *Zhenshchina v obshchestvennykh dvizheniiakh Rossii*. Geneva, p.53.
22. J. Wheelwright (1990) *Amazons and Military Maids: Women Who Dressed as Men in Pursuit of Life, Liberty and Happiness*. London: Pandora, p.30.
23. Bochkareva, *Yashka*, p.116.
24. See I. Rozenthal (1994) "Smertnitsy na fronte", *Argumenty i Fakty*, **31**; A.E. Griesse and R. Stites (1982) "Russia: revolution and war", in N.L. Goldman (ed.), *Female Soldiers – Combatants or Noncombatants? Historical and Contemporary Perspectives*. Westport, CT, Greenwood, ch.3, p.64.
25. See R. Stites (1991) *The Women's Liberation Movement in Russia: Feminism, Nihilism, and Bolshevism, 1860–1930* (2nd edn). Princeton, NJ: Princeton University Press, pp.298–9.
26. A. Bogdanov (1914) *Voina i zhenshchina*. Petrograd, pp.31–2.
27. See B.T. Norton (1989) "The making of a female Social Democrat: E.D. Kuskova's conversion to Russian Social Democracy", *International Review of Social History*, **xxxiv**, pp.227–47.
28. Meyer, "The impact of World War I", p.223.
29. A. Riazanova (1923) *Zhenskii trud*. Moscow, p.34; A.G. Rashin (1958) *Formirovanie rabochego klassa v Rossii: istoriko-economicheskie ocherki*. Moscow, pp.235–6.
30. ibid., p.43.
31. S.O. Zagorsky (1929) *State Control of Industry in Russia during the War*. New Haven, CT: Yale University Press, pp.54–5.
32. Rashin, *Formirovanie rabochego klassa v Rossii*, p.541.
33. *Zhenshchina i voina*, no.1, 1915, pp.13–14.
34. ibid., p.13.
35. The following discussion is based on Rodionova's reminiscences in V. Vavilina (ed.) (1964) *Vsegda s vami: sbornik posviashchennyi 50-letiiu "Rabotnitsy"*. Moscow, pp.98–107: 98–100.

36. The following discussion is taken from *Zhenshchina i voina*, no.1, 1915, p.11.
37. E. Broido (1917) *Zhenshchina-Rabotnitsa*. Petrograd, pp.2–3.
38. A.F. Bessanova (1955) "K istorii izdaniia zhurnala *Rabotnitsa*", *Istoricheskii arkhiv*, **4**, pp.25–53: p.31.
39. ibid., pp.31–9.
40. K. Kondratev (1922) "Vospominaniia", *Krasnaia letopis'* **5**, p.234.
41. E. Bochkareva and S. Liubimova (1967) *Svetlyi put'*. Moscow, pp.49–50.
42. S.N. Serditova (1959) *Bol'sheviki v bor'be za zhenskie proletarskie massy, 1903g.-fevral' 1917g*. Moscow, pp.118–19.
43. V. Bilshai (1956) *Reshenie zhenskogo voprosa v SSSR*. Moscow, pp.83–7.
44. Vavilina, *Vsegda s vami*, pp.206–11; A.M. Kollontai (1921) "Avtobiograficheskii ocherk", *Proletarskaia revoliutsiia* 3, pp.261–302: p.296; K. Samoilova (1920) *Rabotnitsa v rossiisskoi revoliutsii*. Moscow, pp.3–12.
45. Vavilina, *Vsegda s vami*, pp.206–11.
46. Samoilava, *Rabotnitsa v rossiisskoi revoliutsii*, pp.3–12.
47. Broido, *Zhenshchina-Rabotnitsa*, p.7.
48. ibid., p.5.
49. Keep, *The Russian Revolution*, p.45.
50. I.P. Leiberov and S.D. Rudachenko (1990) *Revoliutsiia i khleb*. Moscow, pp.17–20.
51. *Zhenshchiny v revoliutsii*, p.153.
52. R. McKean (1990) *St. Petersburg Between the Revolutions: Workers and Revolutionaries June 1907–February 1917*. New Haven, CT: Yale University Press, pp.223–4.
53. A. Shlyapnikov (1982) *On the Eve of 1917*, R. Chappell (trans.). London: Allison & Busby, p.118.
54. Z. Igumnova (1958) *Zhenshchiny Moskvy v gody grazhdanskoi voiny*. Moscow, p.11.
55. *Rabochee Dvizhenie v Petrograde v 1912–1917gg*. Leningrad 1958, p.277.
56. ibid., pp.281–2.
57. ibid., p.293.
58. ibid., pp.295, 303–5, 410–12.
59. P. Sorokin (1950) *Leaves from a Russian Diary*. London: Hurst & Blackett, p.3.
60. *Rabochee Dvizhenie v Petrograde v 1912–1917gg.*, pp.518–19.
61. T. Hasegawa (1981) *The February Revolution: Petrograd 1917*. Seattle: University of Washington Press, pp.201–3.
62. Blonina, *Bor'ba rabotnits za poslednie gody*, p.29.
63. S.Serditova, *Bol'sheviki v bor'be*, pp.118–19.

64. *Rabochee dvizhenie v Petrograde v 1912–1917gg.*, pp.529–31, 547–9.
65. N.N. Sukhanov (1984) *The Russian Revolution 1917: A Personal Record*, J. Carmichael (ed., trans., abridg.). Princeton, NJ: Princeton University Press, pp.3, 5.
66. Vavilina, *Vsegda s vami*, p.100.

Chapter 6

1. S.N. Serditova (1959) *Bol'sheviki v bor'be za zhenskie proletarskie massy, 1903g.-fevral' 1917g.* Moscow, p.105; E. Bochkareva and S. Liubimova (1967) *Svetlyi put'*. Moscow, pp.47–8; V. Perazich (1927) *Tekstili Leningrada v 1917g.* Leningrad, p.8.
2. See J.L. Keep, *The Russian Revolution: A Study in Mass Mobilization*. London: Weidenfeld & Nicolson, p.58.
3. R. Pipes (1990) *The Russian Revolution, 1899–1919*. London: Fontana pp.275, 278, 280.
4. See, for example, J.D. White (1994) *The Russian Revolution 1917–1921: A Short History*. London: Edward Arnold; T. Hasegawa (1981) *The February Revolution: Petrograd 1917*. Seattle: Washington University Press.
5. I. Gordienko (1957) *Iz boevogo proshlogo, 1914–18gg.* Moscow, pp.56–7.
6. *Rabochee dvizhenie v Petrograde v 1912–1917gg.* Leningrad 1958, pp.547–9.
7. S. Kingsbury and M. Fairchild (1935) *Factory, Family and Women in the Soviet Union*. New York: C.P. Putnam, pp.15–16.
8. A.G. Shliapnikov (1923) *Semnadtsatyi god.* Moscow, pp.60–61.
9. E. Burdzhalov (1987) *Russia's Second Revolution: The February 1917 Uprising in Petrograd*, D.J. Raleigh (trans.) Bloomington Indiana: Indiana University Press, p.105.
10. V. Kaiurov (1923) "Shest' dnei fevral'skoi revoliutsii", *Proletarskaia revoliutsiia*, **1**, pp.157–70: 157–8.
11. See Chapter 2 of this work, and *Geroi Oktiabria*, Leningrad 1967, vol.1, pp.41–3.
12. R.H.B. Lockhart (1967) *The Two Revolutions: An Eye-Witness Study of Russia 1917*. London: Bodley Head, p.70.
13. G. Katkov (1967) *Russia 1917: The February Revolution*. London: Longman, p.249.
14. *Geroi Oktiabria*, pp.318–19.
15. Perazich, *Tekstili Leningrada v 1917g.*, pp.10–18. Burdzhalov, *Russia's Second Revolution*, pp.107, 109.

16. Perazich, *Tekstili Leningrada v 1917g.*, pp.12–13.
17. ibid., pp.1–6.
18. *Zhenshchiny goroda Lenina*, Leningrad 1963, p.89.
19. V. Vavilina (ed.) (1964) *Vsegda s vami: sbornik posviashchennyi 50-letiiu "Rabotnitsy"*. Moscow, p.101.
20. ibid., pp.100–101.
21. A. Shliapnikov (1982) *On the Eve of 1917*, R. Chappell (trans.). London: Allison & Busby, p.7.
22. L. Kunetskaia and K. Mashtakova (1979) *Mariia Ul'ianova*. Moscow, p.170.
23. E.D. Stasova (1988) *Stranitsy zhizni i bor'by*. Moscow, pp.127–8.
24. E. Vechtanova (1981) *Zhenia Egorova*. Leningrad, p.72.
25. Burdzhalov, *Russia's Second Revolution*, pp.114–15.
26. Hasegawa, *The February Revolution*, pp.247–53.
27. O. Figes (1996) *A People's Tragedy: The Russian Revolution 1891–1924*. London: Jonathan Cape, p.310.
28. Gordienko, *Iz boevogo proshlogo*, pp.56–7; Hasegawa, *The February Revolution*, pp.215–24.
29. S.P. Kniazev et al. (eds) (1957) *Petrogradskie Bol'sheviki v Oktiabr'skoi Revoliutsii*. Moscow, pp.38, 117.
30. N.N. Sukhanov (1984) *The Russian Revolution 1917: A Personal Record*, J. Carmichael (ed., abridg. trans.). Princeton, NJ: Princeton University Press, pp.182–3.
31. *Zhenshchiny goroda Lenina*, pp.77–81.
32. M. Donald (1982) "Bolshevik activity amongst the working women of Petrograd in 1917", *International Review of Social History* **xxvii**, pp.129–60, pp.141–3.
33. A.V. Artiukhina (ed.) (1959) *Zhenshchiny v revoliutsii*. Moscow, pp.153–7.
34. See *Rabotnitsa* (19 July 1917), No.7, p.4.
35. E. Broido (1917) *Zhenshchina-Rabotnitsa*. Petrograd, p.8.
36. *Zhenshchiny v revoliutsii*, p.148.
37. Perazich, *Tekstili Leningrada v 1917g.*, p.27.
38. ibid., p.28.
39. ibid., pp.35–6.
40. ibid., p.44.
41. *Revoliutsionerki Rossii*. Moscow 1983, p.105.
42. Donald, "Bolshevik activity amongst the working women of Petrograd in 1917", p.44.
43. D. Koenker and W. Rosenberg (1989) *Strikes and Revolution in Russia, 1917*. Princeton, NJ: Princeton University Press, pp.3–4.
44. ibid., pp.229–32.

45. Figes, *A People's Tragedy*, p.368.
46. A. M. Kollontai (1918) *Rabotnitsa za god revoliutsii*. Moscow, pp.18–19; Koenker and Rosenberg, *Strikes and Revolution in Russia, 1917*, pp.228–9.
47. *Geroi Oktiabria*, p.319.
48. N. Krupskaia (1942) *Memories of Lenin*. London: Lawrence & Wishart, p.268.
49. One example was the leather industry: see *Rabotnitsa*, 30 May 1917, No.7, p.4.
50. *Rabotnitsa*, 18 October 1917, No.11, p.15.
51. Koenker and Rosenberg, *Strikes and Revolution in Russia, 1917*, pp.140, 224.
52. Perazich, *Tekstili Leningrada v 1917g.*, p.44.
53. *Petrogradskie Bol'sheviki v Oktiabr'skoi Revoliutsii*, Moscow 1957, p.44.
54. See, for example, M. Donald (1995) "'What did you do in the Revolution, Mother?' Image, myth and prejudice in Western writing on the Russian Revolution", *Gender and History* **7**, 1, pp.85–99.
55. See C.E. Hayden (1976) "The *Zhenotdel* and the Bolshevik Party", *Russian History* **3**, 2, pp.150–73: 152.
56. See for example, Kollontai, "Lenin i rabotnitsy v 1917 godu", in Vavilina, *Vsegda s vami*, pp.84–6; L. Katasheva (1934) *Natasha: A Bolshevik Woman Organiser*. London, pp.40–45.
57. L. Stal' (1922) "Rabotnitsa v Oktiabre", *Proletarskaia revoliutsiia*, **10**, p.297; *Zhenshchina v revoliutsii*, p.108.
58. Stal', "Rabotnitsa v Oktiabre", p.297.
59. N.D. Karpetskaia (1974) *Rabotnitsy i Velikii Oktiabr'*. Leningrad, pp.44–51.
60. K. Samoilova (1920) *Rabotnitsy v rossiisskoi revoliutsii*. Moscow, pp.7–8.
61. Krupskaia, *Memories of Lenin*, pp.269–70.
62. See Kollontai, *Rabotnitsa za god revoliutsii*, p.4; *Rabotnitsa*, 1 September 1917, No.9, p.9; R. Glickman (1984) *Russian Factory Women: Workplace and Society, 1880–1914*. Berkeley, Calif.: California University Press, p.280; R. Stites (1991) *The Women's Liberation Movement in Russia: Feminism, Nihilism, and Bolshevism, 1860–1930* (2nd edn). Princeton, NJ: Princeton University Press, pp.303–4.
63. Perazich, *Tekstili Leningrada v 1917g.*, p.28.
64. Broido, *Zhenshchina-Rabotnitsa*, p.8.
65. Bochkareva, Liubimova, *Svetlyi put'*, pp.59–69.
66. See Z.V. Stepanov (1956) *Rabochie Petrograda v period podgotovki i provedeniia velikogo oktiabr'skogo voorozhennogo vosstaniia*. Moscow, p.146.

67. Kniazev, *Petrogradskie Bol'sheviki v Oktiabr'skoi Revoliutsii*, pp.237–8.
68. V. Zubkov and Yu. Medvedev (1974) "Liza Pylaeva", *Komsomol'skie Vozhaki*. Moscow, pp.5–30: p.12.
69. Krupskaia, *Memories of Lenin*, p.270.
70. See Karpetskaia, *Rabotnitsy i Velikii Oktiabr'*, p.81.
71. *Zhenshchiny v revoliutsii*, pp.136–7.
72. Samoilova, *Rabotnitsy v rossiisskoi revoliutsii*, p.7; Katasheva, *Natasha*, p.41.
73. Zubkov and Medvedev, "Liza Pylaeva", pp.21–3.
74. Katasheva, *Natasha*, p.42.
75. Kunetskaia and Mashtakova, *Mariia Ul'ianova*, p.179; Stasova, *Stranitsy zhizni i bor'by*, p.15.
76. Stites, *The Women's Liberation Movement*, p.394.
77. E. Broido (1917) *Zhenskaia inspektsiia truda*. Petrograd.
78. Perazich, *Tekstili Leningrada v 1917g.*, p.32.
79. ibid., p.5.
80. Broido, *Zhenshchina-Rabotnitsa*, pp.13–14.
81. Z. Galili (1989) *The Menshevik Leaders in the Russian Revolution: Social Realities and Political Strategies.* Princeton, NJ: Princeton University Press, p.332.
82. Stites, *The Women's Liberation Movement*, p.295.
83. M. Maxwell (1990) *Narodniki Women: Russian Women Who Sacrificed Themselves for the Dream of Freedom.* New York: Pergamon Press, p.229.
84. Quoted in L. Edmondson (1984) *Feminism in Russia 1900–1917.* London: Heinemann, p.167.
85. ibid., p. 168.
86. M.I. Pokrovskaia (1917) "Revoliutsii i gumannost", *Zhenskii vestnik*, Nos5–6, pp.67–9.
87. See Sir George Buchanan (1923) *My Mission to Russia and Other Diplomatic Memories.* London: Cassell, especially vol.2.
88. *Zhenshchiny v revoliutsii*, p.59.
89. Krupskaia, *Memories of Lenin*, p.75.
90. *Yashka: My Life as Peasant, Exile and Soldier*, by Maria Bochkareva, Commander of the Russian Women's Battalion of Death, as set down by Isaac Don Levine (1919). London: Constable, p.162.
91. T. Aleksinskaia (1917) *Zhenshchina v voine i revoliutsii*. Petrograd, np.
92. See I. Rozenthal (1994) "Smertnitsy na fronte", *Argumenty i Fakty*, No.31.
93. See E.S. Pankhurst (1935) *The Life of Emmeline Pankhurst*. London: T. Werner Laurie, pp.159–61; J. Wheelwright (1994) *Amazons and Military Maids: Women Who Dressed as Men in Pursuit of Life, Liberty and Happiness*. London: Pandora, pp.26–7.

94. R. Abraham (1992) "Mariia L. Bochkareva and the Russian Amazons of 1917", in L. Edmondson (ed.) (1992) *Women and Society in Russia and the Soviet Union*. Cambridge: Cambridge University Press, ch.6, p.127.

95. Stites, *The Women's Movement in Russia*, p.299.

96. ibid., p.298.

97. Aleksinskaia, *Zhenshchina v voine i revoliutsii*, np.

98. See Rozenthal, "Smertnitsy na fronte".

99. See, for example, L. Bryant (1918) *Six Red Months in Russia*. London, p.210; A.E. Griesse and R. Stites (1982) "Russia: revolution and war", in N.L. Goldman (ed.), *Female Soldiers – Combatants or Noncombatants? Historical and Contemporary Perspectives*. Westport, CT: Greenwood Press, p.64; Aleksinskaia, *Zhenshchina v voine i revoliutsii*.

100. *Yashka*, pp.184–218; Stites, *The Women's Movement in Russia*, pp.296–7.

101. See, R.V. Daniels (1968) *Red October: The Bolshevik Revolution of 1917*. London: Secker & Warburg, pp.179, 188, 189.

102. Figes, *A People's Tragedy*, p.488.

103. Daniels, *Red October*, p.189.

104. Buchanan, *My Mission to Russia*, vol.2, p.208.

105. H. Pitcher (1994) *Witnesses of the Russian Revolution*. London, p.215.

106. H. Shukman (ed.) (1988) *The Blackwell Encyclopedia of the Russian Revolution*. Oxford: Blackwell, p.36; Rozenthal, "Smertnitsy na fronte".

107. Stites, *The Women's Movement in Russia*, p.299.

108. *Rabotnitsa*, 25 June 1917, No.6, pp.7–8; Karpetskaia, *Rabotnitsy*, p.90.

109. *Zhenshchiny goroda Lenina*, pp.91–2; Bochkareva and Liubimova, *Svetlyi put'*, p.95.

110. J.F. Hutchison (1990) *Politics and Public Health in Revolutionary Russia, 1890–1918*. Baltimore: Johns Hopkins University Press, pp.73, 185.

111. Krupskaia, *Memories of Lenin*, p.279.

112. Vavilina, *Vsegda s vami*, p.106; *Zhenshchiny goroda Lenina*. Leningrad 1963, pp.91–2.

113. *Kommunistka*, 1920, No.5, p.159.

114. See A.R. Bogat (1928) *Rabotnitsa i krest'ianka v Krasnoi Armii*. Moscow, Leningrad.

Chapter 7

1. P. Sorokin (1950) *Leaves from a Russian Diary*. London: Hurst & Blackett, p.3.

2. Konkordia Samoilova (1920) *Rabotnitsa v rossiisskoi revoliutsii*. Moscow, pp.4–5.

3. G.J. Gill (1979) *Peasants and Government in the Russian Revolution*. London, pp.170–86.

4. O. Figes, *Peasant Russia, Civil War: The Volga Countryside in Revolution (1917–1924)*. Oxford: Oxford University Press, p.30.

5. ibid., pp.37–8.

6. D.J. Raleigh (1986) *Revolution on the Volga: 1917 in Saratov*. Ithaca, NY: Cornell University Press, pp.29, 44.

7. ibid., p.133.

8. ibid., p.206.

9. W.J. Chase (1987) *Workers, Society, and the Soviet State: Labour and Life in Moscow 1918–1929*. Urbana: University of Illinois Press, p.7.

10. A.G. Rashin (1958) *Formirovanie rabochego klassa Rossii*. Moscow, p.601.

11. D. Koenker (1981) *Moscow Workers and the 1917 Revolution*. Princeton, NJ: Princeton University Press, p.39.

12. J.H. Bater (1987) "St. Petersburg and Moscow on the eve of revolution", in D.H. Kaiser (ed.) *The Workers' Revolution in Russia, 1917: The View from Below*. Cambridge: Cambridge University Press, ch.2, p.41.

13. D. Koenker "Moscow in 1917: the view from below", ch.4 in ibid., p.83.

14. ibid., pp.87–8.

15. Nadezhda Krupskaia (ed.) (1926) *Pamiati Inessy Armand*. Moscow, pp.24–6, 31.

16. R.C. Elwood (1992) *Inessa Armand: Revolutionary and Feminist*. Cambridge: Cambridge University Press, pp.211–13.

17. See W. Chase and J.A. Getty (1978) "The Moscow Bolshevik cadres of 1917: A prosopographical analysis", *Russian History*, 5, pp.84–105: p.93, n.22.

18. *Revoliutsionerki Rossii*. Moscow 1983, p.115.

19. ibid., pp.179–81.

20. The following discussion is based on A. Litveiko (1953) "V Semnadtsatom", pp.3–18, *Iunost*, 3, 3, pp.3–18.

21. G. Zinov'ev (1919) *Rabotnitsa, krestianka i sovetskaia vlast'*. Petrograd, pp.3, 16.

22. E.A. Wood (1997) *The Baba and the Comrade. Gender and Politics in Revolutionary Russia*. Bloomington, Indiana: Indiana University Press.

23. A. Nove (1962) "Was Stalin Really Necessary?", *Encounter* (April 1962), pp.86–92.

24. R. Slusser (1987) *Stalin in October: The Man Who Missed the Revolution*. Baltimore: Johns Hopkins University Press.

25. N.N. Sukhanov (1984) *The Russian Revolution 1917: A Personal Record*, J. Carmichael (ed., abridg. and trans.). Princeton, NJ: Princeton University Press, p.229.

26. A. Antonov-Ovseyenko (1980) *The Time of Stalin: Portrait of a Tyranny*. New York: Harper & Row, p.250.

27. See, for example, M. Donald (1982) "Bolshevik activity amongst the working women of Petrograd in 1917", *International Review of Social History*, **27**, pp.129–60.

28. A. Bobroff (1974) "The Bolsheviks and working women, 1905–20", *Soviet Studies*, **26**, 4, pp.540–65: 561.

29. D.P. Koenker and W.G. Rosenberg (1992) "Perceptions and Realities of Labour Protest, March to October 1917", in E.R. Frankel, J. Frankel and B. Knei-Paz (eds) *Revolution in Russia: Reassessments of 1917*. Cambridge: Cambridge University Press, ch.7, pp.142–3.

30. Koenker, *Moscow Workers in 1917*, pp.207–8.

31. ibid., p.208.

32. E. Acton (1990) *Rethinking the Russian Revolution*. London: Edward Arnold, pp.156–66.

33. Z. Galili (1989) *The Menshevik Leaders in the Russian Revolution: Social Realities and Political Strategies*. Princeton, NJ: Princeton University Press, p.125.

34. Sukhanov, *The Russian Revolution*, pp.182–3.

35. A.V. Stepanov (1965) *Rabochie Petrograda v period podgotovki i provedeniia oktiabr'skogo vooruzhennogo vosstaniia, avgust-oktiabr', 1917g.* Moscow & Leningrad, pp.54–5.

36. Acton, *Rethinking the Russian Revolution*, p.186.

37. ibid., p.187.

38. See S.A. Smith (1983) *Red Petrograd: Revolution in the Factories 1917–1918*. Cambridge: Cambridge University Press; D. Mandel (1983) *The Petrograd Workers and the Fall of the Old Regime*. London: Macmillan. and D. Mandel (1984) *The Petrograd Workers and the Soviet Seizure of Power*. London: Macmillan.

39. See *Moskovskaia zastava v 1917*. Leningrad 1959, pp.35, 52–3.

40. V. Vavilina (ed.) (1964) *Vsegda s vami: sbornik, posviashchennyi 50-letiiu zhurnala "Rabotnitsa"*. Moscow, p.139.

Select Bibliography

Acton, E. (1990) *Rethinking the Russian Revolution*. London: Edward Arnold

Amfiteatrov, A. (1905) *Zhenshchiny v obshchestvennykh dvizheniiakh Rossii*. Geneva

Atkinson, D., Dallin, A. and Lapidus, G.W. (eds) (1977) *Women in Russia*. Palo Alto: Stanford University Press

Bergman, J. (1983) *Vera Zasulich: A Biography*. Palo Alto: Stanford University Press

Bessanova, A.F. (ed.) (1955) "K istorii izdaniia zhurnala *Rabotnitsa* (1914)". *Istoricheskyi arkhiv*, **4**, pp.25–54

Blackwell, A.S. (1919) *The Little Grandmother of the Russian Revolution: Reminiscences and Letters of Catherine Breshkovsky*. Boston: Little Brown

Bobroff, A. (1974) "The Bolsheviks and Working Women, 1905–1920", *Soviet Studies*, **26**, 4, pp.540–65

Bobrovskaia, C. (1934) *Twenty Years in Underground Russia*. New York: International Publishers

Bochkareva, E. and Liubimova, S. (1967) *Svetlyi put'*. Moscow

Bochkareva, M. (1919) *Yashka: My Life as Peasant, Officer and Exile*, as set down by Isaac Don Levine. London: Constable

Bonnell, V.E. (1983) *Roots of Rebellion: Workers' Politics and organisations in St. Petersburg and Moscow, 1900–1914*. Berkeley, Calif.: California University Press

Bonnell, V.E. (ed.) (1983) *The Russian Worker: Life and Labour Under the Old Regime*. Berkeley, Calif.: California University Press

Broido, E. (1967) *Memoirs of a Revolutionary*. V. Broido (trans. and ed.). London: Oxford University Press

Burdzhalov, E.N. (1987) *Russia's Second Revolution: the February 1917 Uprising in Petrograd*. D.J. Raleigh (trans.). Bloomington, Indiana: Indiana University Press

Chirkov, P.M. (1978) *Reshenie zhenskogo voprosa v SSSR 1917–1939*. Moscow

Clements, B.E. (1979) *Bolshevik Feminist: the Life of Alexandra Kollontai*. Bloomington, Indiana: Indiana University Press

Clements, B.E. (1994) *Daughters of the Revolution: A History of Women in the U.S.S.R.* Arlington Heights, Illinois: Harlan Davidson

Clements, B.E. (1997) *Bolshevik Women*. Cambridge: Cambridge University Press

Donald, M. (1982) "Bolshevik Activity Amongst The Working Women of Petrograd in 1917", *International Review of Social History*, **xxvii**, pp.129–60

Donald, M. (1995) "'What did you do in the Revolution, Mother?' Image, Myth and Prejudice in Western Writing on the Russian Revolution", *Gender and History*, **7**, 1, pp.85–99

Edmondson, L.H. (1984) *Feminism in Russia, 1900–1917*. London: Heinemann Educational

Elwood, R.C. (1992) *Inessa Armand: revolutionary and feminist*. Cambridge: Cambridge University Press

Engel, B.A. (1983) *Mothers and Daughters: Women of the Intelligentsia in Nineteenth-Century Russia*. Cambridge: Cambridge University Press

Engel, B.A. (1994) *Between the Fields and the City: Women, Work and Family in Russia, 1861–1914*. Cambridge: Cambridge University Press

Engel, B.A. and Rosenthal, C.N. (eds) (1975) *Five Sisters: Women against the Tsar. The Memoirs of Five Revolutionaries*. London: Weidenfeld & Nicolson

Engelstein, L. (1991) *The Keys to Happiness: Sex and the Search for Modernity in fin-de-siècle Russia*. Ithaca, NY: Cornell University Press

Farnsworth, B. (1980) *Aleksandra Kollontai: Socialism, Feminism and the Bolshevik Revolution*. Palo Alto: Stanford University Press

Figes, O. (1996) *A People's Tragedy: The Russian Revolution, 1890–1924*. London: Jonathan Cape

Figner, V. (1929) *Memoirs of a Revolutionist*. New York: International Publishers

Figner, V. (1964) *Zapechatlennyi trud: vospominaniia* (2 volumes). Moscow

Frankel, E.R., Frankel, J. and Knei-Paz, B. (eds) (1992) *Revolution in Russia: Reassessments of 1917*. Cambridge: Cambridge University Press

Geifman, A. (1993) *Thou Shalt Kill: Revolutionary Terrorism in Russia, 1894–1917*. Princeton, NJ: Princeton University Press

Glickman, R. (1984) *Russian Factory Women: Workplace and Society, 1880–1914*. Berkeley, Calif.: California University Press

Gordienko, I. (1957) *Iz boevogo proshlogo, 1914–1918gg*. Moscow

Hasegawa, T. (1981) *The February Revolution: Petrograd 1917*. Seattle: Washington University Press

Hayden, C.E. (1976) "The *Zhenotdel* and the Bolshevik Party", *Russian History*, **3**, 2, pp.150–73

Heimen, J. (1978) "Kollontai and the History of Women's Oppression", *New Left Review*, **110**, pp.43–65

Horsbrugh-Porter, A. (ed.) (1993) *Memories of Revolution: Russian Women Remember.* London: Routledge

Itkina, A. (1970) *Revoliutsioner, tribun, diplomat: stranitsy zhizni Aleksandry Mikhailovny Kollontai.* Moscow

Kaiser, D.H. (ed.) (1987) *The Workers' Revolution in Russia, 1917: The View from Below.* Cambridge: Cambridge University Press

Kaiurov, V. (1923) "Shest' dnei fevral'skoi revoliutsii", *Proletarskaia revoliutsiia*, **1**, pp.150–70

Karelina, V. (1922) "Vospominaniia: na zare rabochego dvizheniia v S-Peterburge", *Krasnaia letopis'*, **4**, pp.12–21

Karpetskaia, N.D. (1974) *Rabotnitsy i Velikii Oktiabr'.* Leningrad

Katasheva, L. (1934) *Natasha: A Bolshevik Woman Organiser.* London

Knight, A. (1975) "The Fritsche: A Study of Female Radicals in the Russian Populist Movement", *Canadian-American Slavic Studies*, **9**, 1, pp.1–17

Knight, A. (1979) "Female Terrorists in the Russian Socialist Revolutionary Party", *Russian Review*, **38**, 2, pp.139–59

Koenker, D. (1981) *Moscow Workers and the 1917 Revolution.* Princeton, NJ: Princeton University Press

Koenker, D. and Rosenberg, W. (1989) *Strikes and Revolution in Russia, 1917.* Princeton, NJ: Princeton University Press

Kollontai, A.M. (1918) *Novaia moral' i rabochii klass.* Moscow

Kollontai, A.M. (1921) "Avtobiograficheskii ocherk", *Proletarskaia revoliutsiia*, **3**, pp.261–302

Kollontai, A.M. (1945) "Iz vospominanii", *Oktiabr'*, **9**, pp.59–89

Kollontai, A.M. (1972) *The Autobiography of a Sexually Emancipated Communist Woman*, I. Fetscher (ed.). London: Orbach & Chambers

Kollontai, A.M. (1974) *Iz moei zhizni i raboty.* Moscow

Kollontai, A.M. (1977) *Selected Writings*, translated, with an introduction and commentaries by Alix Holt. London: Allison & Busby

Krupskaia, K.N. (1901) *Zhenshchina-rabotnitsa.* Geneva

Krupskaia, K.N. (1920) *Pamiati Inessy Armand.* Moscow

Krupskaia, K.N. (1942) *Memories of Lenin.* London: Lawrence & Wishart

Kudelli, P.F. (ed.) (1926) *Rabotnitsa v 1905g v S-Peterburge: sbornik statei i vospominanii.* Leningrad

McDermid, J. & Hillyar, A. (1998) *Women and Work in Russia, 1880–1930: A Study in Continuity through Change.* Harlow, Essex: Longman

McKean, R. (1990) *St. Petersburg Between the Revolutions: Workers and Revolutionaries June 1907–February 1917.* New Haven, CT: Yale University Press

McNeal, R. (1971–2) "Women in the Russian Radical Movement", *Journal of Social History*, **5**, 2, pp.143–63

McNeal, R. (1973) *Bride of the Revolution: Krupskaia and Lenin*. London: Victor Gollancz

Marsh, R. (ed.) (1996) *Women in Russia and Ukraine*. Cambridge: Cambridge University Press

Mitskevich, S.I. (1932) *Na zare rabochego dvizheniia v Moskve*. Moscow

Pushkareva, N. (1997) *Women in Russian History From the Tenth to the Twentieth Century*, translated and edited by Eve Levin. New York: M.E. Sharpe

Read, C. (1990) *Culture and Power in Revolutionary Russia: the intelligentsia and the transition from tsarism to socialism*. New York: St Martin's Press

Read, C. (1996) *From Tsar to Soviets: The Russian people and their revolution, 1917–21*. London: UCL Press

Reynalds, S. (ed.) (1986) *Women, State and Revolution*. Brighton: Wheatsheaf

Samoilova, K. (1920) *Rabotnitsa v rossiisskoi revoliutsii*. Moscow

Serditova, S.N. (1959) *Bol'sheviki v bor'be za zhenskie proletarskie massy, 1903g.-fevral' 1917g*. Moscow

Service, R. (ed.) (1992) *Society and Politics in the Russian Revolution*. London: Macmillan

Slaughter, J. & Kern, R. (eds) (1981) *European Women on the Left*. Westport, CT: Greenwood Press

Smith, S.A. (1984) *Red Petrograd: Revolution in the Factories, 1917–1918*. Cambridge: Cambridge University Press

Stal', L. (1992) "Rabotnitsa v Oktiabre", *Proletarskaia revoliutsiia*, **10**, pp.299–302

Stepanov, Z.V. (1956) *Rabochie Petrograda v period podgotovki i provedeniia velikogo oktiabr'skogo vooruzhennogo vosstaniia*. Moscow

Stites, R. (1991) *The Women's Liberation Movement in Russia: Feminism, Nihilism, and Bolshevism, 1860–1930* (2nd edn). Princeton, NJ: Princeton, University Press

Sukhanov, N.N. (1984) *The Russian Revolution 1917: A Personal Record*, J. Carmichael (ed., trans., abridg.). Princeton, NJ: Princeton University Press

Suny, R. (1993) "Towards a social history of the October revolution", *American Historical Review*, **88**, 1, pp.31–52

Tsederbaum, S. (1927) *Zhenshchina v russkom revoliutsionnom dvizhenii 1870–1905*. Leningrad

Vavilina, V. (ed.) (1964) *Vsegda s vami: sbornik posviashchennyi 50-letiiu Zhurnala "Rabotnitsa"*. Moscow

Wallace, D.M. (1961) *Russia on the Eve of War and Revolution*, edited, introduced and abridged by C.E. Black. New York: Vintage Books

White, J.D. (1994) *The Russian Revolution 1917–1921: A Short History*. London: Edward Arnold

Wolfe, B. (1963) "Lenin and Inessa Armand", *Slavic Review*, **22**, 1, pp.96–114

Wood, E.A. (1997) *The Baba and the Comrade: Gender and Politics in Revolutionary Russia*. Bloomington, Indiana: Indiana University Press

Zhenshchiny goroda Lenina (Leningrad 1963)

Zhenshchiny v revoliutsii (Moscow 1959)

Index